A WAVE BLUE WORLD
EST. 2005
AWBW

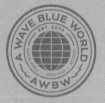

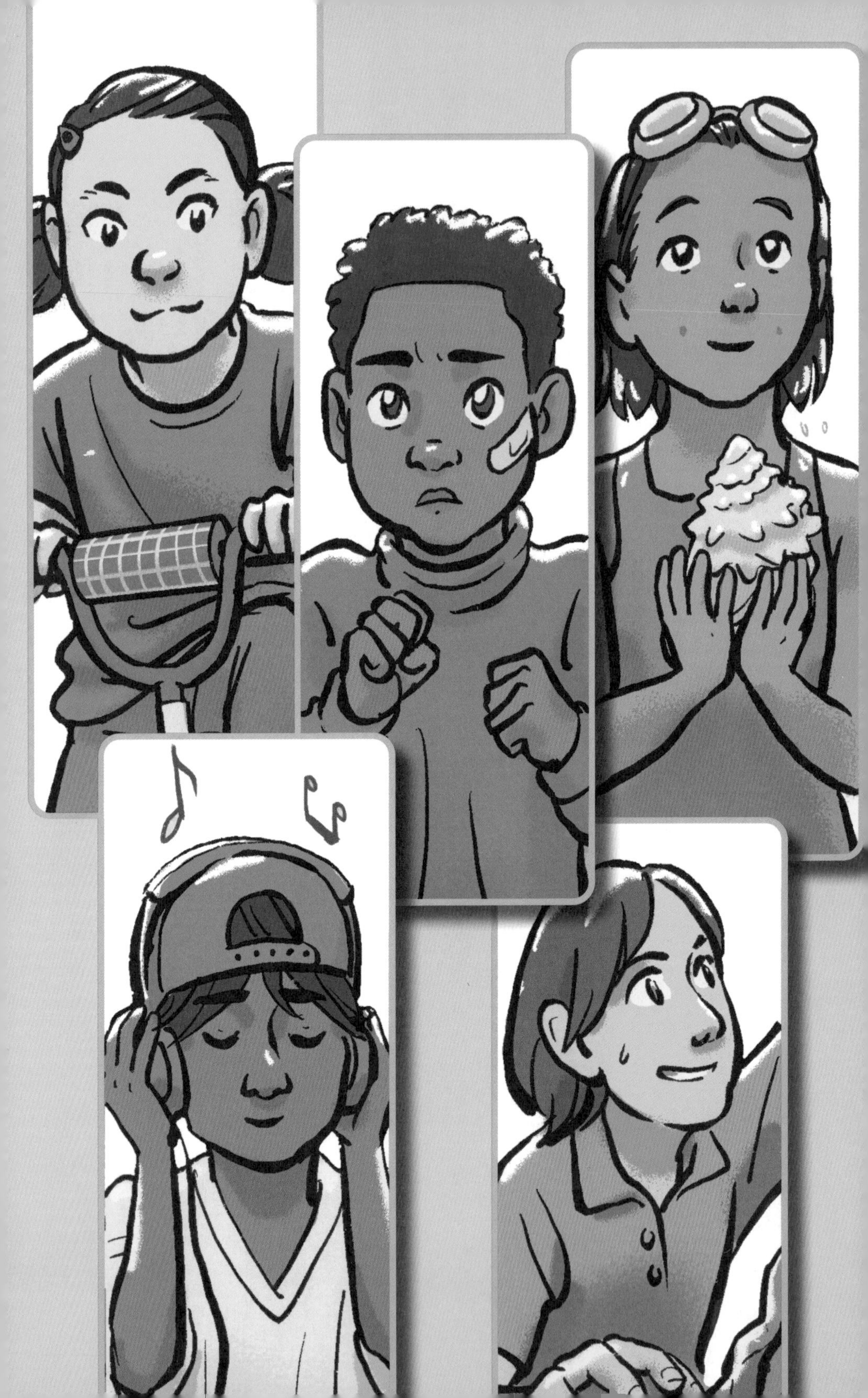

BECOMING

WHO WE ARE

REAL STORIES ABOUT GROWING UP TRANS

EDITED BY SAMMY LISEL
AND HAZEL NEWLEVANT

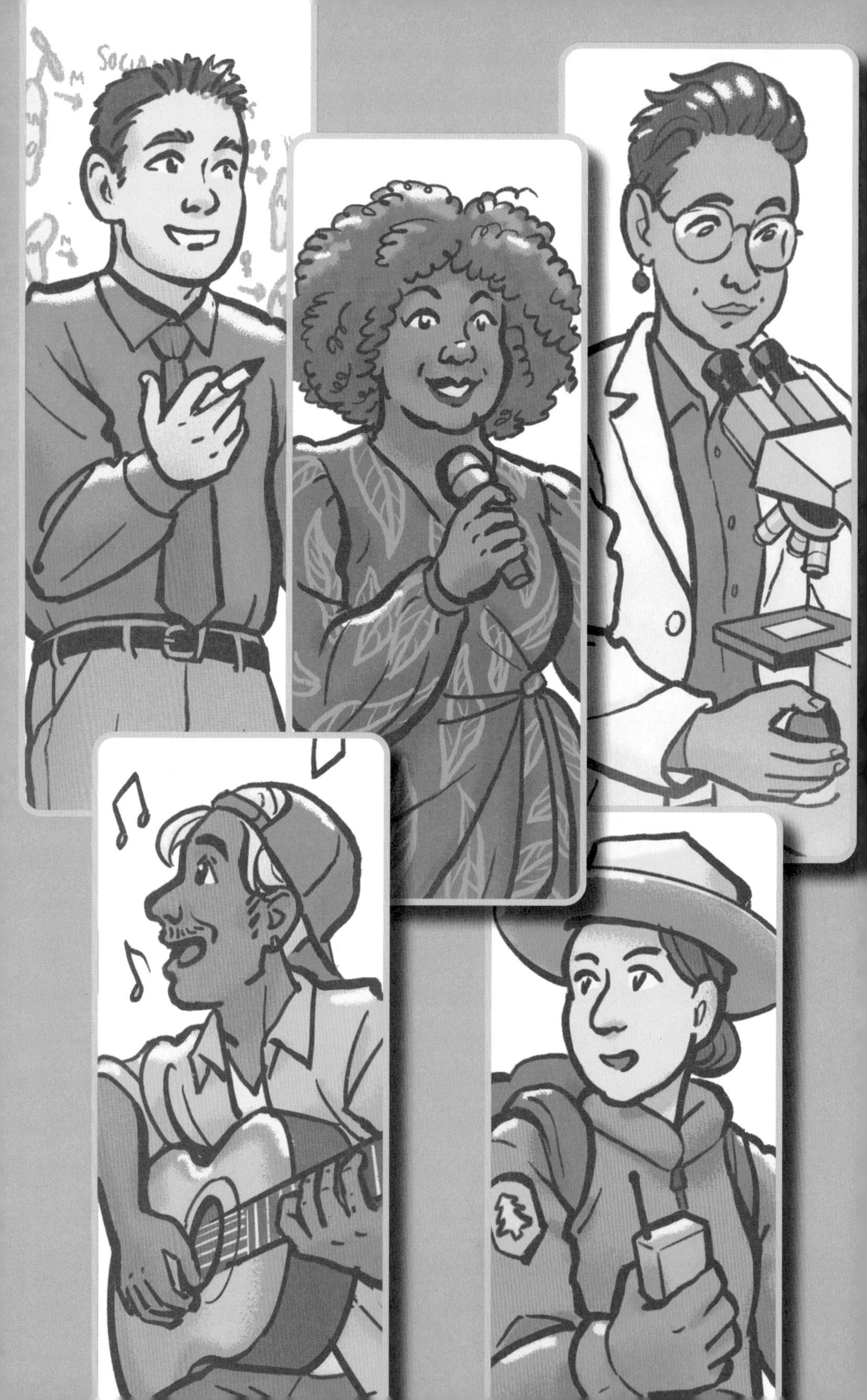

CONSULTING EDITOR:
STEFAN PETRUCHA
COVER ART & LOGO:
HAZEL NEWLEVANT
BOOK DESIGN:
PETE CARLSSON

A WAVE BLUE WORLD
CO-PUBLISHER
TYLER CHIN-TANNER

CO-PUBLISHER
WENDY CHIN-TANNER

ART DIRECTOR
PETE CARLSSON

DIRECTOR OF MARKETING
DIANA KOU

BOOK PUBLICIST
JESSE POST

SOCIAL MEDIA &
COMMUNITY MANAGER
HAZEL NEWLEVANT

SALES DEVELOPMENT MANAGER
MEGAN MARSDEN

Publisher's Cataloging-in-Publication
(Provided by Cassidy Cataloguing Services, Inc.)

Names: Lisel, Sammy, author, editor. | Newlevant, Hazel, editor, artist. | Petrucha, Stefan, editor. | Carlsson, Pete, designer. | Chin-Tanner, Tyler, publisher. | Chin-Tanner, Wendy, publisher.

Title: Becoming who we are : real stories about growing up trans / [written by Sammy Lisel] ; edited by Sammy Lisel and Hazel Newlevant ; consulting editor: Stefan Petrucha ; cover art & logo: Hazel Newlevant ; book design: Pete Carlsson ; co-publisher: Tyler Chin-Tanner ; co-publisher: Wendy Chin-Tanner.

Description: [Rhinebeck, New York] : A Wave Blue World, 2024. | Interest grade level: 6-8. | Summary: A collection of stories by members of the trans community about their childhoods, specifically their life goals and how they achieved them, including musicians, actors, teachers, scientists, forest rangers, and activists.--Publisher.

Identifiers: ISBN: 978-1-949518-26-9

Subjects: LCSH: Transgender people--Biography--Comic books, strips, etc. | CYAC: Transgender people--Biography--Cartoons and comics. | LCGFT: Graphic novels. | Biographical comics. | BISAC: JUVENILE NONFICTION / Comics & Graphic Novels / Biography & Memoir. | JUVENILE NONFICTION / Comics & Graphic Novels / Social Topics. | JUVENILE NONFICTION / Biography & Autobiography / LGBTQ+.

Classification: LCC: HQ77.7 .L57 2024 | DDC: 306.768--dc23

ISBN 978-1-949518-26-9   Printed in Canada   AWBW.com

EDITORS' NOTE

Years ago, I read somewhere that Zulu parents whisper in their sleeping children's ears *"Become who you already are."* I don't know if it's true, but it stayed with me. I borrowed it, telling my kids on their birthdays that I couldn't wait to see them grow into who they already are. I'm struck by the tension between the forward motion of becoming, of all that shapes us into who we are and become, and the simple truth that we are already whole. Perhaps the very best we can wish for is to allow our truest self to shine through. We too often waste time comparing ourselves to others, wishing to be what we are not, instead of honoring and celebrating our very special uniqueness. It takes a lot of courage to be who we are, and by doing so, to share our very special gifts with the world.

In *Becoming Who We Are,* nine people show us their unique path to becoming themselves. They, like all of us, face hardships: divorce, loneliness, bullying, disability, discrimination, among many others. And they, like all of us, are wonderful and unique individuals: funny, interesting, resilient, smart, capable and so courageous. If there is one thing I'd like all of us to feel in these pages it's the underlying truth that we are deserving of love, acceptance and a bright future exactly the way we are, that each one of us is precious, loveable, and whole. Let's support all the children to be who they are and to take their place in the world.

- Sammy Lisel

Sammy came to me with a plan for a graphic novel. She had interviewed some amazing transgender people about their lives, and she wanted to turn their stories into comics, so they could entertain and inspire readers everywhere. Sammy wanted this book to exist for her own kids, to show them that they're not alone, and help them imagine exciting possible futures.

My idea was: a diversity of stories needs a diversity of artists. To illustrate comics, even with reference photos, we're all drawing on our own experiences— literally! Fortunately, I know some brilliant cartoonists who also happen to be trans, and they were just as excited to draw these stories as I was. That's how *Becoming Who We Are* became an anthology! It was a joy to help bring the creators together and see their comics develop.

- Hazel Newlevant

We thank Sam, Robbi, Brooke, Kate, Robbie, Diamond, Marli, Robin, and Rebekah for being so generous with sharing their stories and letting the world get to know them. We also thank A Wave Blue World for seeing the vision and publishing this book beautifully.

TABLE OF CONTENTS

All stories written by Sammy Lisel

A NOTE ABOUT NAMES AND PRONOUNS:

To stay true to our stars' childhood experiences, we show other characters calling them by the pronouns that were used when they were growing up.

However, to be respectful and make the stories easier to follow, we've used everyone's chosen names throughout the comics.

BECOMING SAM LONG

Sam Long (he/him) is a first-generation Chinese-American-Canadian, scientist, and educator. He's the proud recipient of awards in civil rights advocacy and excellence in teaching and loves playing drums in the concert band.

Written by Sammy Lisel
Illustrated by Cynthia Yuan Cheng

Cynthia (they/them) is a Taiwanese American cartoonist who loves creating funny-bittersweet stories about connection, identity, and belonging. Their favorite activities include making their friends laugh and eating spicy Szechuan food.

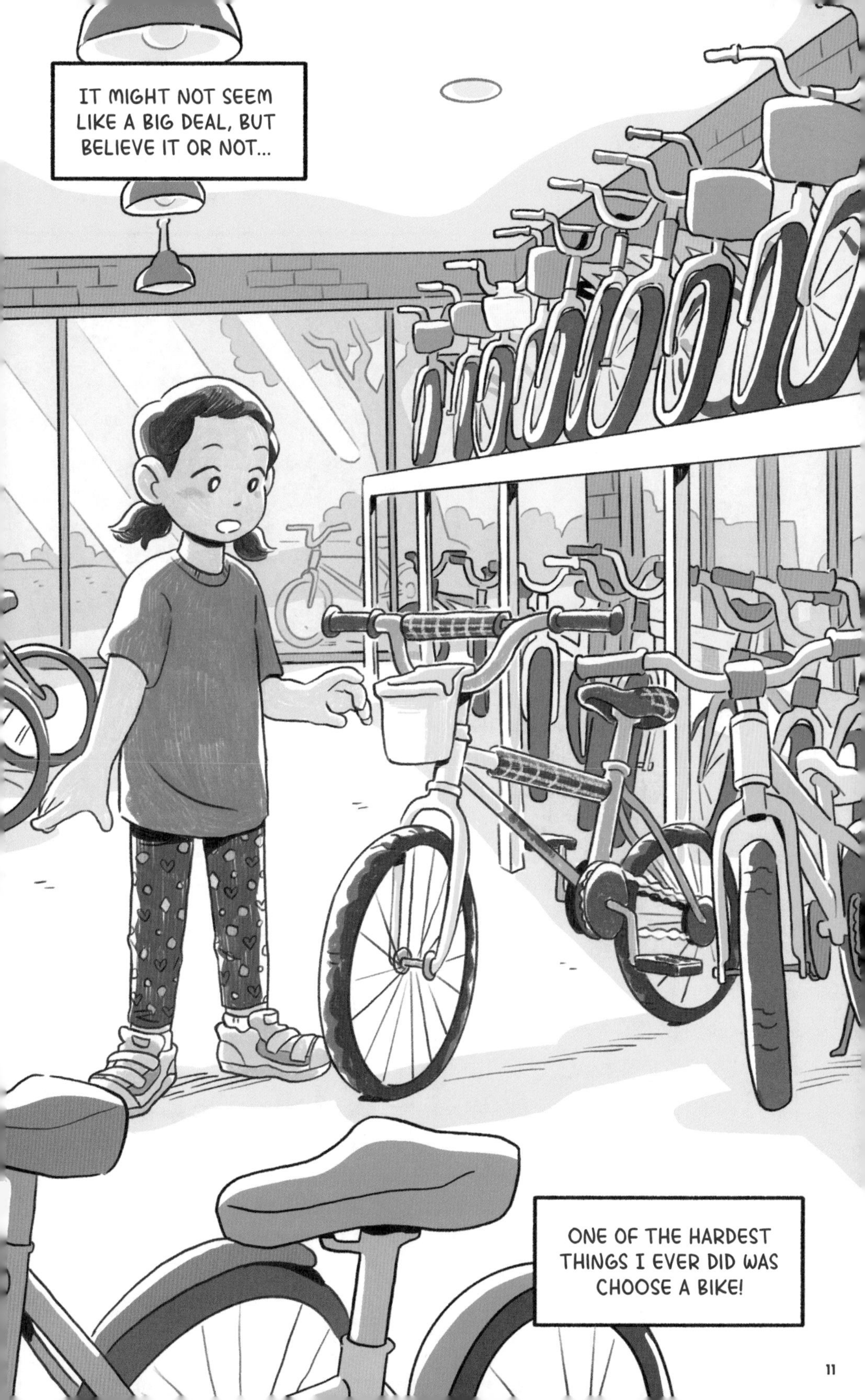
IT MIGHT NOT SEEM LIKE A BIG DEAL, BUT BELIEVE IT OR NOT...
ONE OF THE HARDEST THINGS I EVER DID WAS CHOOSE A BIKE!

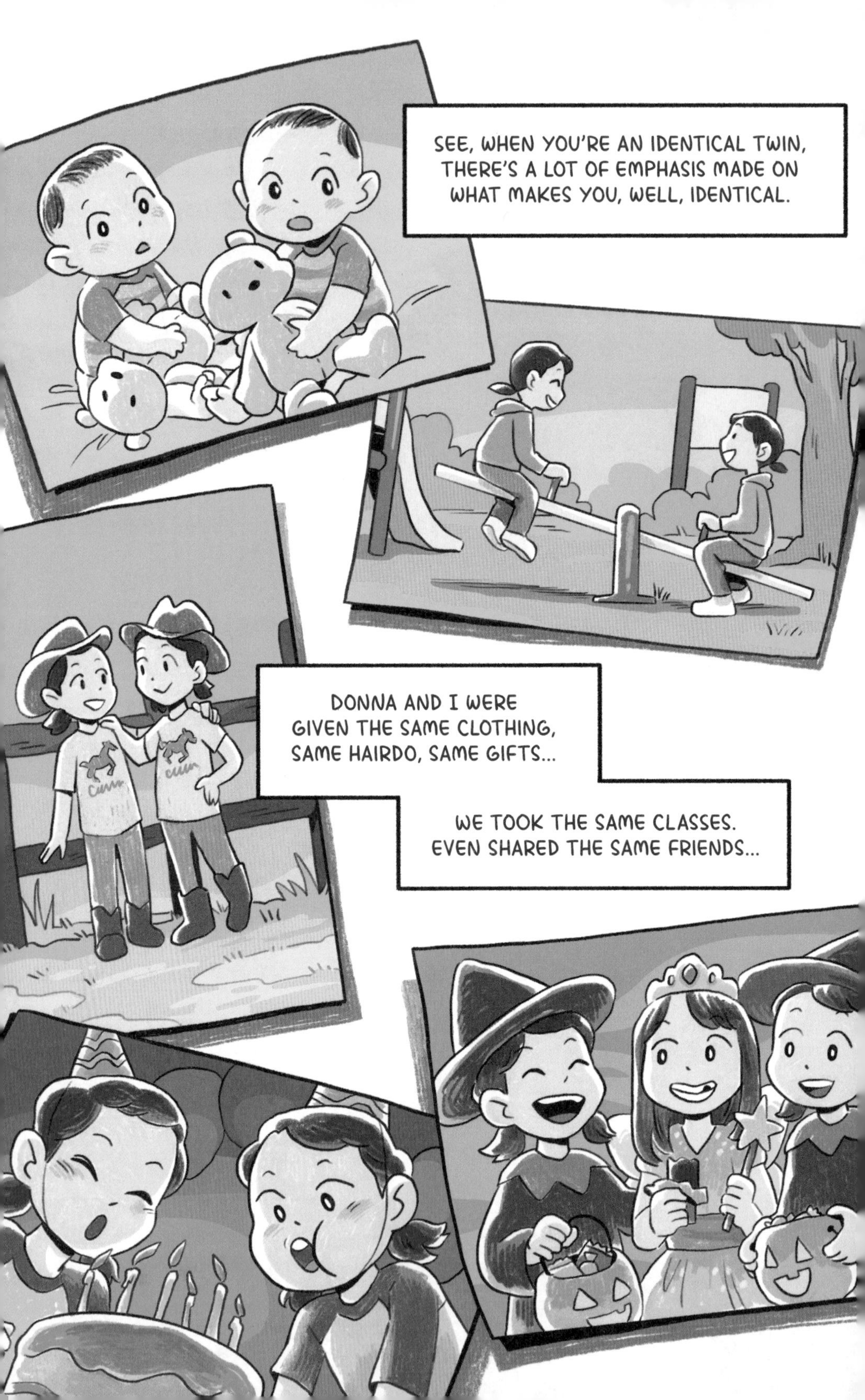
SEE, WHEN YOU'RE AN IDENTICAL TWIN, THERE'S A LOT OF EMPHASIS MADE ON WHAT MAKES YOU, WELL, IDENTICAL.
DONNA AND I WERE GIVEN THE SAME CLOTHING, SAME HAIRDO, SAME GIFTS...
WE TOOK THE SAME CLASSES. EVEN SHARED THE SAME FRIENDS...

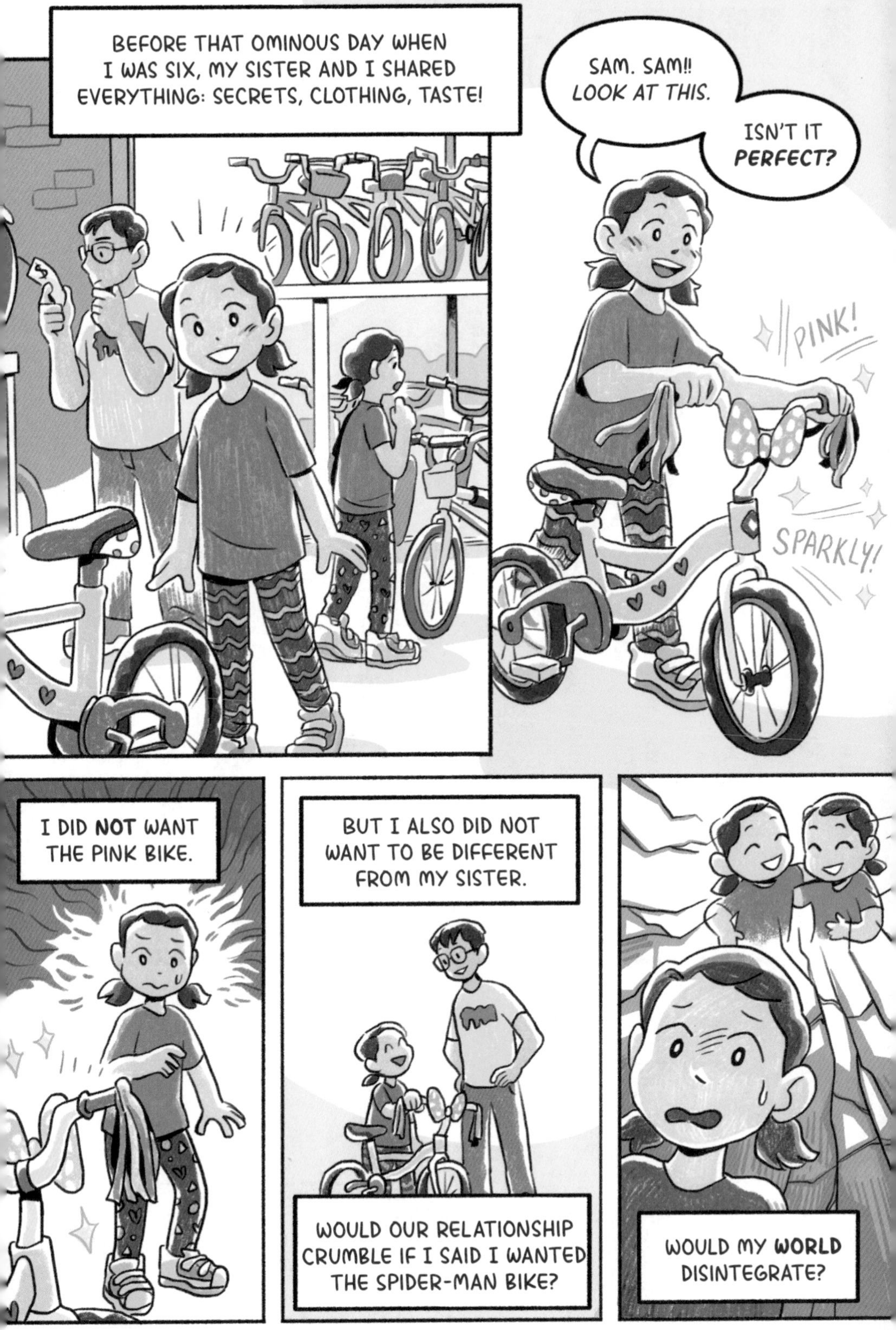
BEFORE THAT OMINOUS DAY WHEN I WAS SIX, MY SISTER AND I SHARED EVERYTHING: SECRETS, CLOTHING, TASTE!
SAM. SAM!! LOOK AT THIS.
ISN'T IT PERFECT?
PINK!
SPARKLY!
I DID NOT WANT THE PINK BIKE.
BUT I ALSO DID NOT WANT TO BE DIFFERENT FROM MY SISTER.
WOULD OUR RELATIONSHIP CRUMBLE IF I SAID I WANTED THE SPIDER-MAN BIKE?
WOULD MY WORLD DISINTEGRATE?

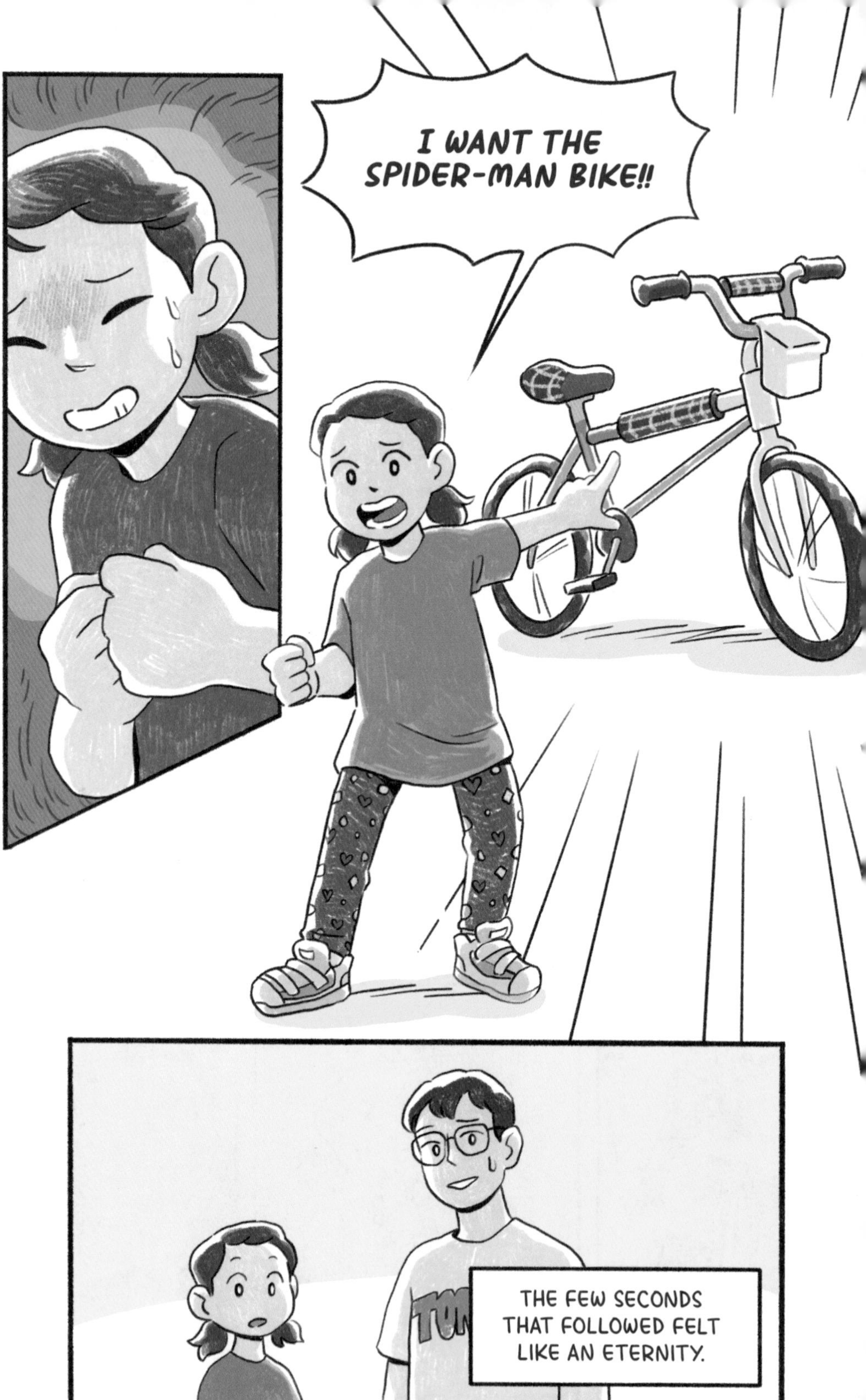
I WANT THE SPIDER-MAN BIKE!!
THE FEW SECONDS THAT FOLLOWED FELT LIKE AN ETERNITY.

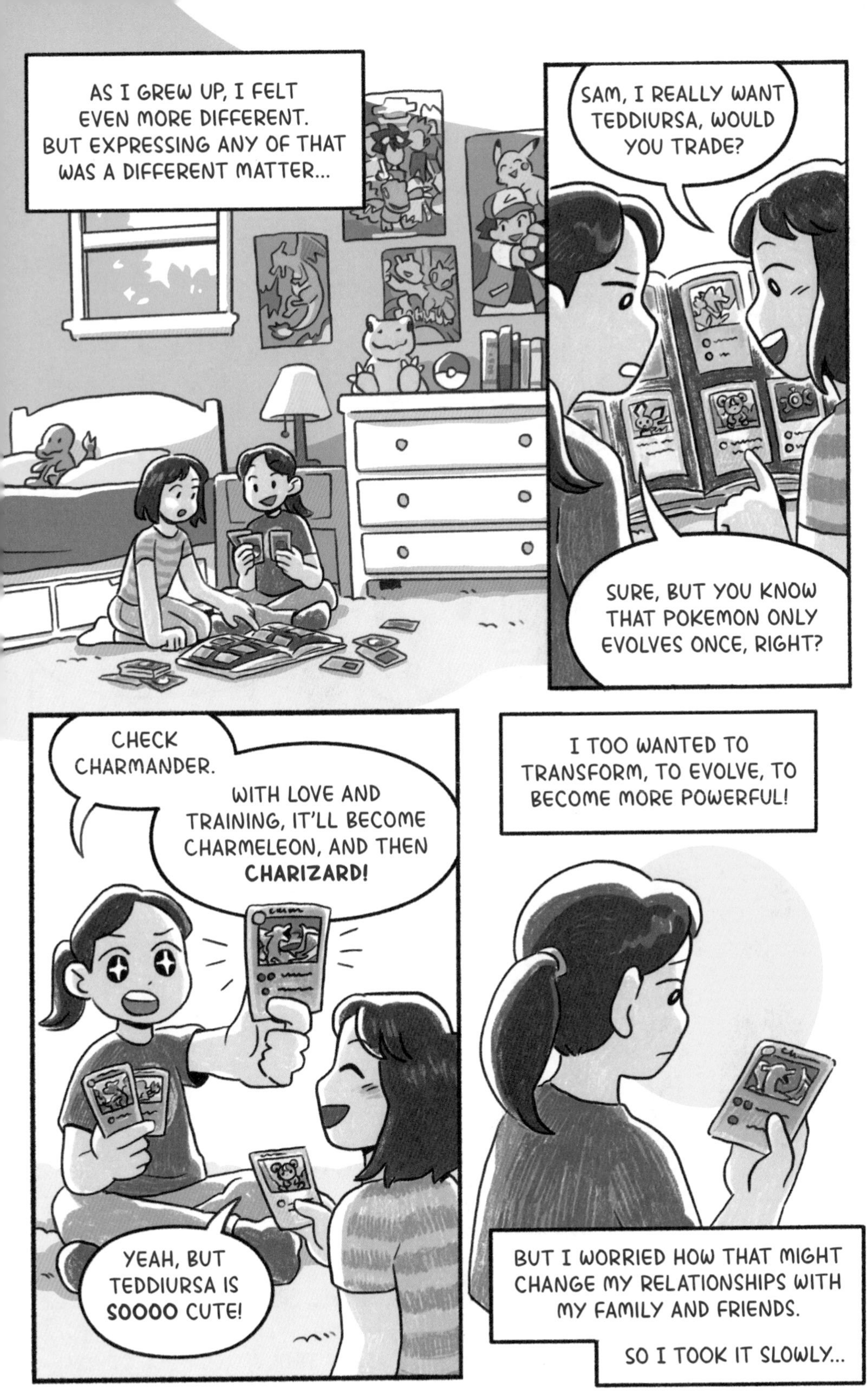
AS I GREW UP, I FELT EVEN MORE DIFFERENT. BUT EXPRESSING ANY OF THAT WAS A DIFFERENT MATTER...
SAM, I REALLY WANT TEDDIURSA, WOULD YOU TRADE?
SURE, BUT YOU KNOW THAT POKEMON ONLY EVOLVES ONCE, RIGHT?
CHECK CHARMANDER.
WITH LOVE AND TRAINING, IT'LL BECOME CHARMELEON, AND THEN **CHARIZARD!**
YEAH, BUT TEDDIURSA IS **SOOOO** CUTE!
I TOO WANTED TO TRANSFORM, TO EVOLVE, TO BECOME MORE POWERFUL!
BUT I WORRIED HOW THAT MIGHT CHANGE MY RELATIONSHIPS WITH MY FAMILY AND FRIENDS.
SO I TOOK IT SLOWLY...

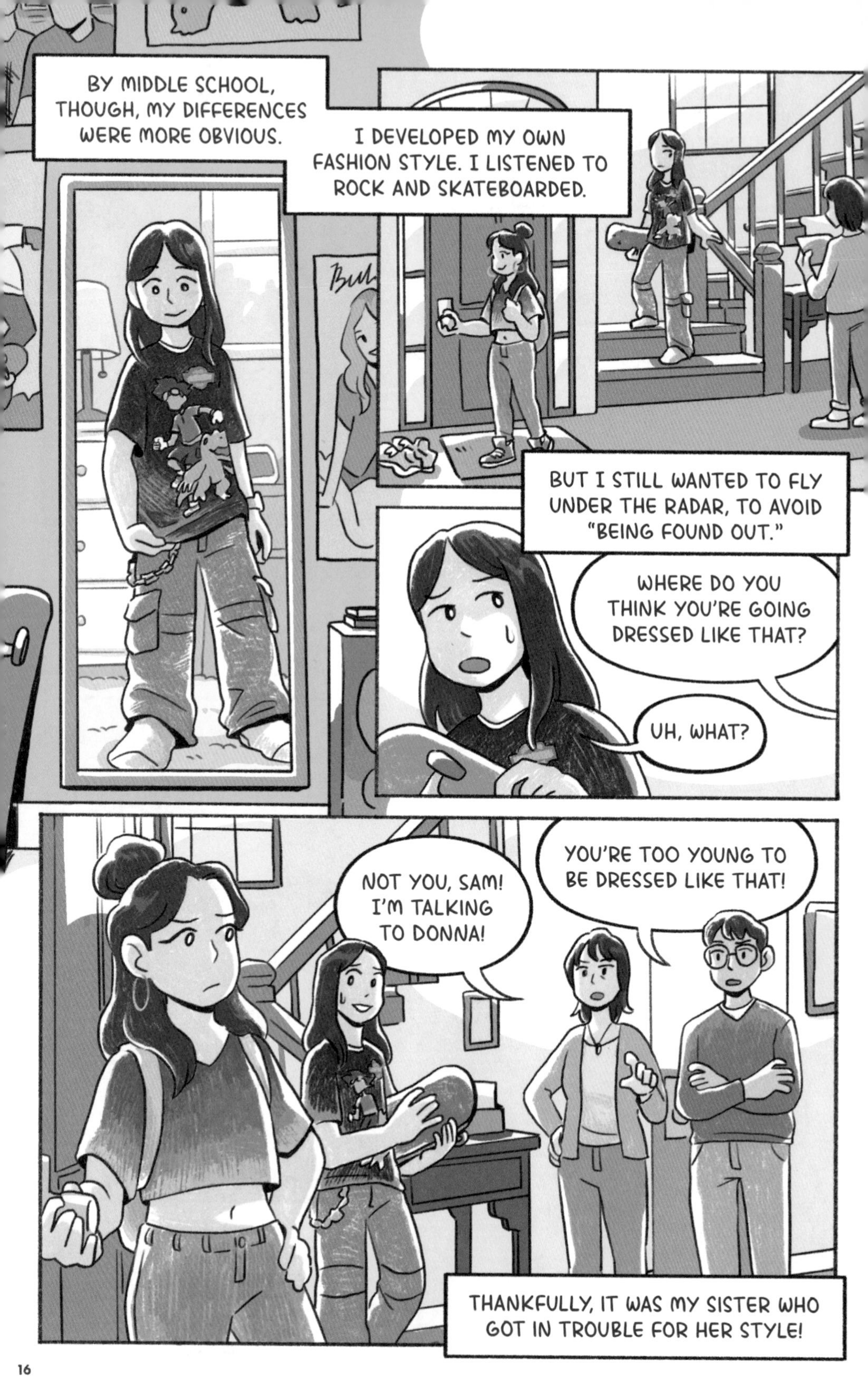
BY MIDDLE SCHOOL, THOUGH, MY DIFFERENCES WERE MORE OBVIOUS.
I DEVELOPED MY OWN FASHION STYLE. I LISTENED TO ROCK AND SKATEBOARDED.
BUT I STILL WANTED TO FLY UNDER THE RADAR, TO AVOID "BEING FOUND OUT."
WHERE DO YOU THINK YOU'RE GOING DRESSED LIKE THAT?
UH, WHAT?
YOU'RE TOO YOUNG TO BE DRESSED LIKE THAT!
NOT YOU, SAM! I'M TALKING TO DONNA!
THANKFULLY, IT WAS MY SISTER WHO GOT IN TROUBLE FOR HER STYLE!

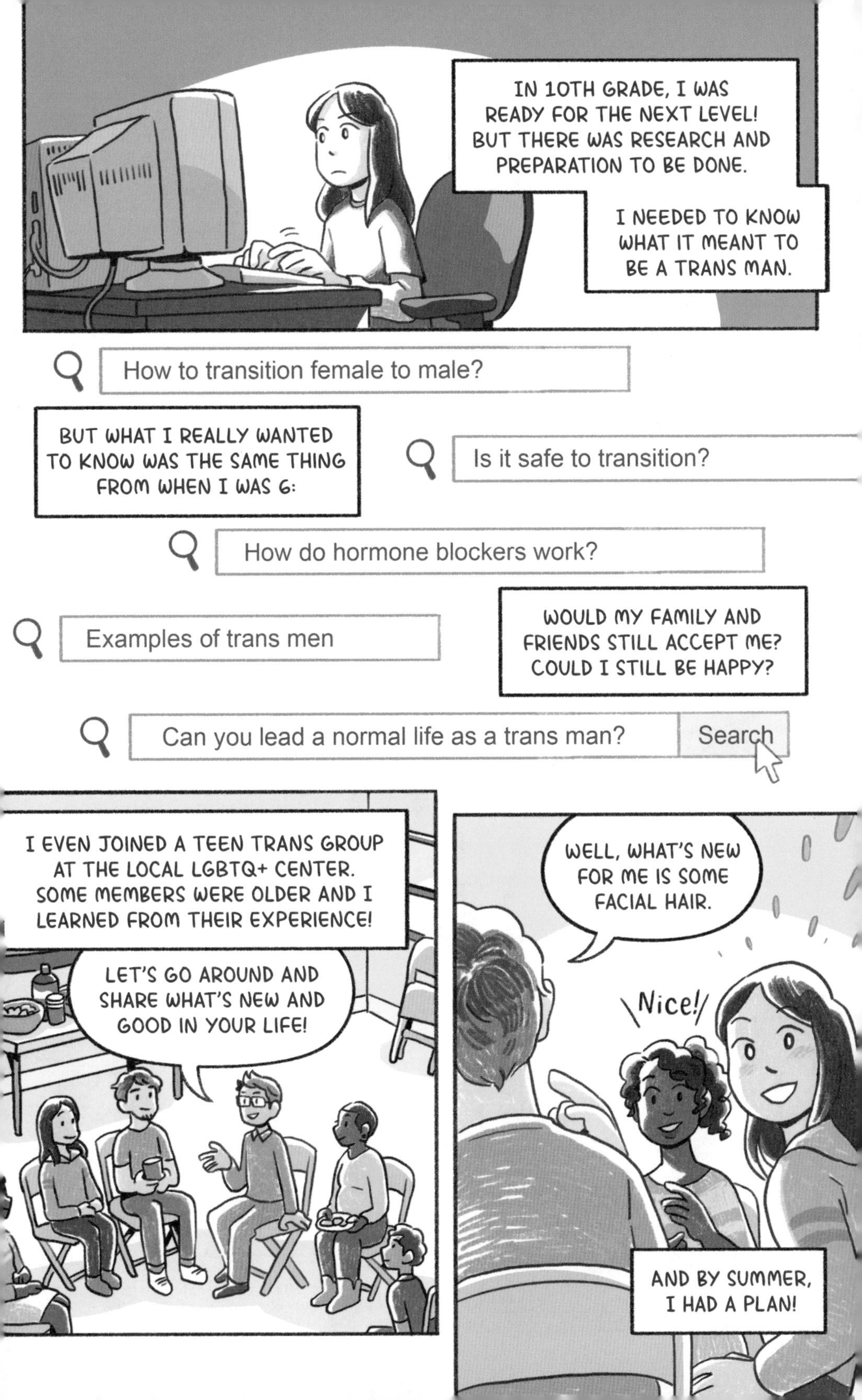
IN 10TH GRADE, I WAS READY FOR THE NEXT LEVEL! BUT THERE WAS RESEARCH AND PREPARATION TO BE DONE.
I NEEDED TO KNOW WHAT IT MEANT TO BE A TRANS MAN.
How to transition female to male?
BUT WHAT I REALLY WANTED TO KNOW WAS THE SAME THING FROM WHEN I WAS 6:
Is it safe to transition?
How do hormone blockers work?
Examples of trans men
WOULD MY FAMILY AND FRIENDS STILL ACCEPT ME? COULD I STILL BE HAPPY?
Can you lead a normal life as a trans man?
Search
I EVEN JOINED A TEEN TRANS GROUP AT THE LOCAL LGBTQ+ CENTER. SOME MEMBERS WERE OLDER AND I LEARNED FROM THEIR EXPERIENCE!
LET'S GO AROUND AND SHARE WHAT'S NEW AND GOOD IN YOUR LIFE!
WELL, WHAT'S NEW FOR ME IS SOME FACIAL HAIR.
Nice!
AND BY SUMMER, I HAD A PLAN!

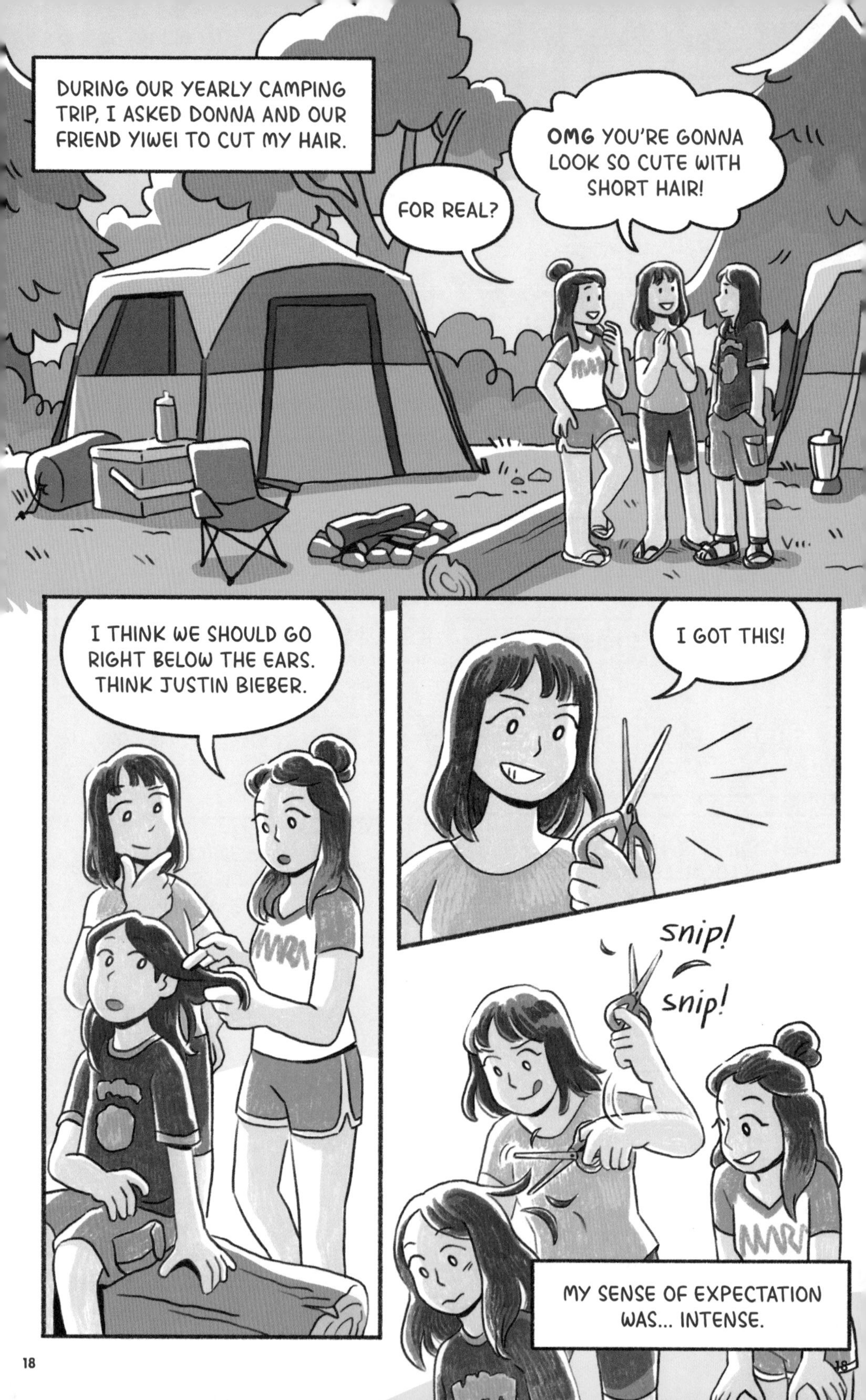
DURING OUR YEARLY CAMPING TRIP, I ASKED DONNA AND OUR FRIEND YIWEI TO CUT MY HAIR.
OMG YOU'RE GONNA LOOK SO CUTE WITH SHORT HAIR!
FOR REAL?
I THINK WE SHOULD GO RIGHT BELOW THE EARS. THINK JUSTIN BIEBER.
I GOT THIS!
snip!
snip!
MY SENSE OF EXPECTATION WAS... INTENSE.

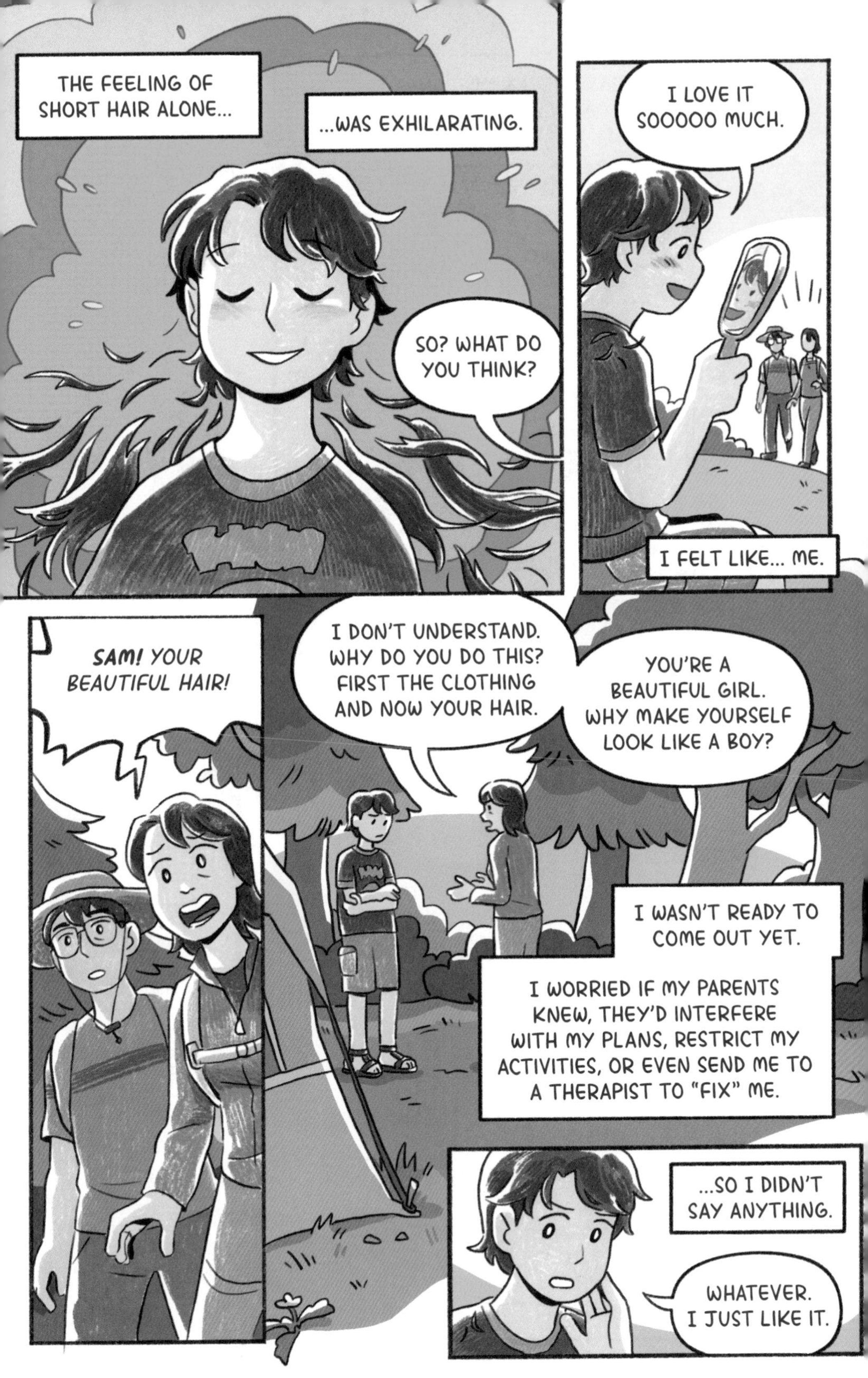
THE FEELING OF SHORT HAIR ALONE...
...WAS EXHILARATING.
SO? WHAT DO YOU THINK?
I LOVE IT SOOOOO MUCH.
I FELT LIKE... ME.
SAM! YOUR BEAUTIFUL HAIR!
I DON'T UNDERSTAND. WHY DO YOU DO THIS? FIRST THE CLOTHING AND NOW YOUR HAIR.
YOU'RE A BEAUTIFUL GIRL. WHY MAKE YOURSELF LOOK LIKE A BOY?
I WASN'T READY TO COME OUT YET.
I WORRIED IF MY PARENTS KNEW, THEY'D INTERFERE WITH MY PLANS, RESTRICT MY ACTIVITIES, OR EVEN SEND ME TO A THERAPIST TO "FIX" ME.
...SO I DIDN'T SAY ANYTHING.
WHATEVER. I JUST LIKE IT.

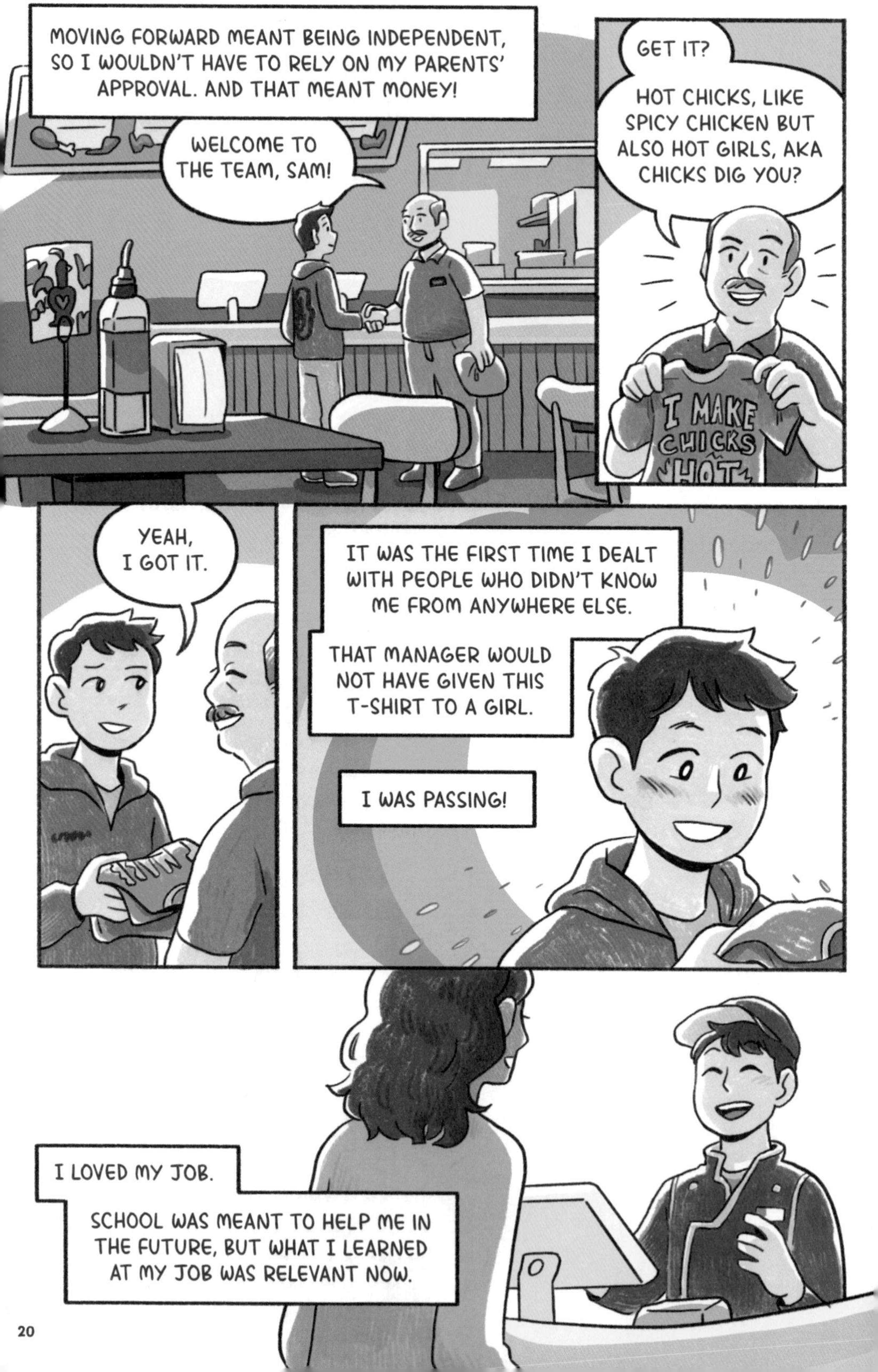
MOVING FORWARD MEANT BEING INDEPENDENT, SO I WOULDN'T HAVE TO RELY ON MY PARENTS' APPROVAL. AND THAT MEANT MONEY!
WELCOME TO THE TEAM, SAM!
GET IT?
HOT CHICKS, LIKE SPICY CHICKEN BUT ALSO HOT GIRLS, AKA CHICKS DIG YOU?
I MAKE CHICKS HOT
YEAH, I GOT IT.
IT WAS THE FIRST TIME I DEALT WITH PEOPLE WHO DIDN'T KNOW ME FROM ANYWHERE ELSE.
THAT MANAGER WOULD NOT HAVE GIVEN THIS T-SHIRT TO A GIRL.
I WAS PASSING!
I LOVED MY JOB.
SCHOOL WAS MEANT TO HELP ME IN THE FUTURE, BUT WHAT I LEARNED AT MY JOB WAS RELEVANT NOW.

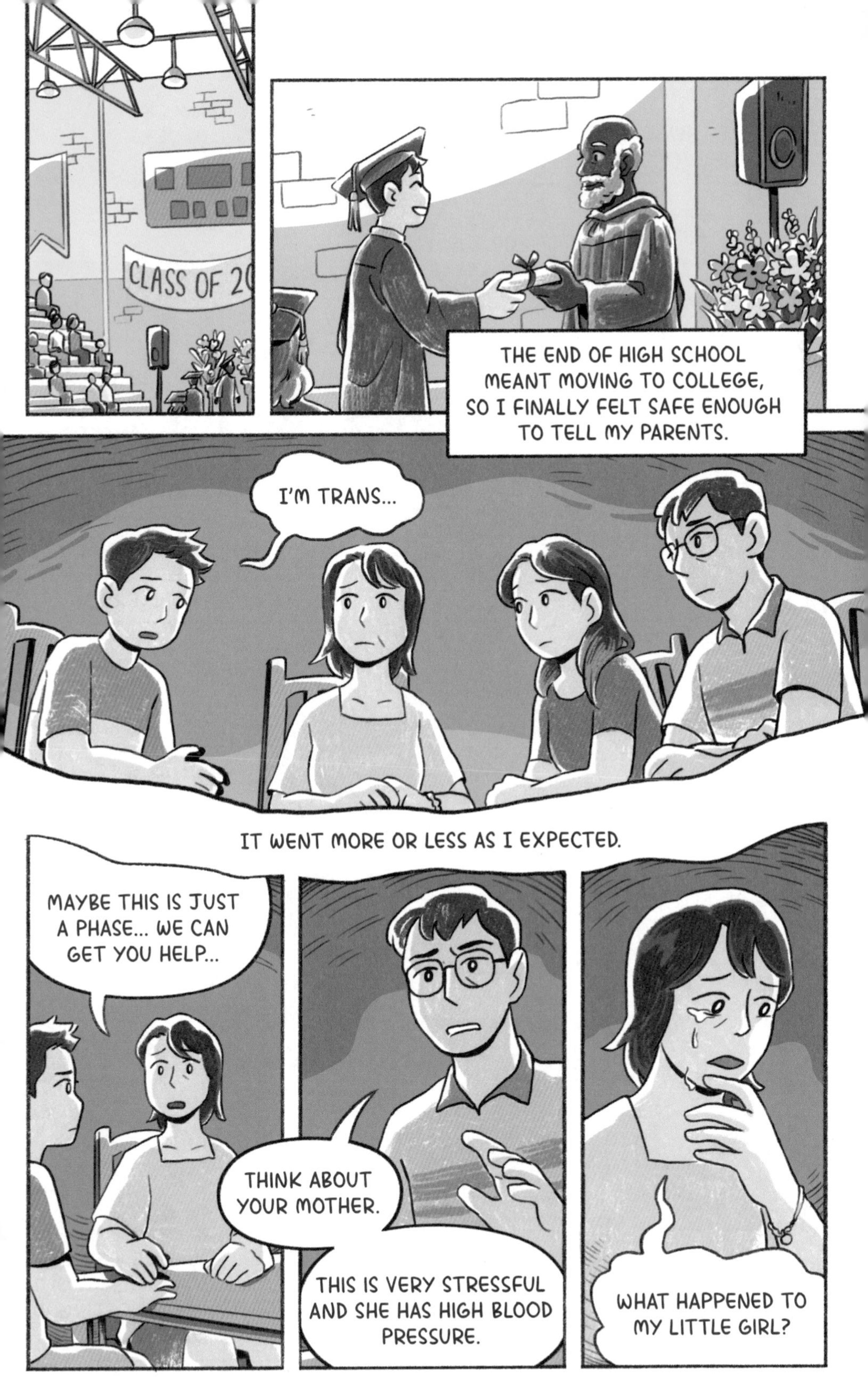
CLASS OF 20
THE END OF HIGH SCHOOL MEANT MOVING TO COLLEGE, SO I FINALLY FELT SAFE ENOUGH TO TELL MY PARENTS.
I'M TRANS...
IT WENT MORE OR LESS AS I EXPECTED.
MAYBE THIS IS JUST A PHASE... WE CAN GET YOU HELP...
THINK ABOUT YOUR MOTHER.
THIS IS VERY STRESSFUL AND SHE HAS HIGH BLOOD PRESSURE.
WHAT HAPPENED TO MY LITTLE GIRL?

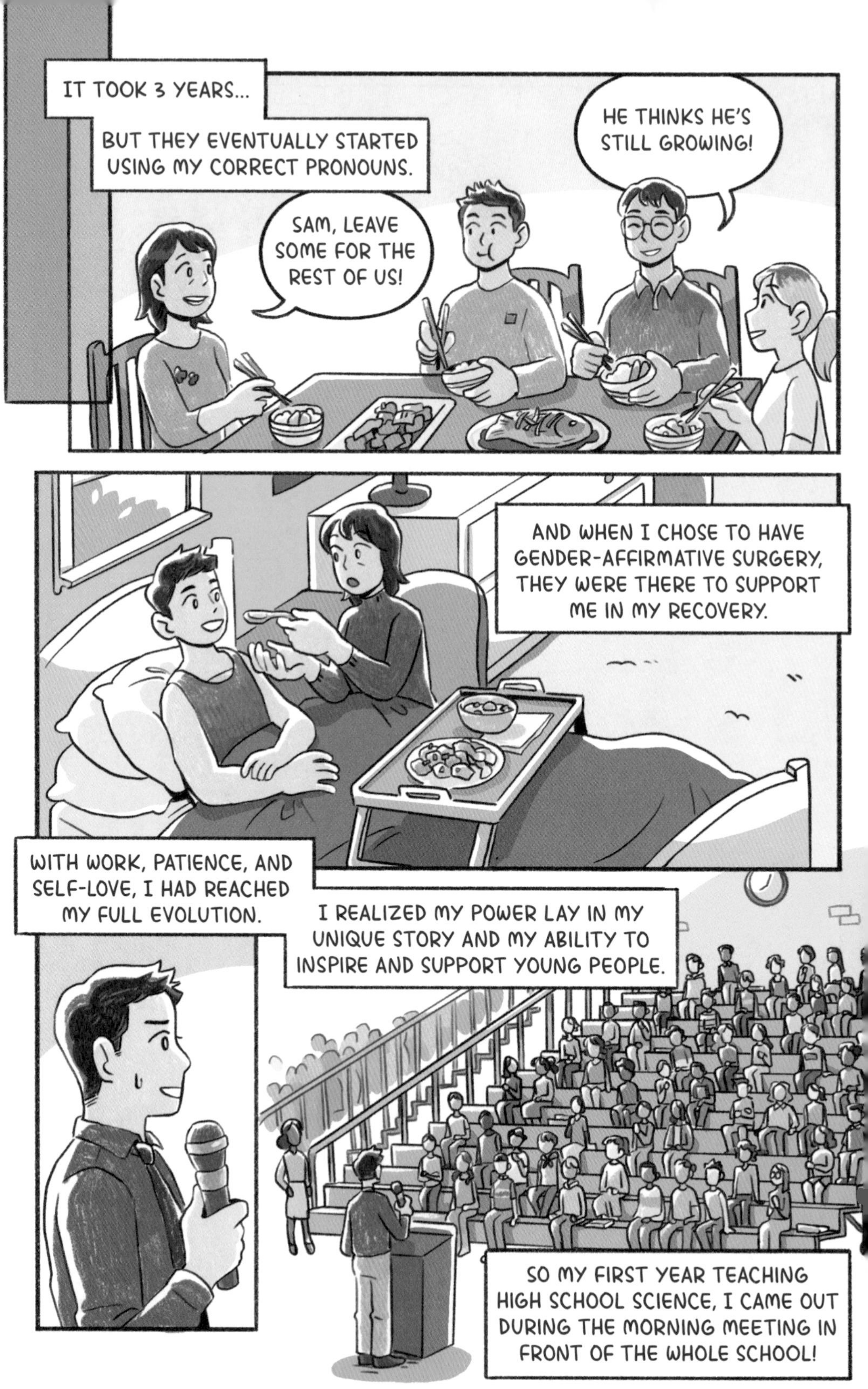
IT TOOK 3 YEARS...
BUT THEY EVENTUALLY STARTED USING MY CORRECT PRONOUNS.
SAM, LEAVE SOME FOR THE REST OF US!
HE THINKS HE'S STILL GROWING!
AND WHEN I CHOSE TO HAVE GENDER-AFFIRMATIVE SURGERY, THEY WERE THERE TO SUPPORT ME IN MY RECOVERY.
WITH WORK, PATIENCE, AND SELF-LOVE, I HAD REACHED MY FULL EVOLUTION.
I REALIZED MY POWER LAY IN MY UNIQUE STORY AND MY ABILITY TO INSPIRE AND SUPPORT YOUNG PEOPLE.
SO MY FIRST YEAR TEACHING HIGH SCHOOL SCIENCE, I CAME OUT DURING THE MORNING MEETING IN FRONT OF THE WHOLE SCHOOL!

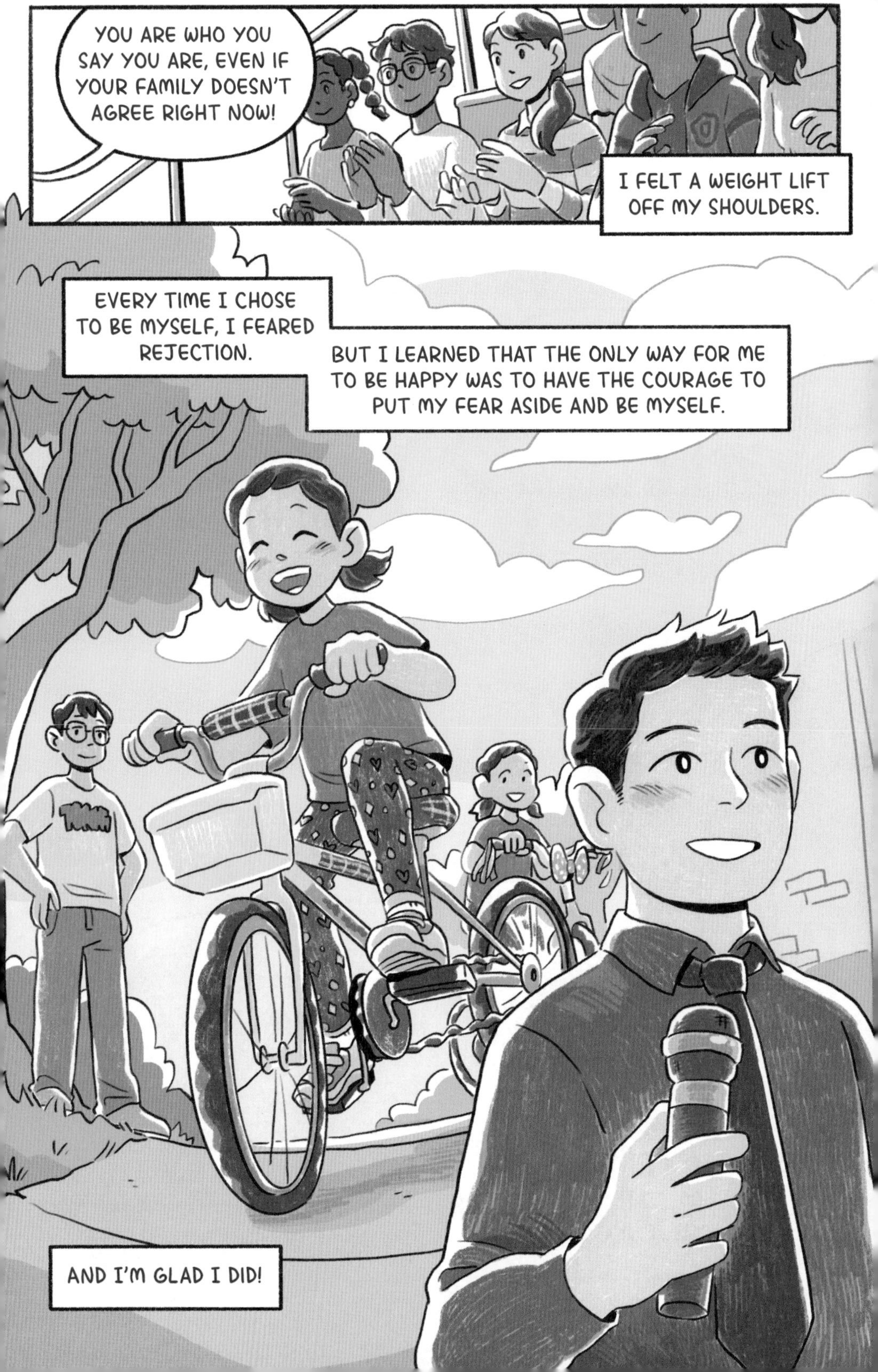
YOU ARE WHO YOU SAY YOU ARE, EVEN IF YOUR FAMILY DOESN'T AGREE RIGHT NOW!
I FELT A WEIGHT LIFT OFF MY SHOULDERS.
EVERY TIME I CHOSE TO BE MYSELF, I FEARED REJECTION.
BUT I LEARNED THAT THE ONLY WAY FOR ME TO BE HAPPY WAS TO HAVE THE COURAGE TO PUT MY FEAR ASIDE AND BE MYSELF.
AND I'M GLAD I DID!

BECOMING ROBBI MECUS

Robbi Mecus (she/her/hers) is a forest ranger and rock climber in New York's Adirondack Mountains. She works with her local Pride, and organized the first ever queer ice climbing festival.

Written by **Lilah Sturges**
and **Sammy Lisel**
Illustrated by **Naomi Rubin**

Naomi (she/her/hers) is a comic artists who creates stories about self-understanding in a fantasy world. She used to be kinda good at *Dance Dance Revolution*. Naomi loves cooking and being out in nature.

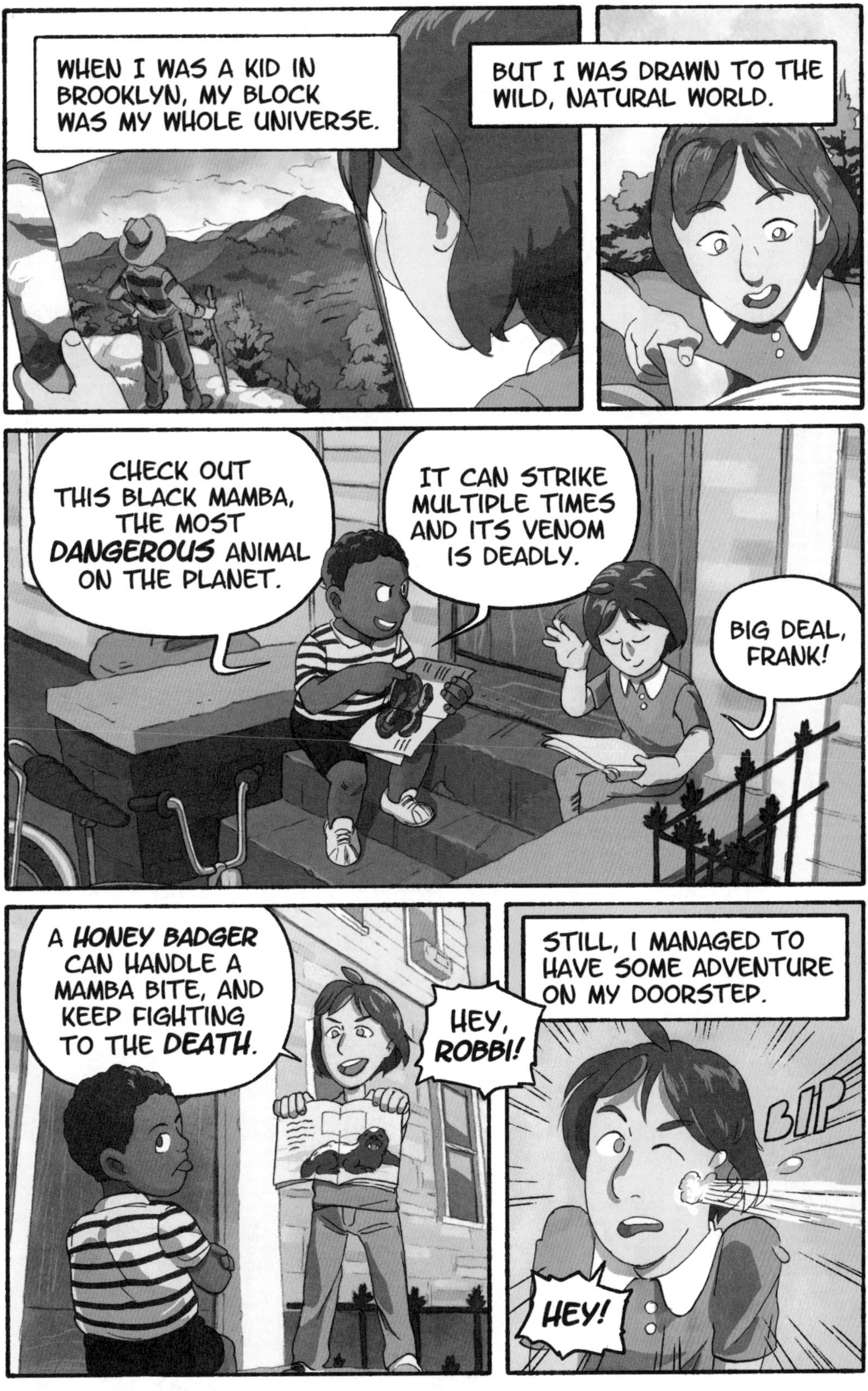
WHEN I WAS A KID IN BROOKLYN, MY BLOCK WAS MY WHOLE UNIVERSE.
BUT I WAS DRAWN TO THE WILD, NATURAL WORLD.
CHECK OUT THIS BLACK MAMBA, THE MOST DANGEROUS ANIMAL ON THE PLANET.
IT CAN STRIKE MULTIPLE TIMES AND ITS VENOM IS DEADLY.
BIG DEAL, FRANK!
A HONEY BADGER CAN HANDLE A MAMBA BITE, AND KEEP FIGHTING TO THE DEATH.
HEY, ROBBI!
STILL, I MANAGED TO HAVE SOME ADVENTURE ON MY DOORSTEP.
BIP
HEY!

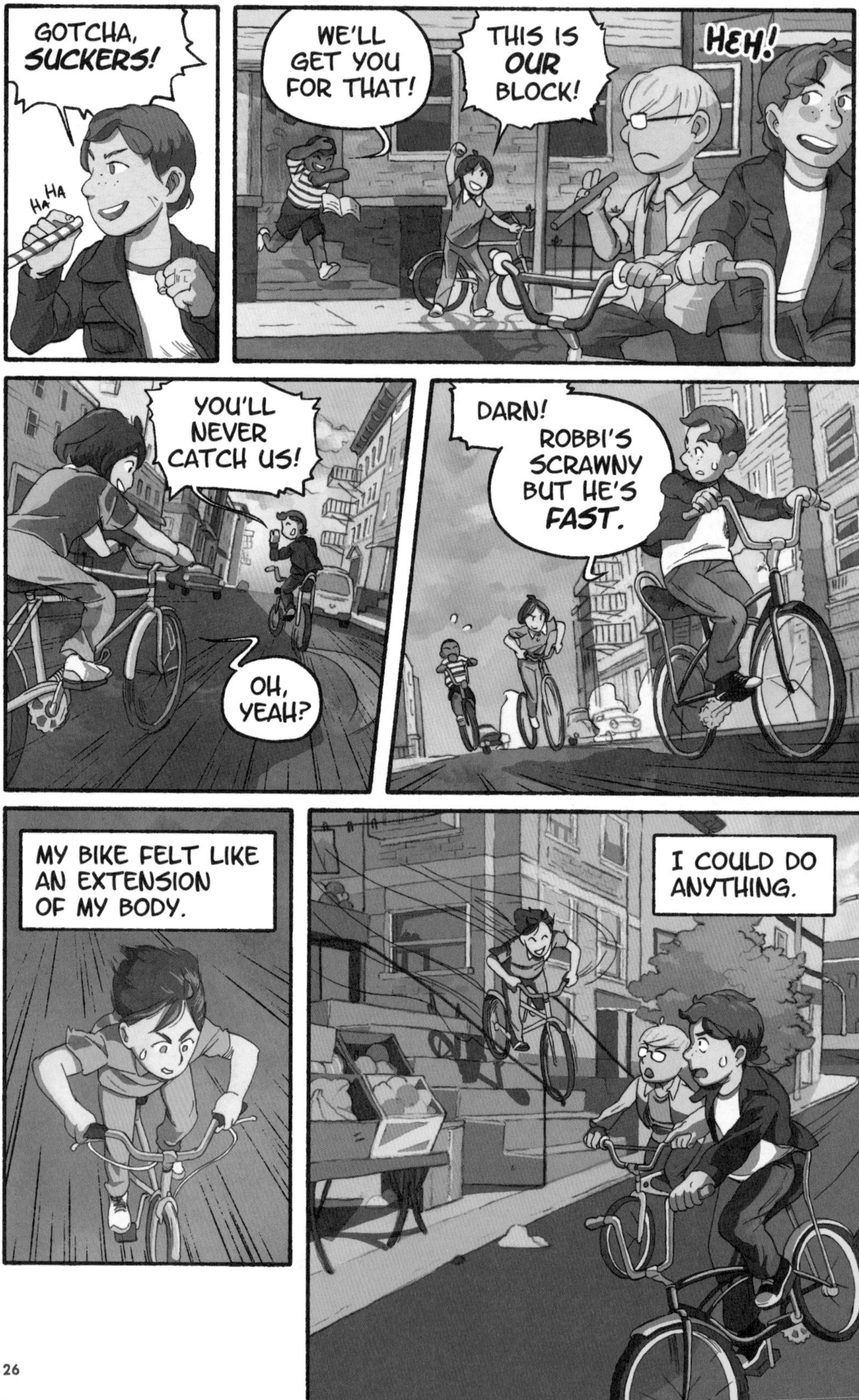
GOTCHA, SUCKERS!
HA HA HA
WE'LL GET YOU FOR THAT!
THIS IS OUR BLOCK!
HEH!
YOU'LL NEVER CATCH US!
OH, YEAH?
DARN! ROBBI'S SCRAWNY BUT HE'S FAST.
MY BIKE FELT LIKE AN EXTENSION OF MY BODY.
I COULD DO ANYTHING.

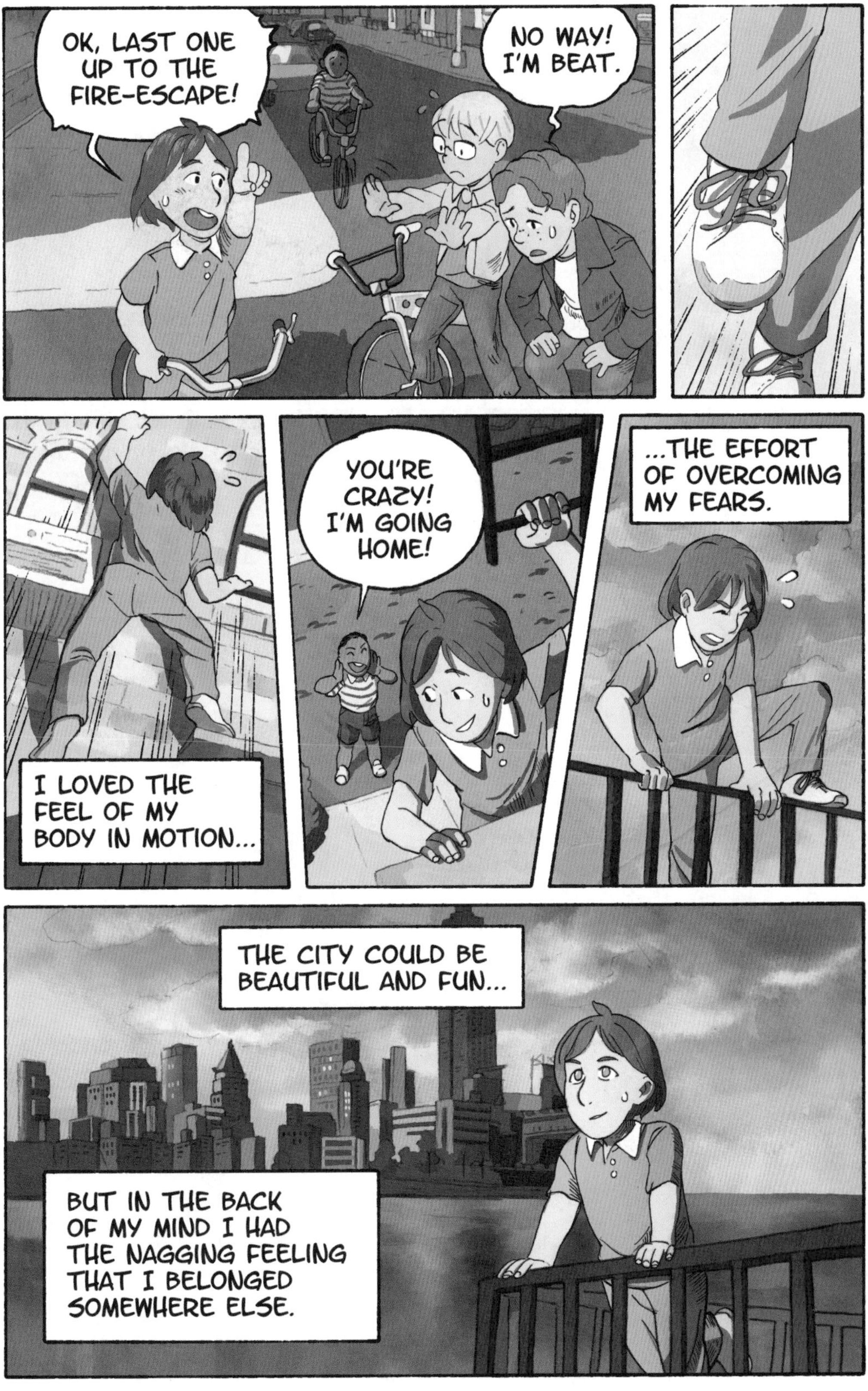
OK, LAST ONE UP TO THE FIRE-ESCAPE!
NO WAY! I'M BEAT.
I LOVED THE FEEL OF MY BODY IN MOTION...
YOU'RE CRAZY! I'M GOING HOME!
...THE EFFORT OF OVERCOMING MY FEARS.
THE CITY COULD BE BEAUTIFUL AND FUN...
BUT IN THE BACK OF MY MIND I HAD THE NAGGING FEELING THAT I BELONGED SOMEWHERE ELSE.

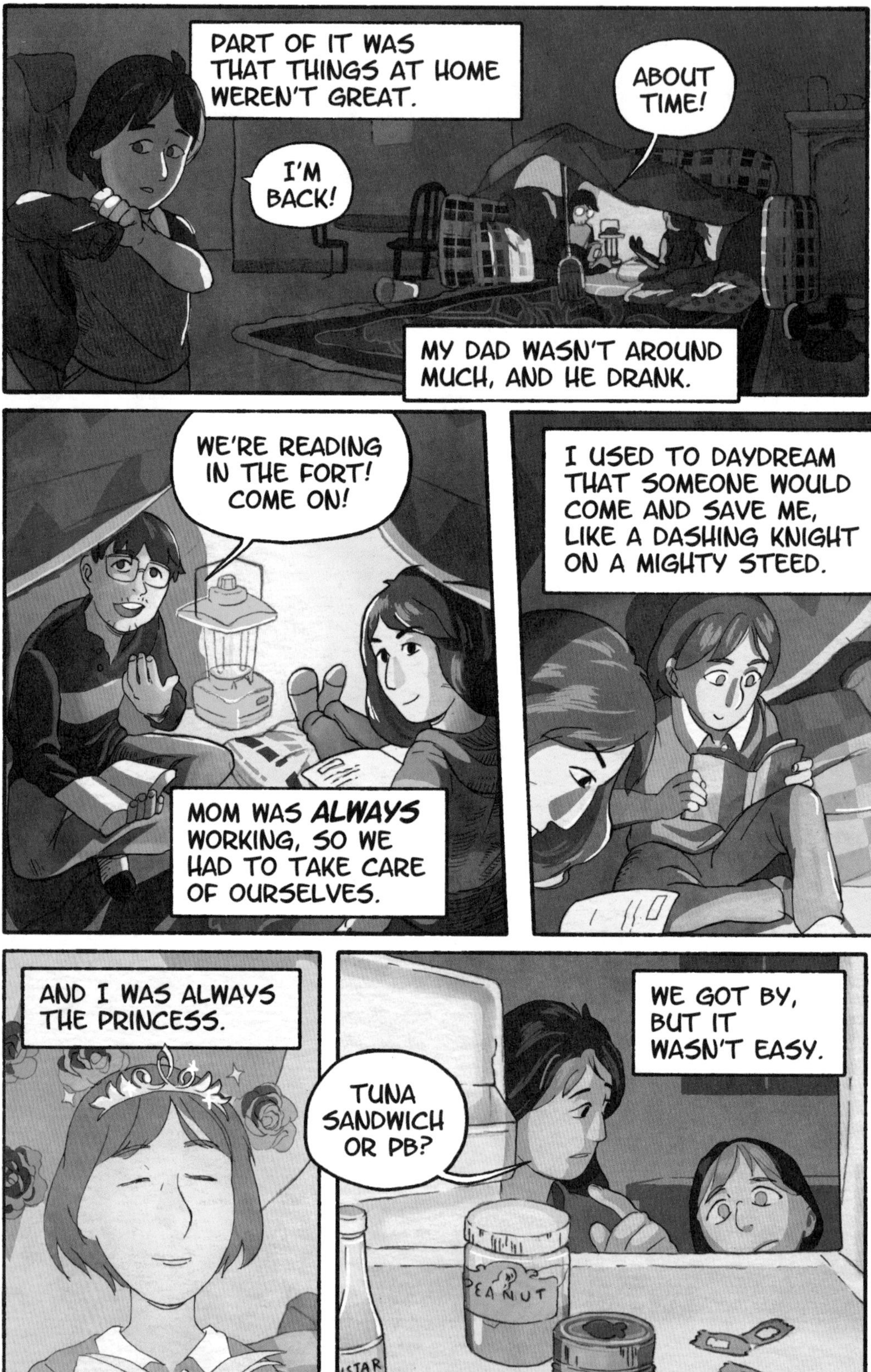
PART OF IT WAS THAT THINGS AT HOME WEREN'T GREAT.
I'M BACK!
ABOUT TIME!
MY DAD WASN'T AROUND MUCH, AND HE DRANK.
WE'RE READING IN THE FORT! COME ON!
MOM WAS ***ALWAYS*** WORKING, SO WE HAD TO TAKE CARE OF OURSELVES.
I USED TO DAYDREAM THAT SOMEONE WOULD COME AND SAVE ME, LIKE A DASHING KNIGHT ON A MIGHTY STEED.
AND I WAS ALWAYS THE PRINCESS.
WE GOT BY, BUT IT WASN'T EASY.
TUNA SANDWICH OR PB?
EANUT
USTAR

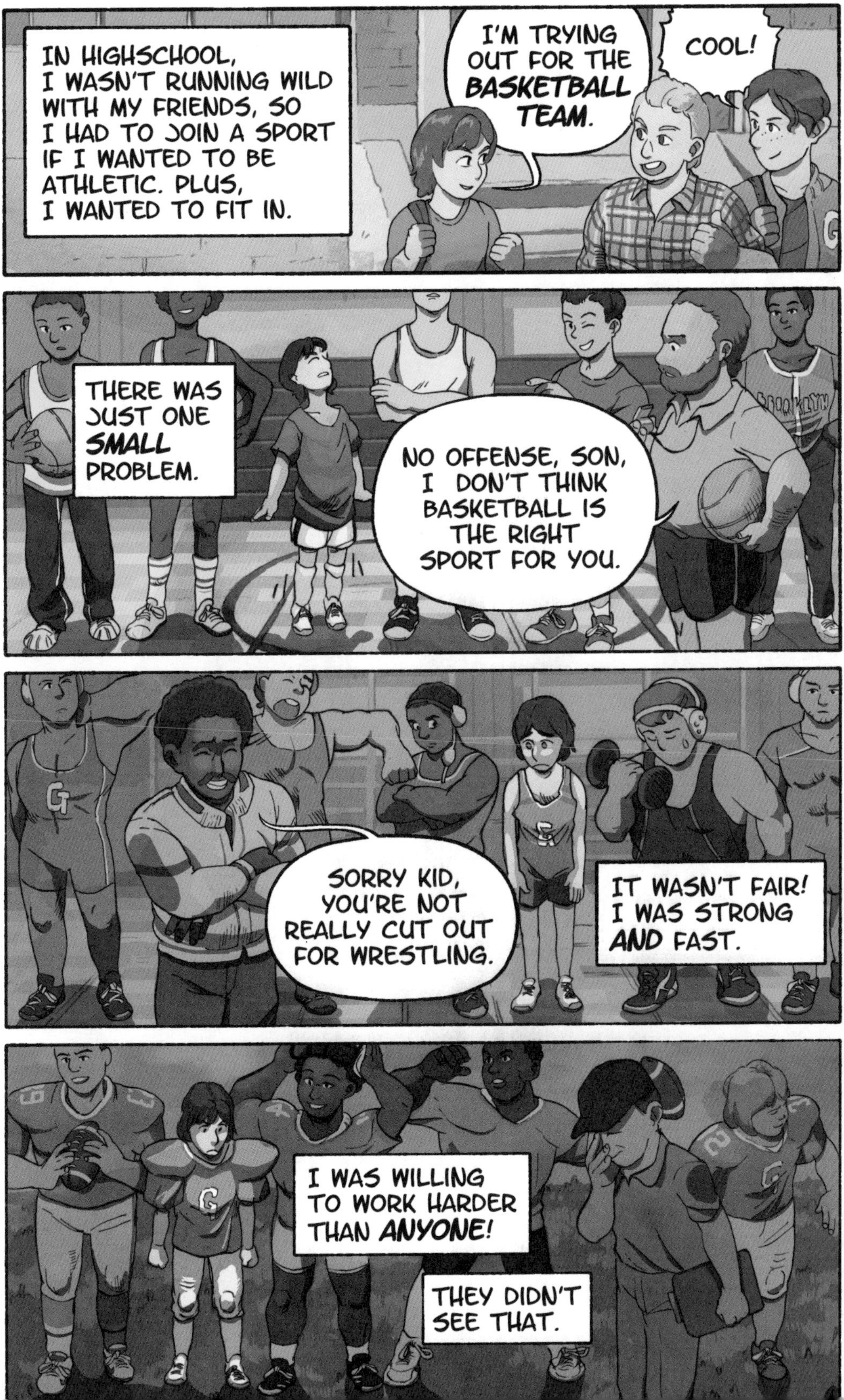
IN HIGHSCHOOL, I WASN'T RUNNING WILD WITH MY FRIENDS, SO I HAD TO JOIN A SPORT IF I WANTED TO BE ATHLETIC. PLUS, I WANTED TO FIT IN.
I'M TRYING OUT FOR THE BASKETBALL TEAM.
COOL!
THERE WAS JUST ONE SMALL PROBLEM.
NO OFFENSE, SON, I DON'T THINK BASKETBALL IS THE RIGHT SPORT FOR YOU.
SORRY KID, YOU'RE NOT REALLY CUT OUT FOR WRESTLING.
IT WASN'T FAIR! I WAS STRONG AND FAST.
I WAS WILLING TO WORK HARDER THAN ANYONE!
THEY DIDN'T SEE THAT.

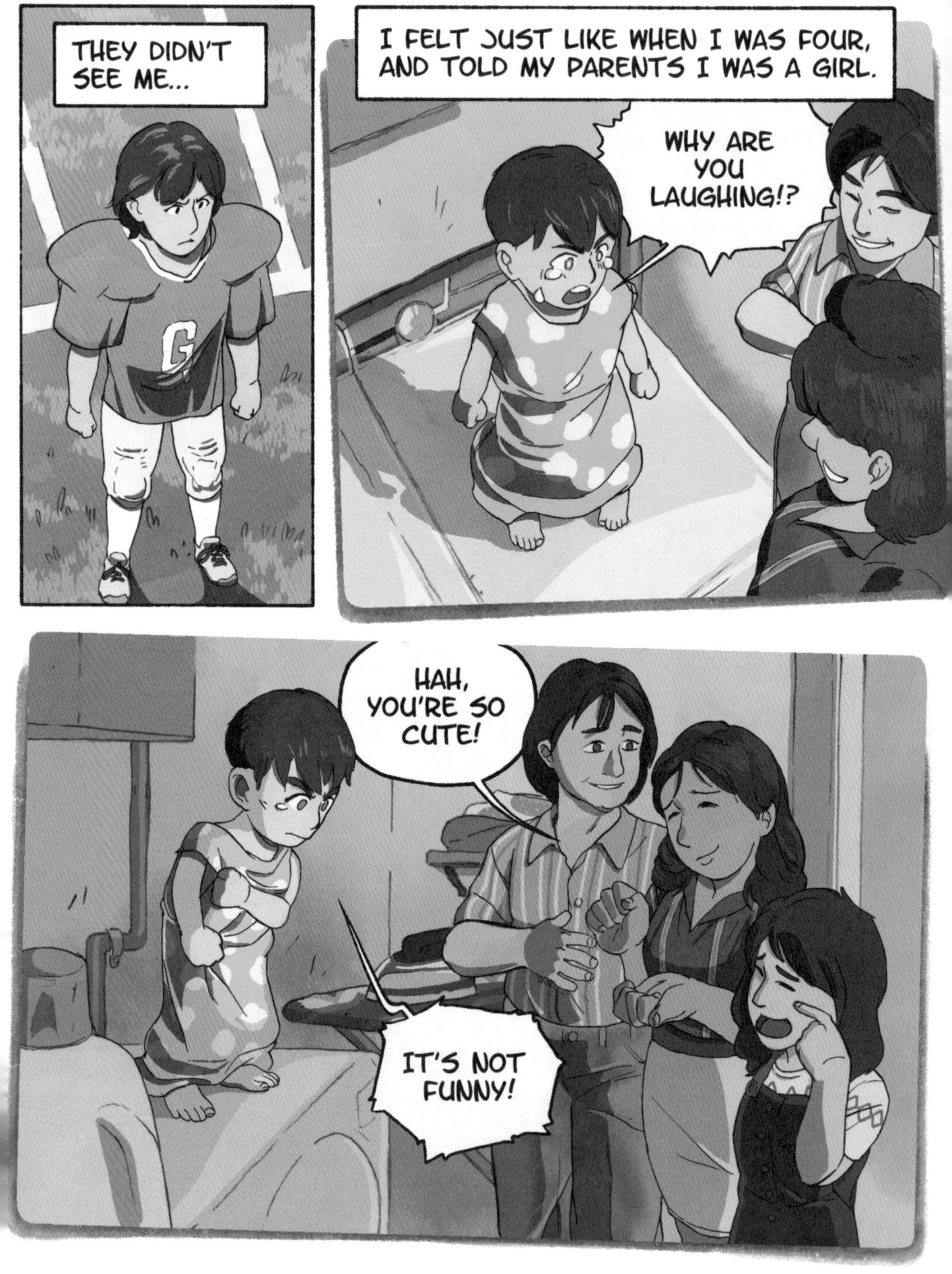
THEY DIDN'T SEE ME...
I FELT JUST LIKE WHEN I WAS FOUR, AND TOLD MY PARENTS I WAS A GIRL.
WHY ARE YOU LAUGHING!?
HAH, YOU'RE SO CUTE!
IT'S NOT FUNNY!

THEY DIDN'T SEE ME,
EITHER.

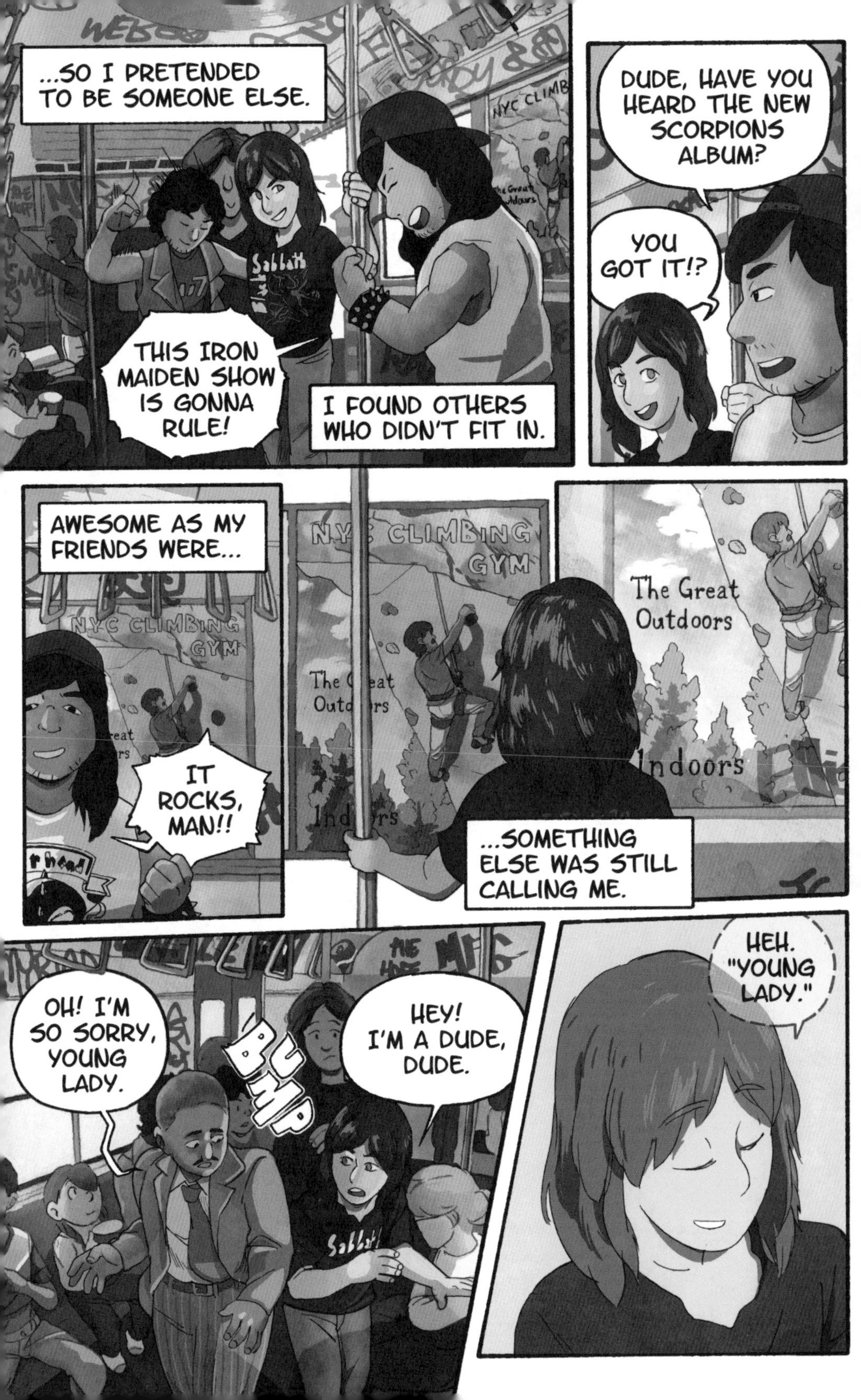
...SO I PRETENDED TO BE SOMEONE ELSE.
THIS IRON MAIDEN SHOW IS GONNA RULE!
I FOUND OTHERS WHO DIDN'T FIT IN.
DUDE, HAVE YOU HEARD THE NEW SCORPIONS ALBUM?
YOU GOT IT!?
AWESOME AS MY FRIENDS WERE...
NYC CLIMBING GYM
The Great Outdoors
IT ROCKS, MAN!!
Indoors
...SOMETHING ELSE WAS STILL CALLING ME.
OH! I'M SO SORRY, YOUNG LADY.
BUMP
HEY! I'M A DUDE, DUDE.
HEH. "YOUNG LADY."

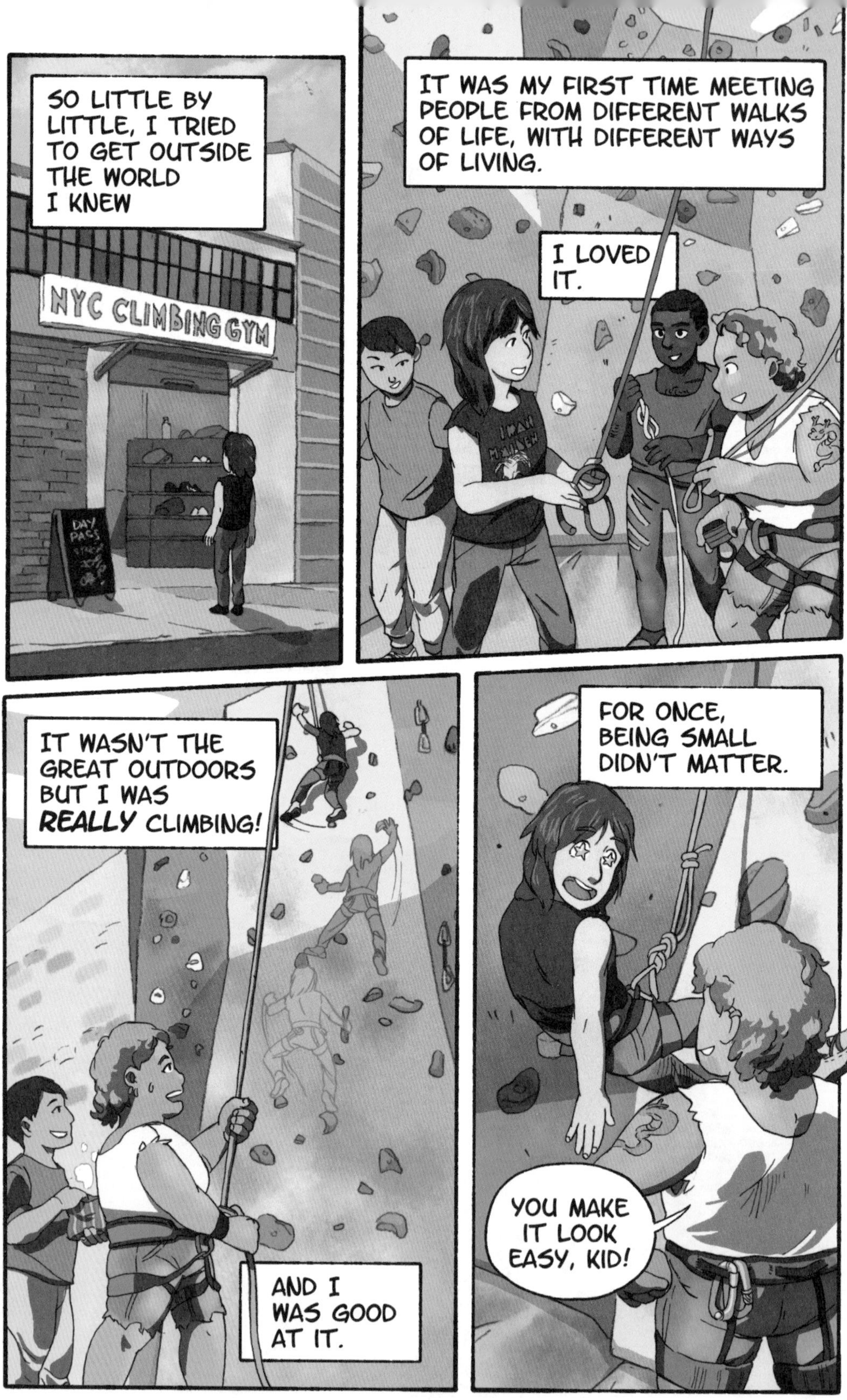
SO LITTLE BY LITTLE, I TRIED TO GET OUTSIDE THE WORLD I KNEW
NYC CLIMBING GYM
IT WAS MY FIRST TIME MEETING PEOPLE FROM DIFFERENT WALKS OF LIFE, WITH DIFFERENT WAYS OF LIVING.
I LOVED IT.
IT WASN'T THE GREAT OUTDOORS BUT I WAS ***REALLY*** CLIMBING!
AND I WAS GOOD AT IT.
FOR ONCE, BEING SMALL DIDN'T MATTER.
YOU MAKE IT LOOK EASY, KID!

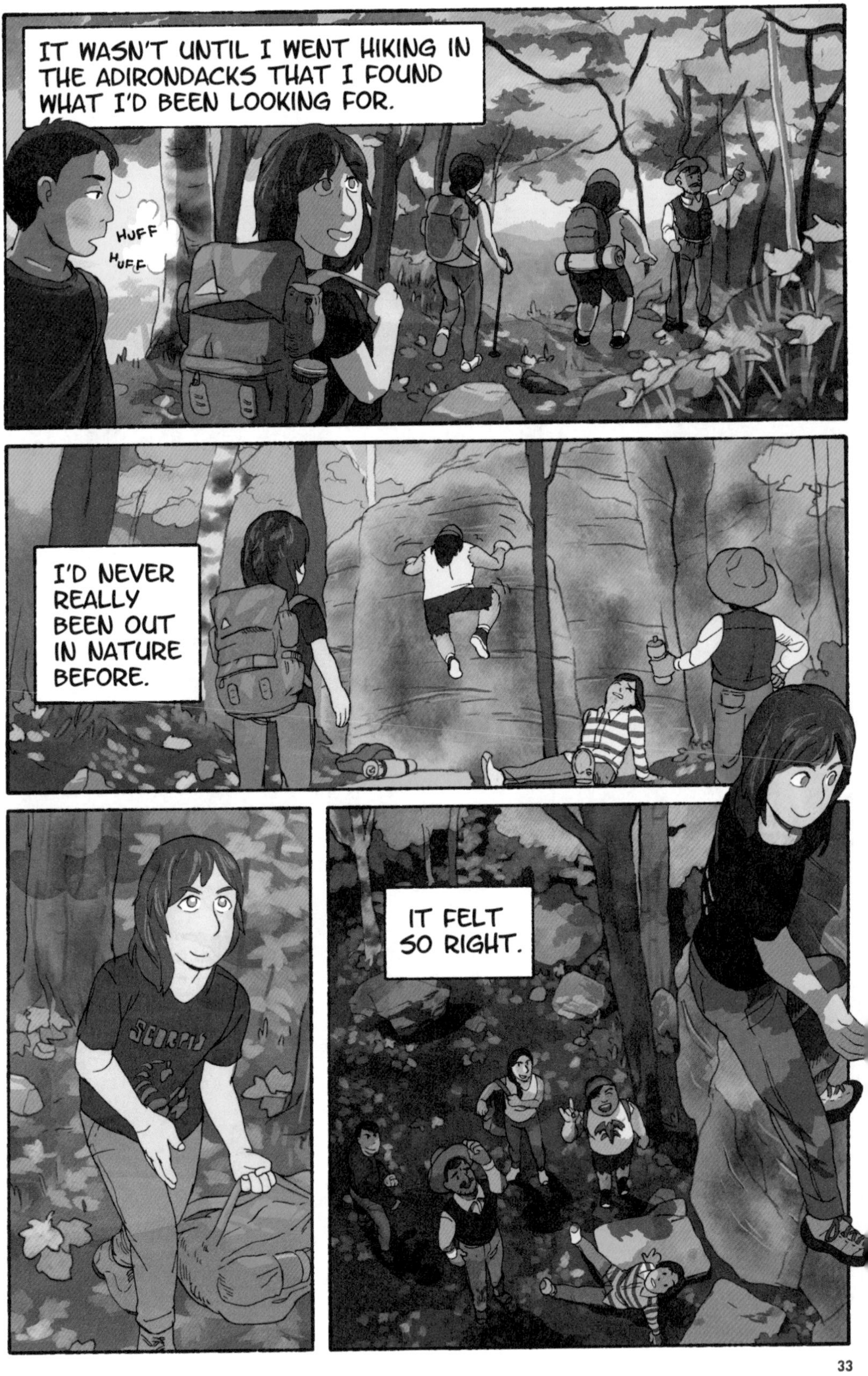
IT WASN'T UNTIL I WENT HIKING IN THE ADIRONDACKS THAT I FOUND WHAT I'D BEEN LOOKING FOR.
HUFF
HUFF
I'D NEVER REALLY BEEN OUT IN NATURE BEFORE.
SCORPIO
IT FELT SO RIGHT.

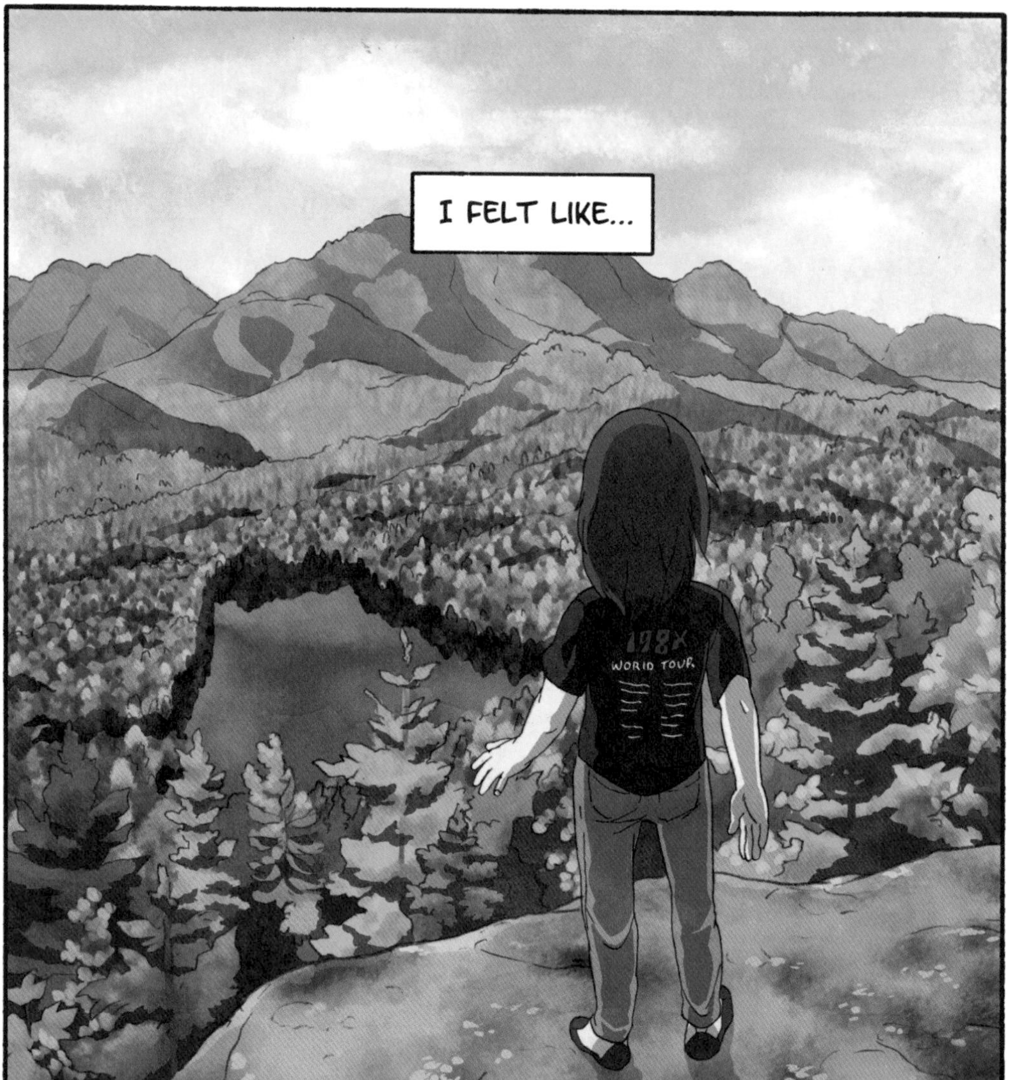
I FELT LIKE...
198X
WORLD TOUR

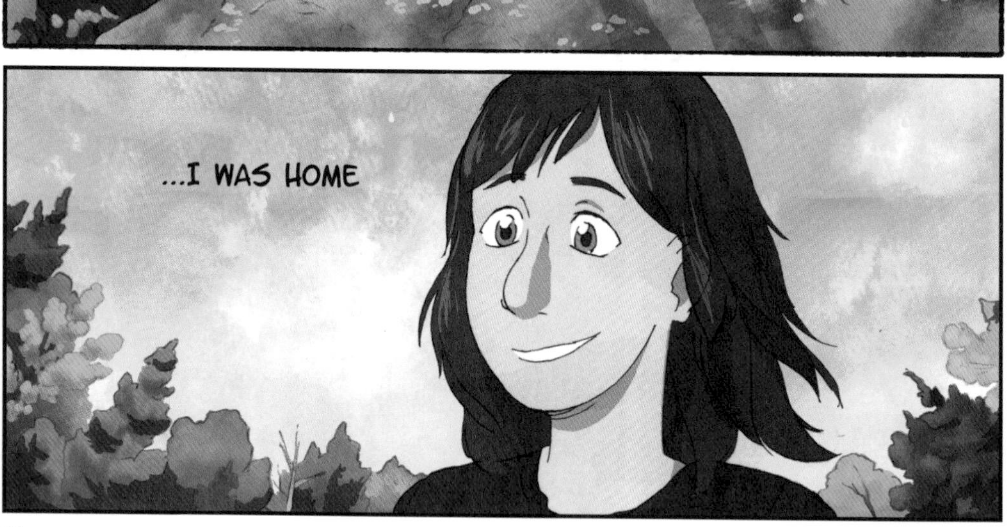
...I WAS HOME

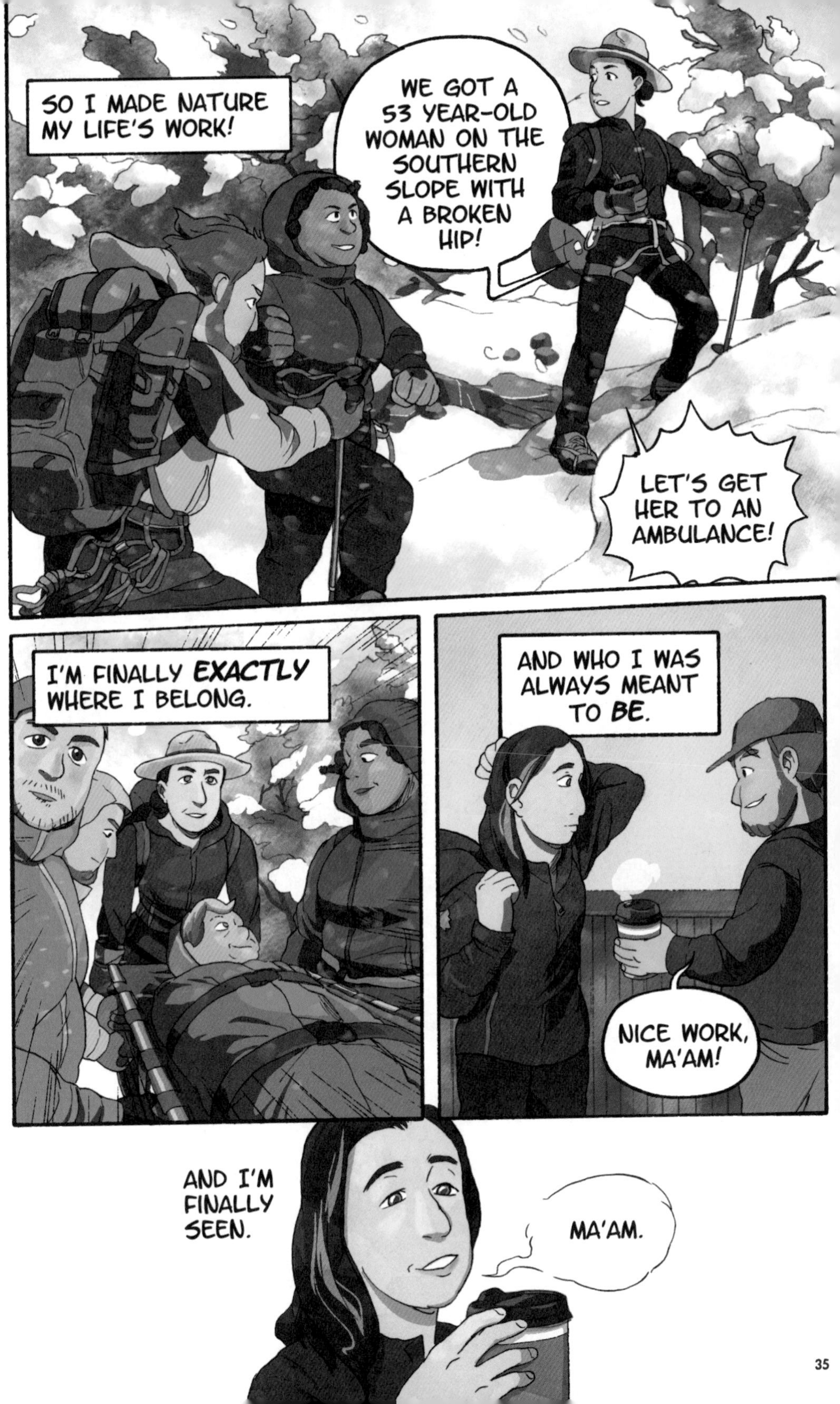
SO I MADE NATURE MY LIFE'S WORK!
WE GOT A 53 YEAR-OLD WOMAN ON THE SOUTHERN SLOPE WITH A BROKEN HIP!
LET'S GET HER TO AN AMBULANCE!
I'M FINALLY **EXACTLY** WHERE I BELONG.
AND WHO I WAS ALWAYS MEANT TO **BE**.
NICE WORK, MA'AM!
AND I'M FINALLY SEEN.
MA'AM.

BECOMING BROOKE GUINAN

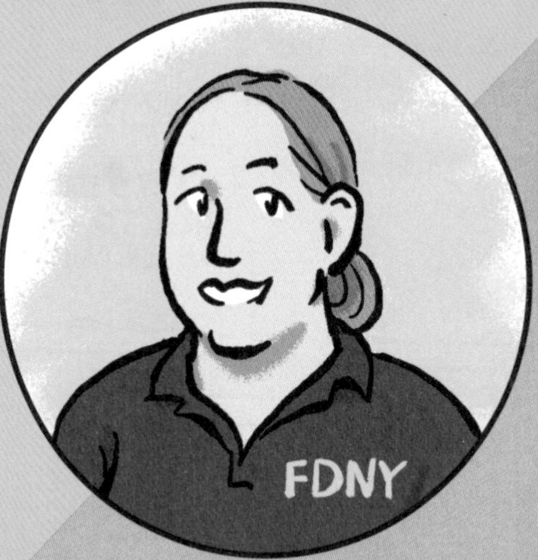
FDNY

Brooke Guinan is a non-binary firefighting nerd born and raised in New York. When she is not hanging about at home with their husband and furry kids in the woods of New York State, they can be found playing *Pokémon Go* or spending time with her supportive family.

Written by Sammy Lisel
Illustrated by Hazel Newlevant

Hazel Newlevant is a cartoonist and comics editor who lives in Brooklyn with their two cats, Xanthippe and Calypso. When they're not drawing, Hazel likes doing karaoke, watching drag shows, and learning about queer history and gender justice.

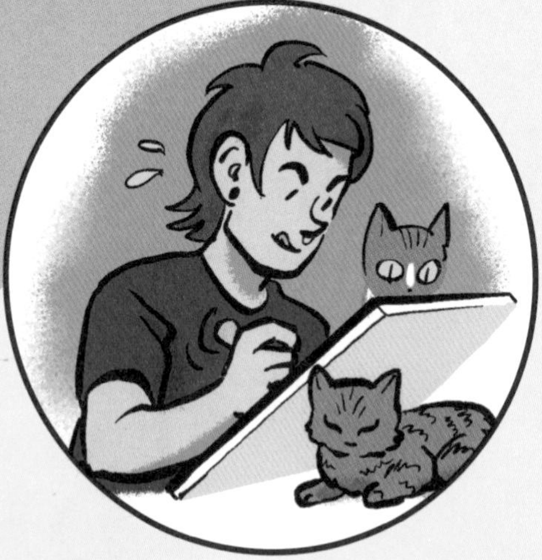

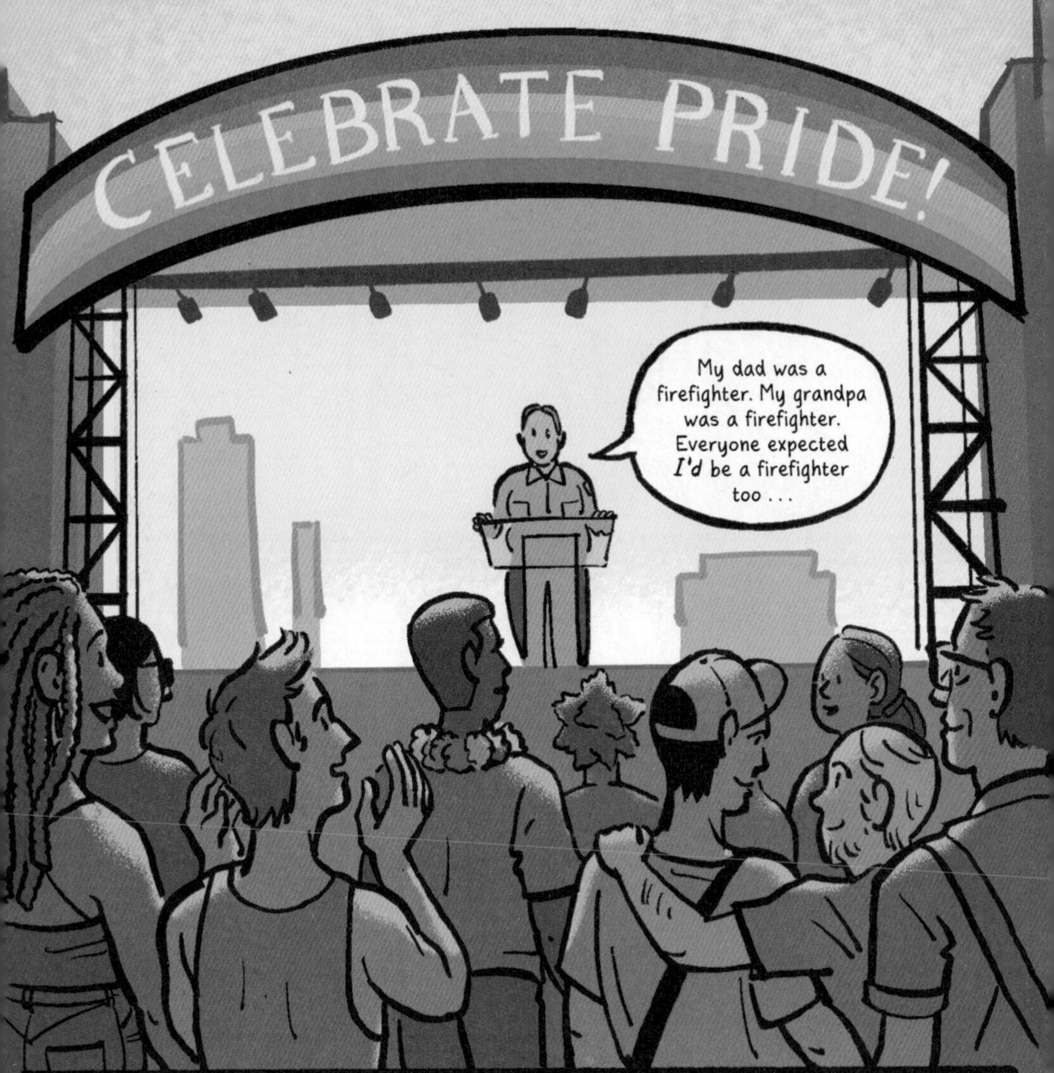
CELEBRATE PRIDE!
My dad was a firefighter. My grandpa was a firefighter. Everyone expected *I'd* be a firefighter too . . .

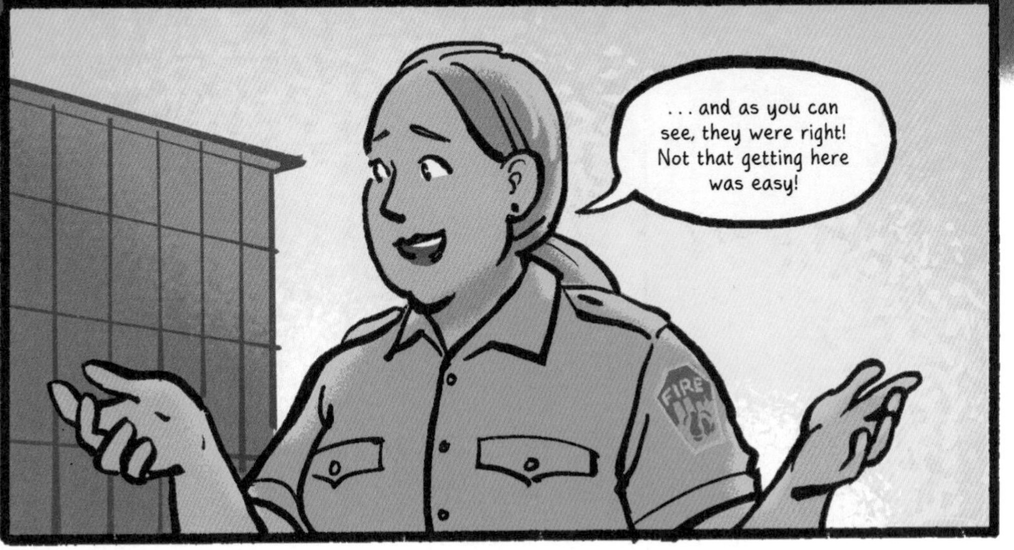
. . . and as you can see, they were right! Not that getting here was easy!
FIRE

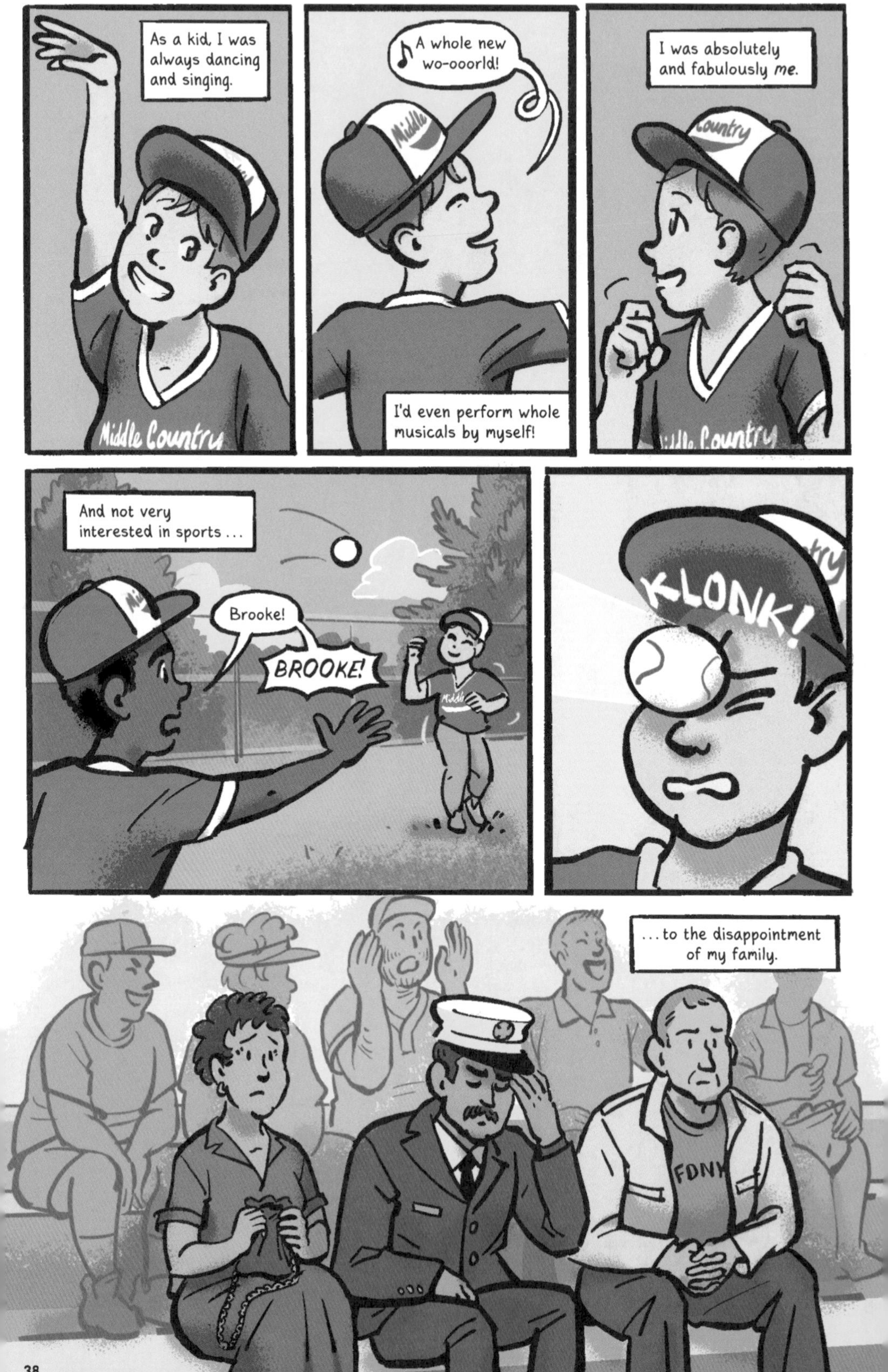
As a kid, I was always dancing and singing.
Middle Country
A whole new wo-ooorld!
Middle
I'd even perform whole musicals by myself!
I was absolutely and fabulously *me*.
Country
And not very interested in sports . . .
Brooke!
BROOKE!
KLONK!
. . . to the disappointment of my family.
FDNY

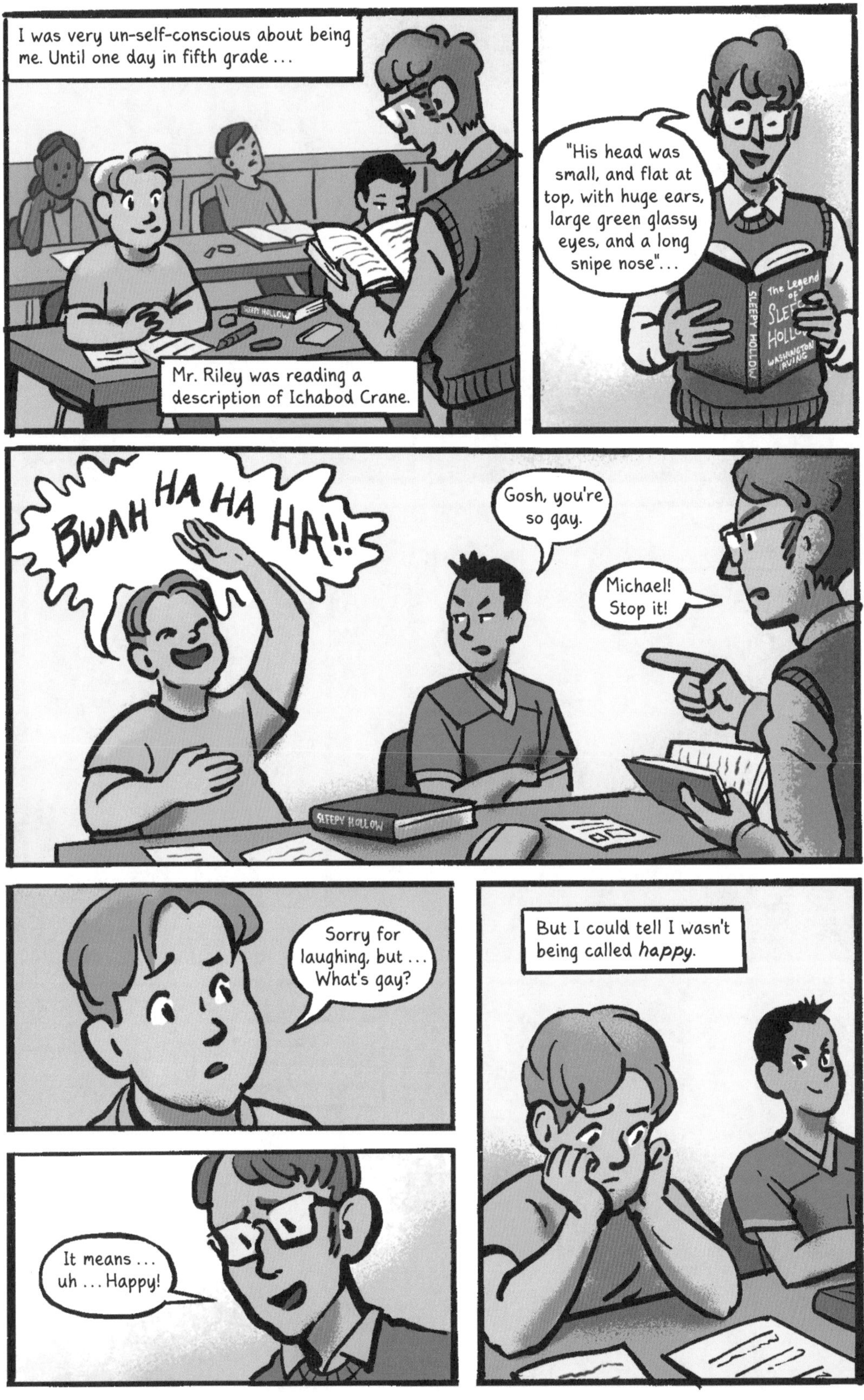

I was very un-self-conscious about being me. Until one day in fifth grade . . .
SLEEPY HOLLOW
Mr. Riley was reading a description of Ichabod Crane.
"His head was small, and flat at top, with huge ears, large green glassy eyes, and a long snipe nose". . .
The Legend of
SLEEPY HOLLOW
WASHINGTON IRVING
BWAH HA HA HA!!
Gosh, you're so gay.
Michael! Stop it!
SLEEPY HOLLOW
Sorry for laughing, but . . . What's gay?
It means . . . uh . . . Happy!
But I could tell I wasn't being called *happy*.

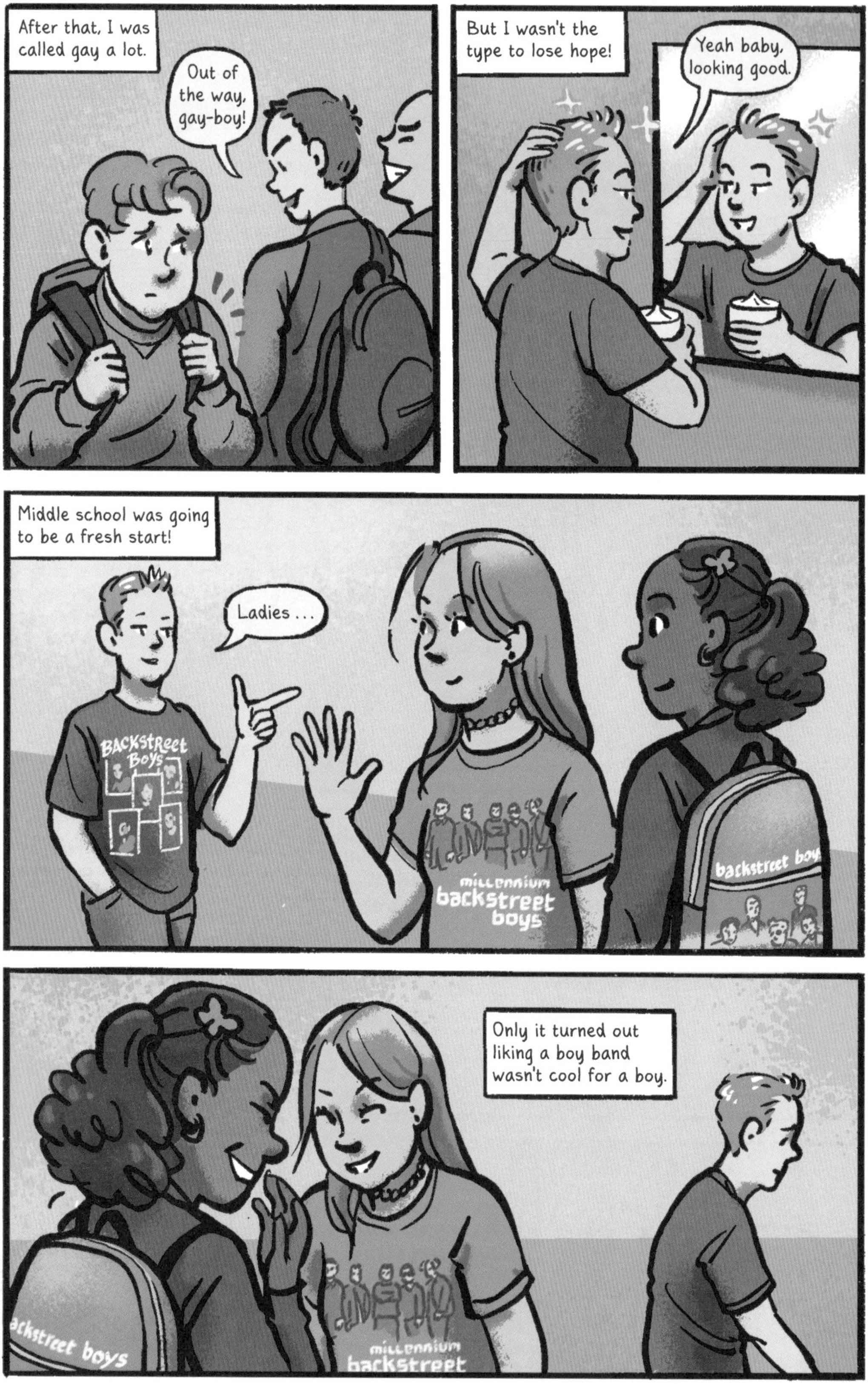
After that, I was called gay a lot.
Out of the way, gay-boy!
But I wasn't the type to lose hope!
Yeah baby, looking good.
Middle school was going to be a fresh start!
Ladies ...
BACKSTREET Boys
millennium backstreet boys
backstreet boys
Only it turned out liking a boy band wasn't cool for a boy.
ackstreet boys
millennium backstreet

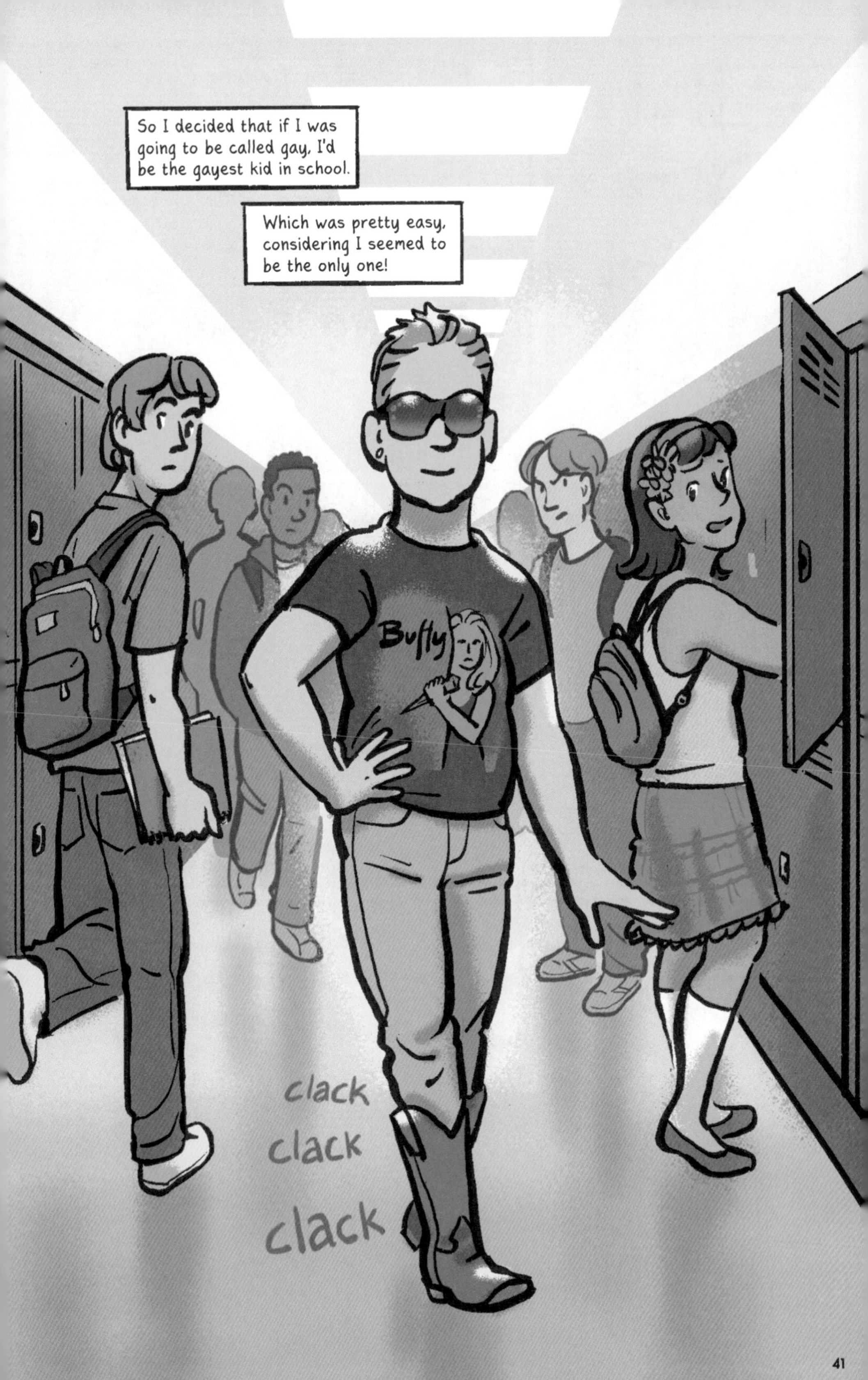
So I decided that if I was going to be called gay, I'd be the gayest kid in school.
Which was pretty easy, considering I seemed to be the only one!
Buffy
clack
clack
clack

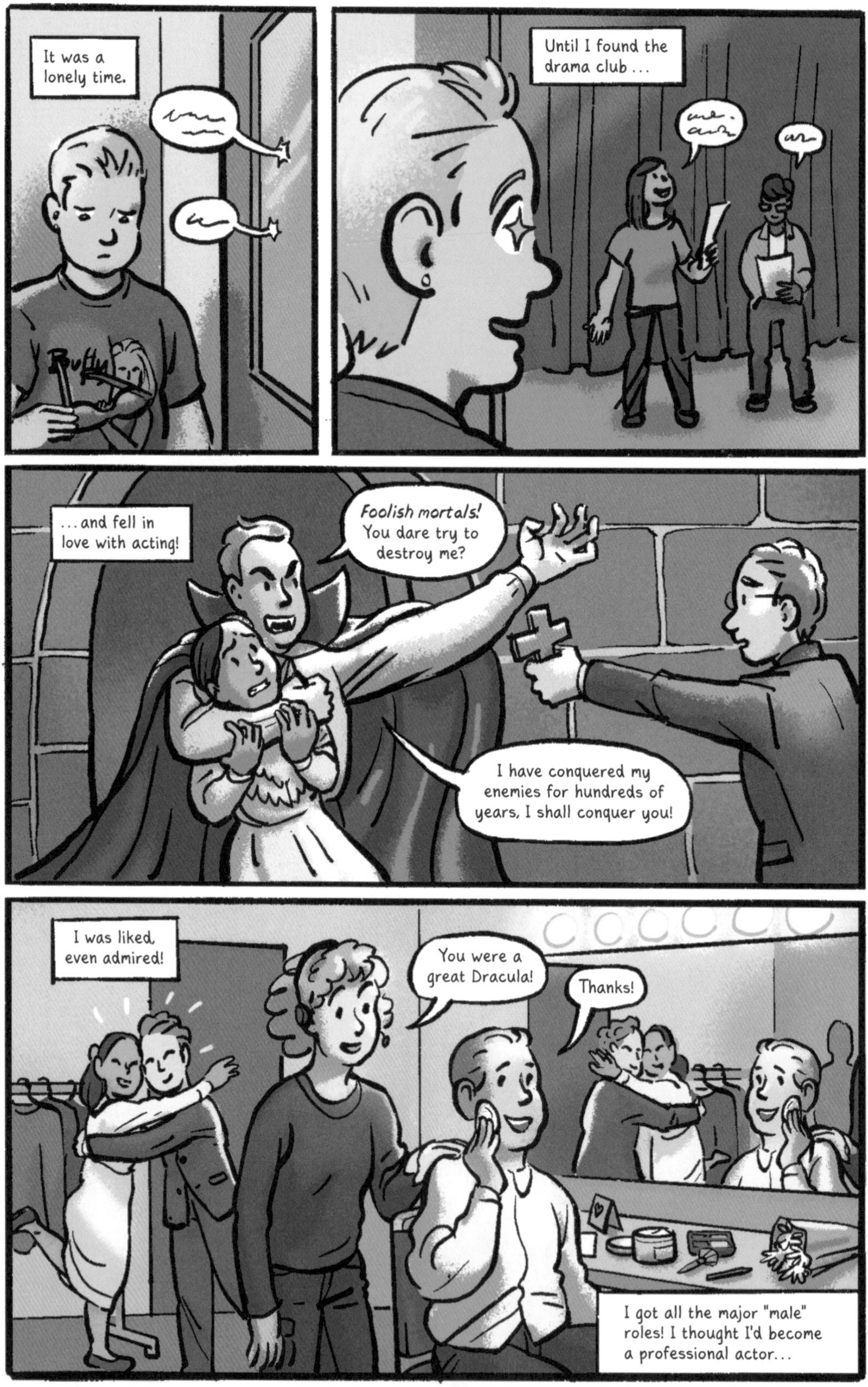
It was a lonely time.
Until I found the drama club . . .
. . . and fell in love with acting!
Foolish mortals! You dare try to destroy me?
I have conquered my enemies for hundreds of years, I shall conquer you!
I was liked, even admired!
You were a great Dracula!
Thanks!
I got all the major "male" roles! I thought I'd become a professional actor . . .

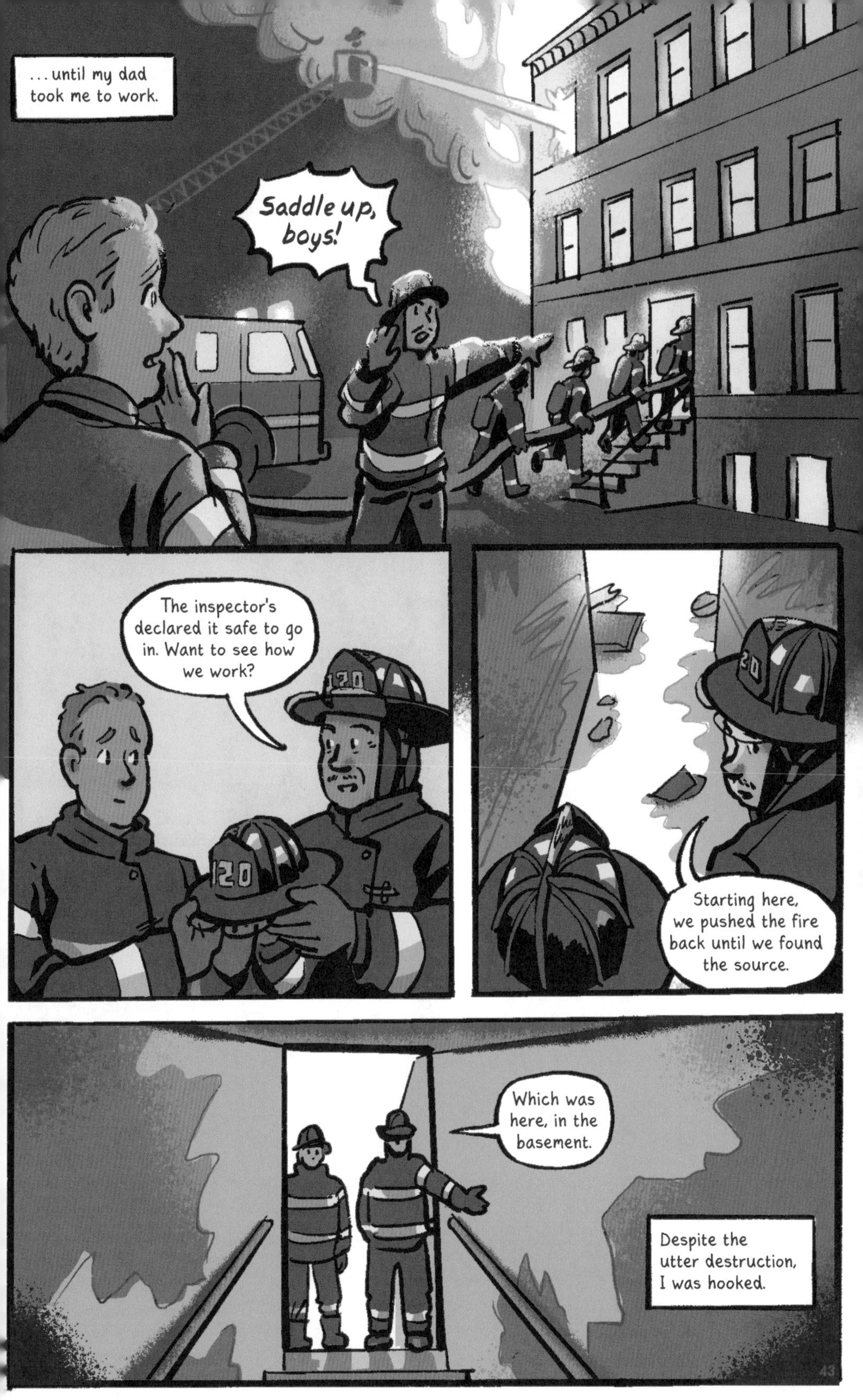
...until my dad took me to work.
Saddle up, boys!
The inspector's declared it safe to go in. Want to see how we work?
Starting here, we pushed the fire back until we found the source.
Which was here, in the basement.
Despite the utter destruction, I was hooked.

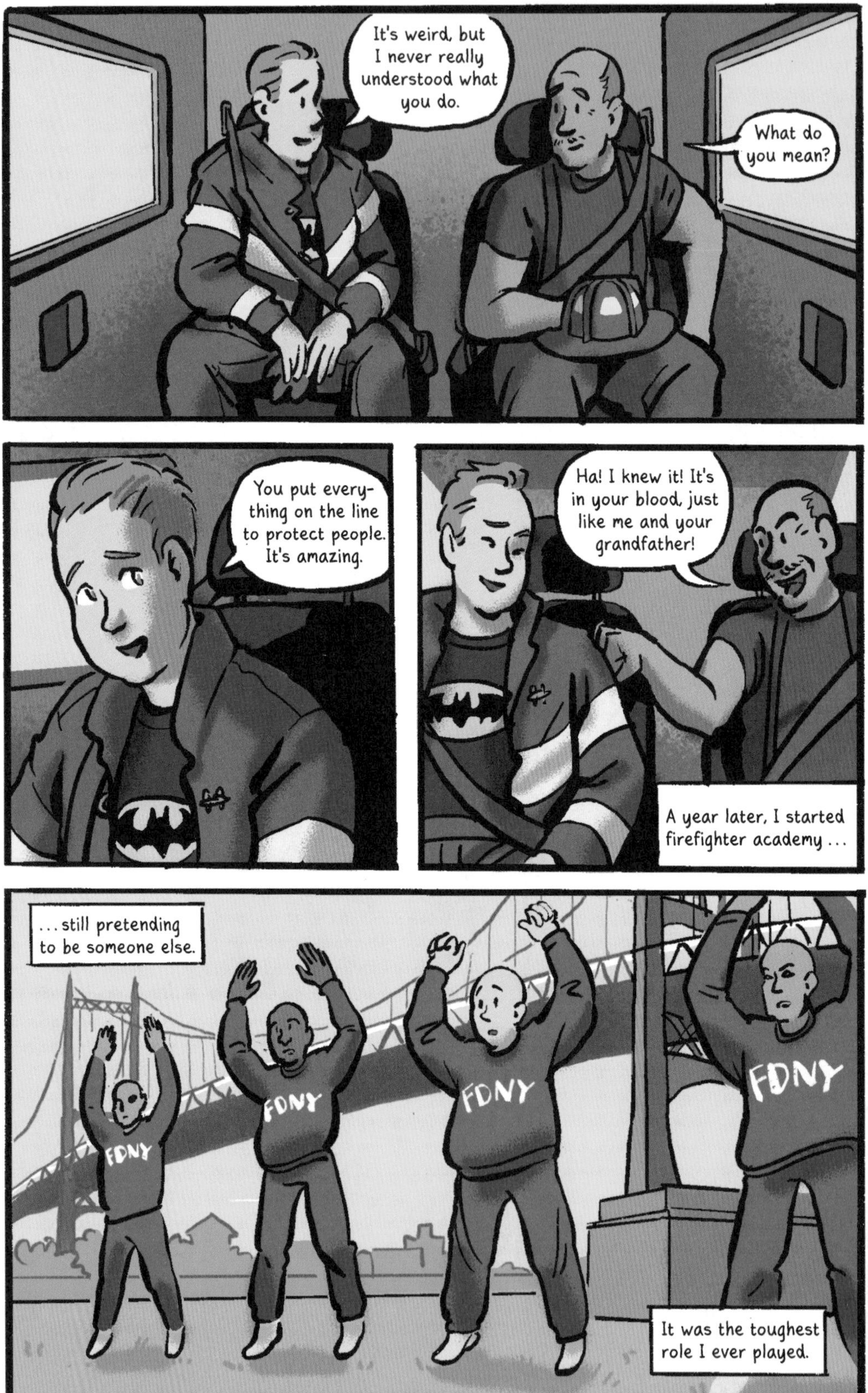
It's weird, but I never really understood what you do.
What do you mean?
You put everything on the line to protect people. It's amazing.
Ha! I knew it! It's in your blood, just like me and your grandfather!
A year later, I started firefighter academy . . .
. . . still pretending to be someone else.
FDNY
FDNY
FDNY
FDNY
It was the toughest role I ever played.

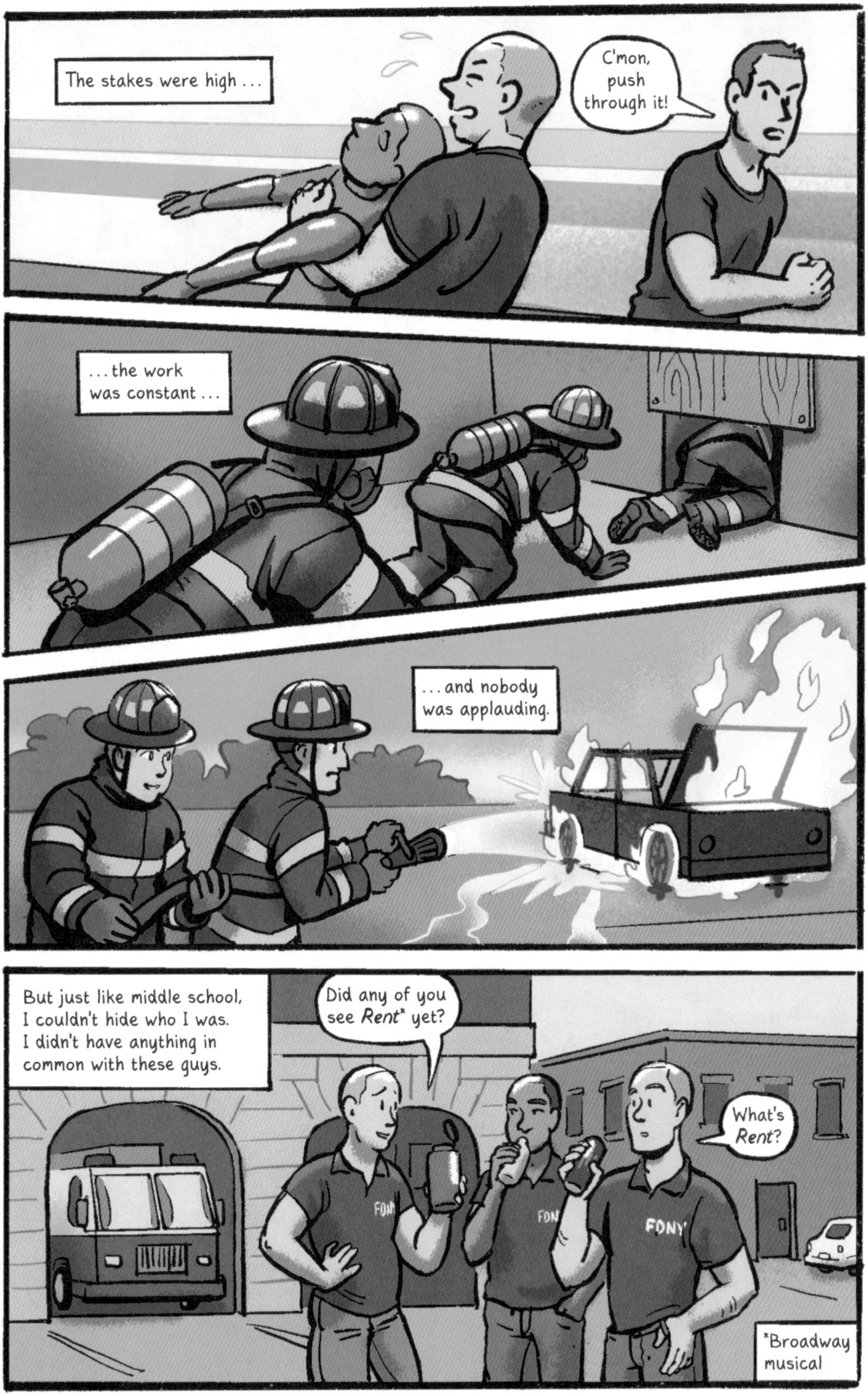
The stakes were high . . .
C'mon, push through it!
. . . the work was constant . . .
. . . and nobody was applauding.
But just like middle school, I couldn't hide who I was. I didn't have anything in common with these guys.
Did any of you see *Rent** yet?
What's *Rent*?
FDNY
FDNY
FDNY
*Broadway musical

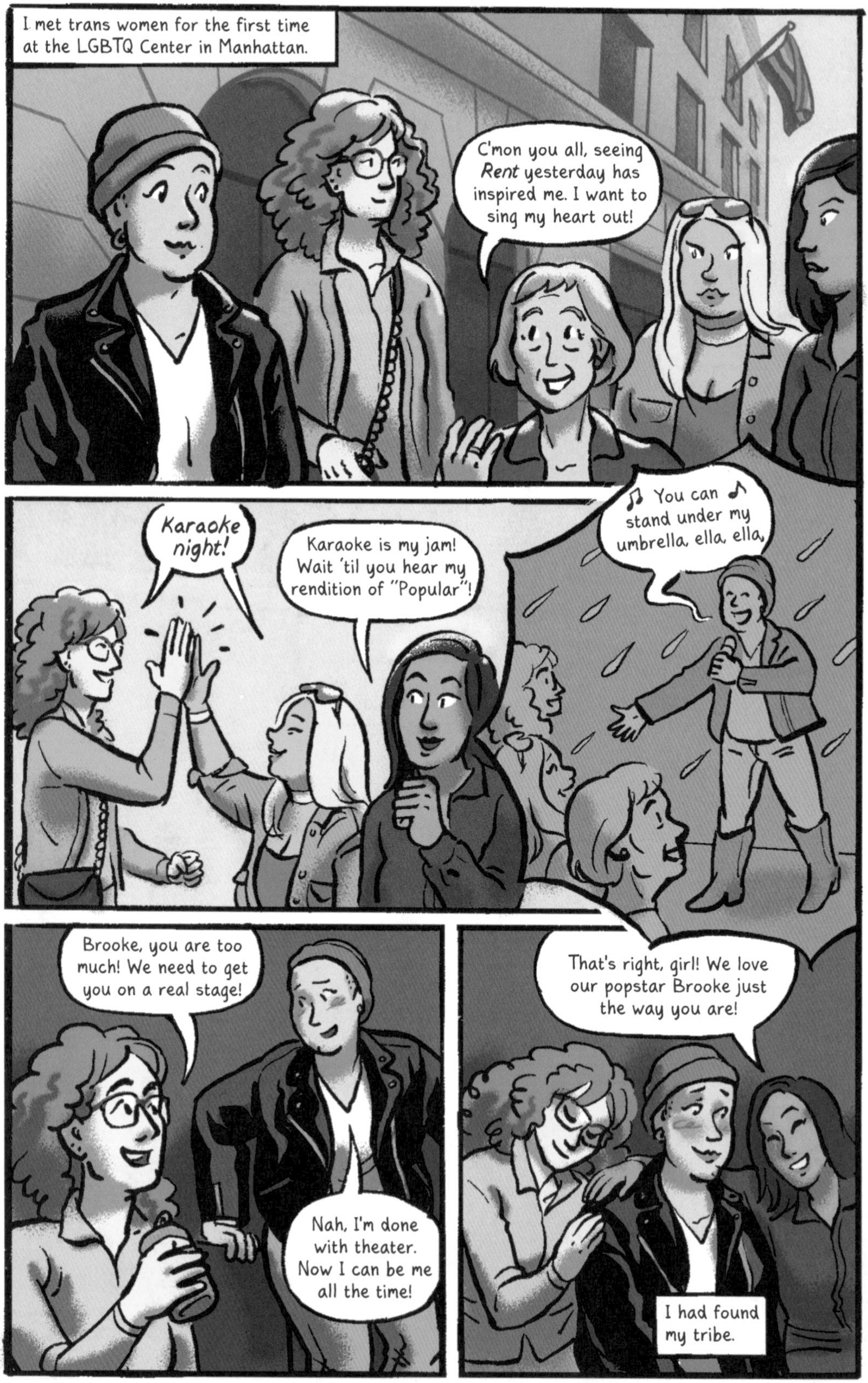
I met trans women for the first time at the LGBTQ Center in Manhattan.
C'mon you all, seeing *Rent* yesterday has inspired me. I want to sing my heart out!
Karaoke night!
Karaoke is my jam! Wait 'til you hear my rendition of "Popular"!
♫ You can ♪ stand under my umbrella, ella, ella,
Brooke, you are too much! We need to get you on a real stage!
Nah, I'm done with theater. Now I can be me all the time!
That's right, girl! We love our popstar Brooke just the way you are!
I had found my tribe.

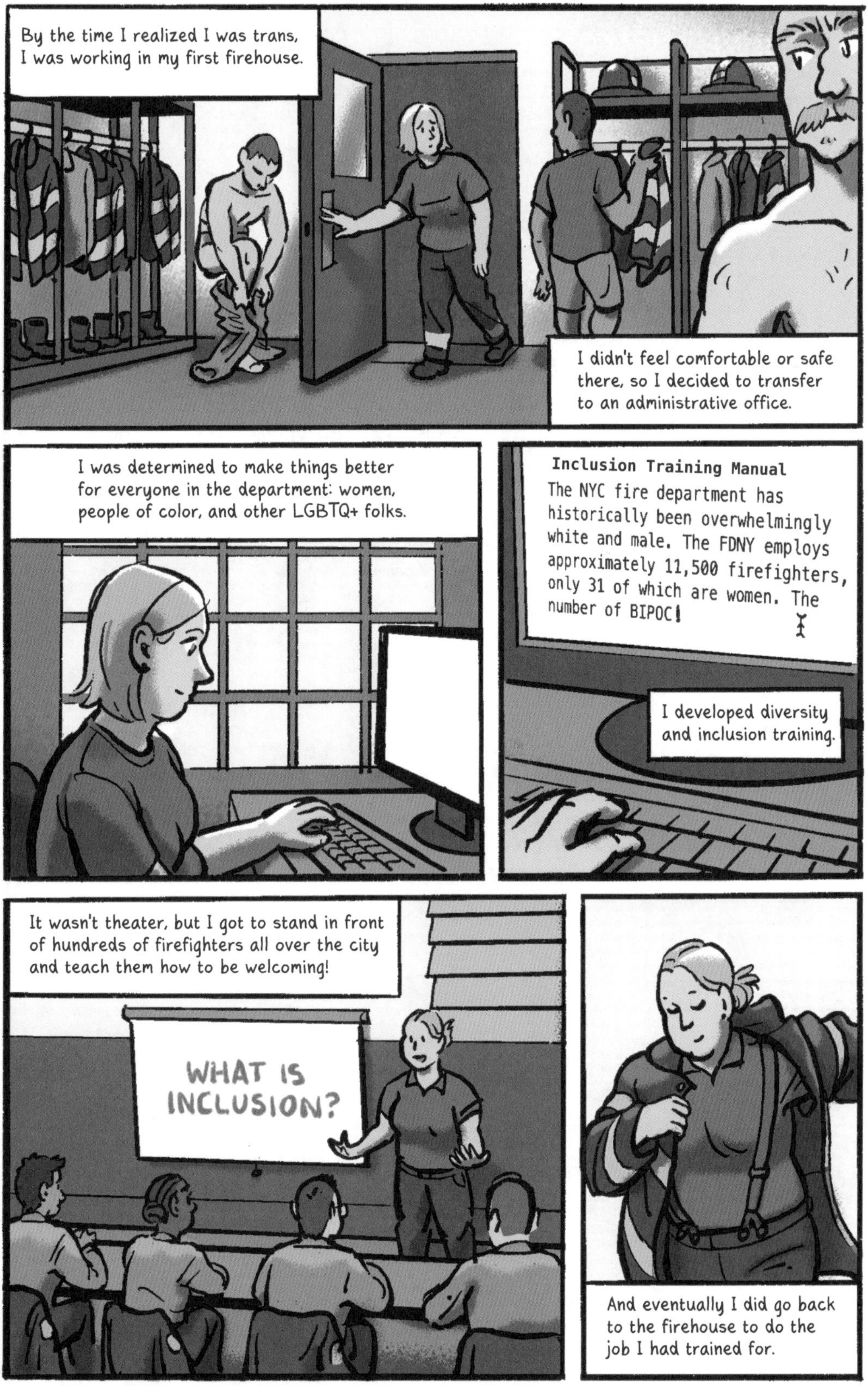
By the time I realized I was trans, I was working in my first firehouse.
I didn't feel comfortable or safe there, so I decided to transfer to an administrative office.
I was determined to make things better for everyone in the department: women, people of color, and other LGBTQ+ folks.
Inclusion Training Manual
The NYC fire department has historically been overwhelmingly white and male. The FDNY employs approximately 11,500 firefighters, only 31 of which are women. The number of BIPOC
I developed diversity and inclusion training.
It wasn't theater, but I got to stand in front of hundreds of firefighters all over the city and teach them how to be welcoming!
WHAT IS INCLUSION?
And eventually I did go back to the firehouse to do the job I had trained for.

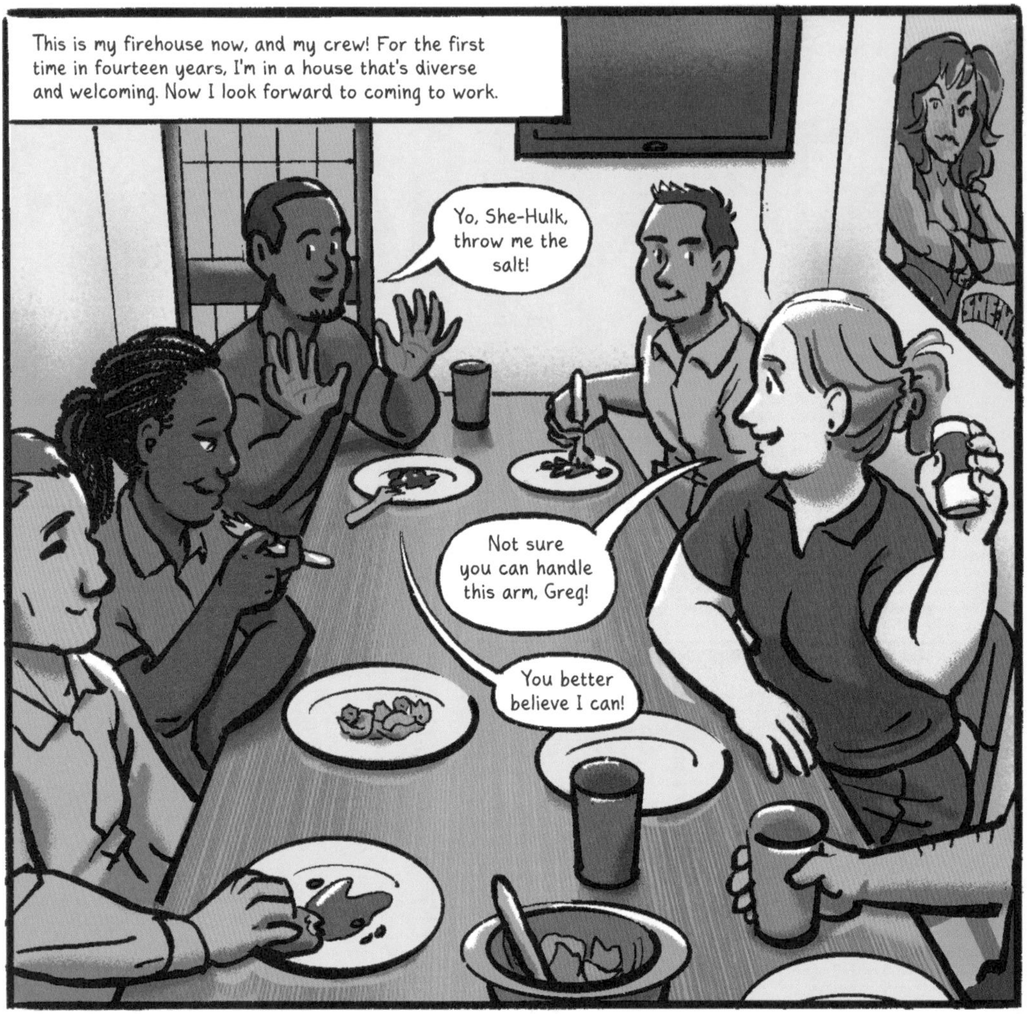
This is my firehouse now, and my crew! For the first time in fourteen years, I'm in a house that's diverse and welcoming. Now I look forward to coming to work.
Yo, She-Hulk, throw me the salt!
Not sure you can handle this arm, Greg!
You better believe I can!

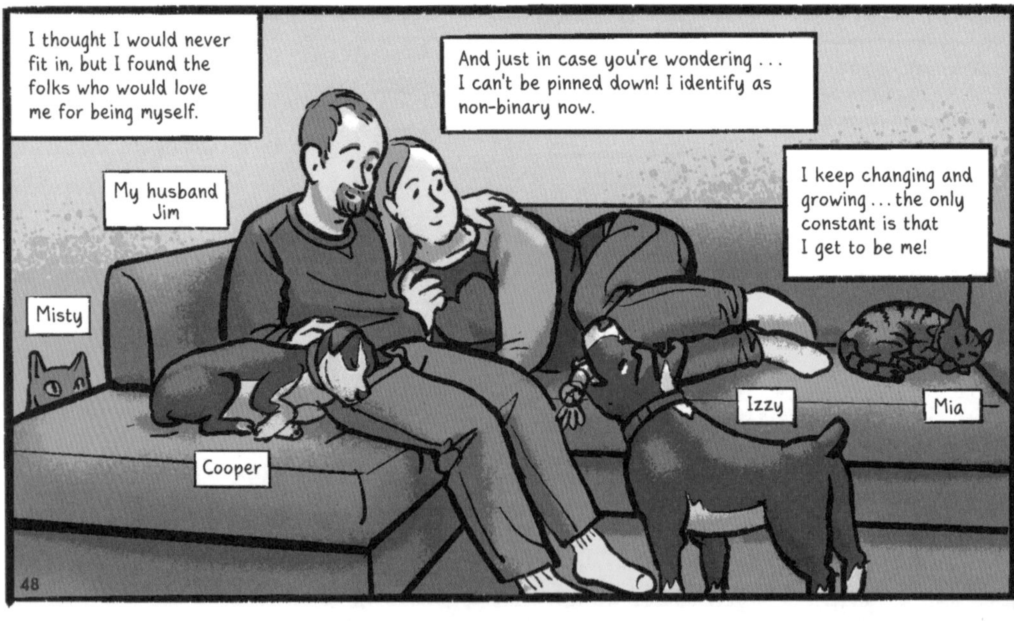
I thought I would never fit in, but I found the folks who would love me for being myself.
And just in case you're wondering . . . I can't be pinned down! I identify as non-binary now.
My husband Jim
I keep changing and growing . . . the only constant is that I get to be me!
Misty
Cooper
Izzy
Mia

BECOMING KATE STONE

Dr. Kate Stone is an English engineer and founder and CEO of the company Novalia, which develops lots of cool products using "interactive Printed Media." When she's not coming up with new inventions, Kate likes to explore the wilderness!

Written by Sammy Lisel
Illustrated by Ravi Teixeira

Ravi Teixeira is a city-slicking cowboy and cartoonist who spends most of his time drawing silly comic books about other city-slicking cowboys. He lives happily in Canada with his partner, a cat named Charlie, and a dog named Sahara.

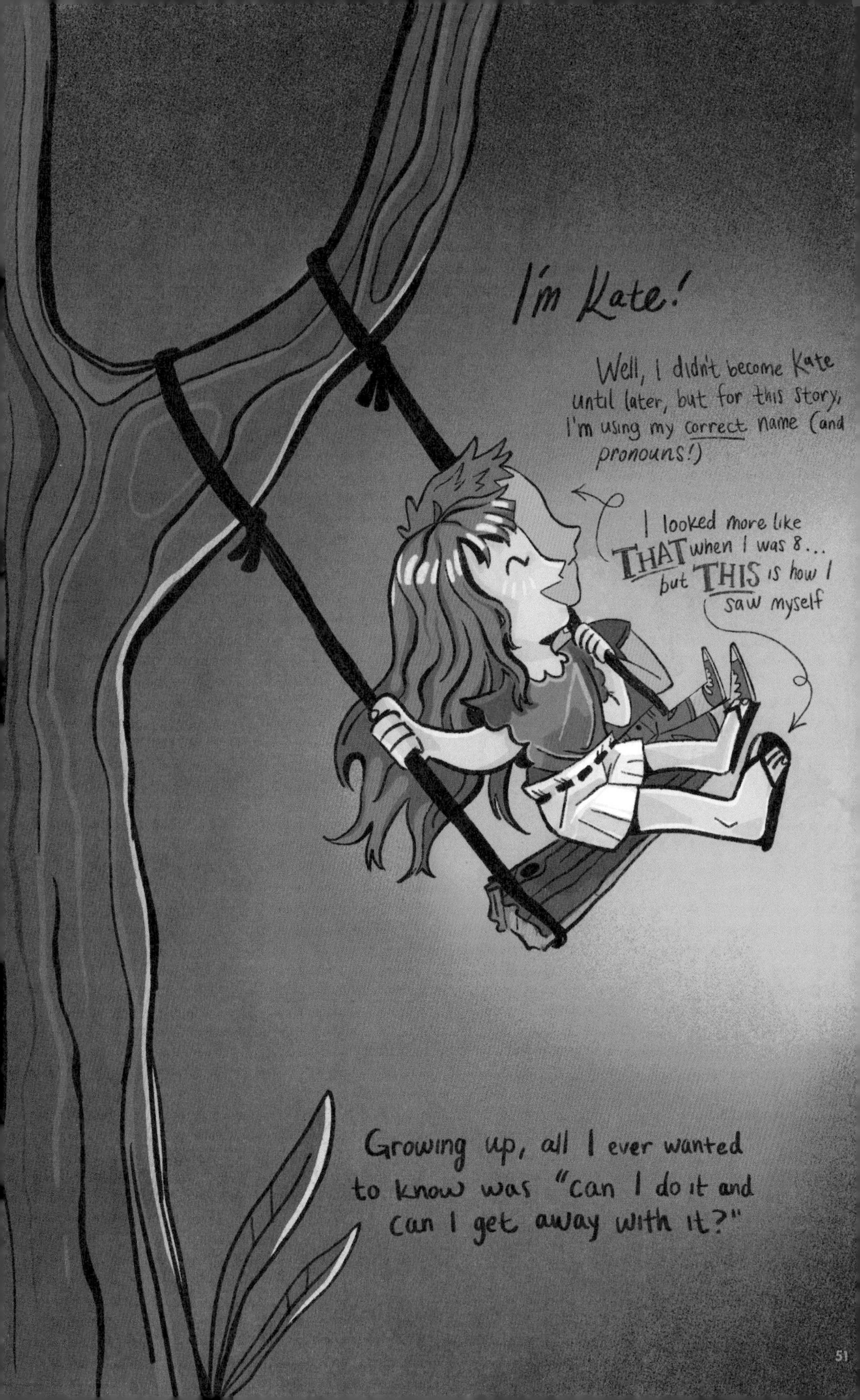
I'm Kate!
Well, I didn't become Kate until later, but for this story, I'm using my correct name (and pronouns!)
I looked more like THAT when I was 8... but THIS is how I saw myself
Growing up, all I ever wanted to know was "can I do it and can I get away with it?"

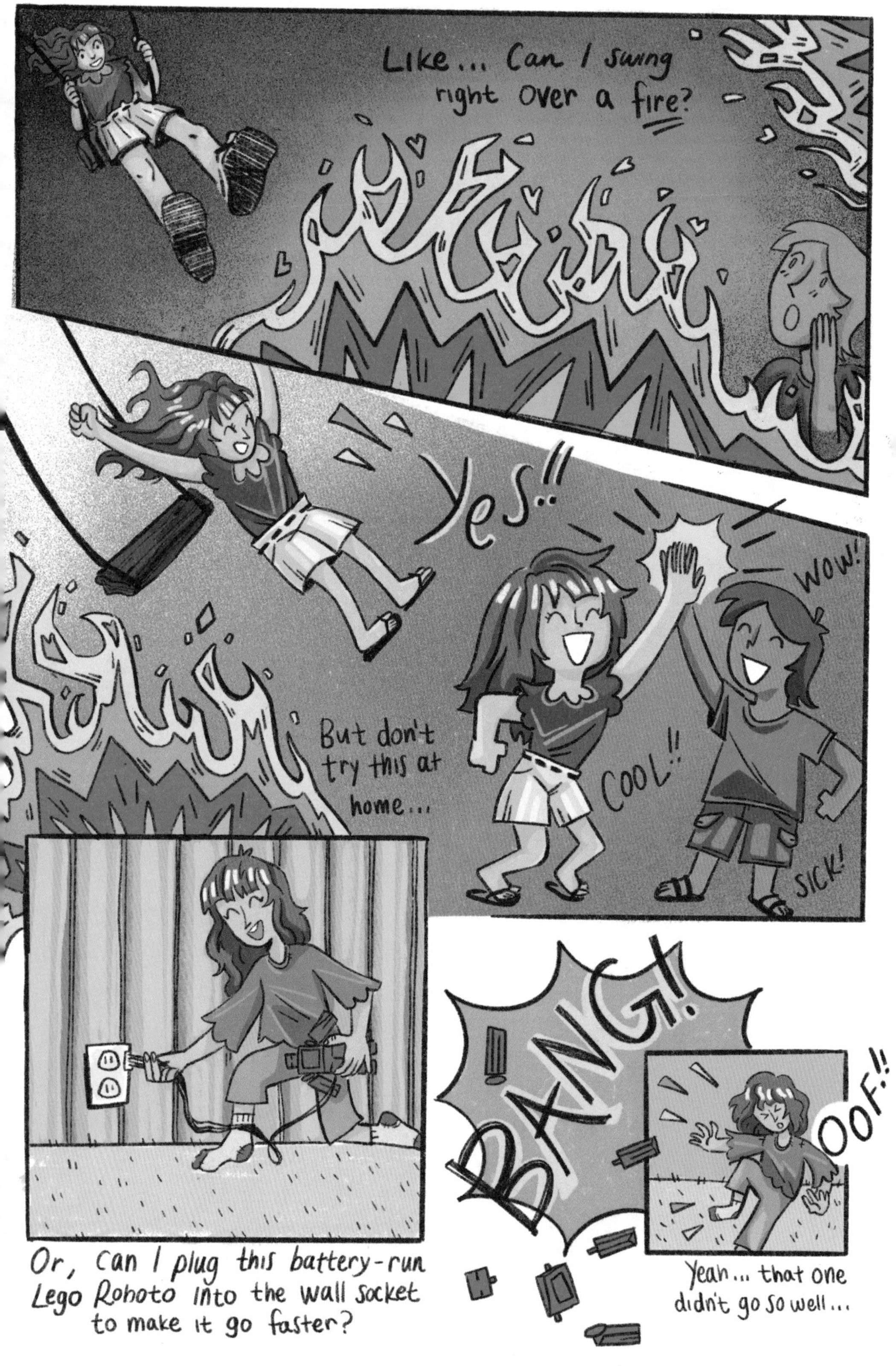
Like... Can I swing right over a fire?
Yes!!
WOW!
COOL!!
SICK!
But don't try this at home...
Or, can I plug this battery-run Lego Roboto into the wall socket to make it go faster?
BANG!
OOF!!
Yeah... that one didn't go so well...

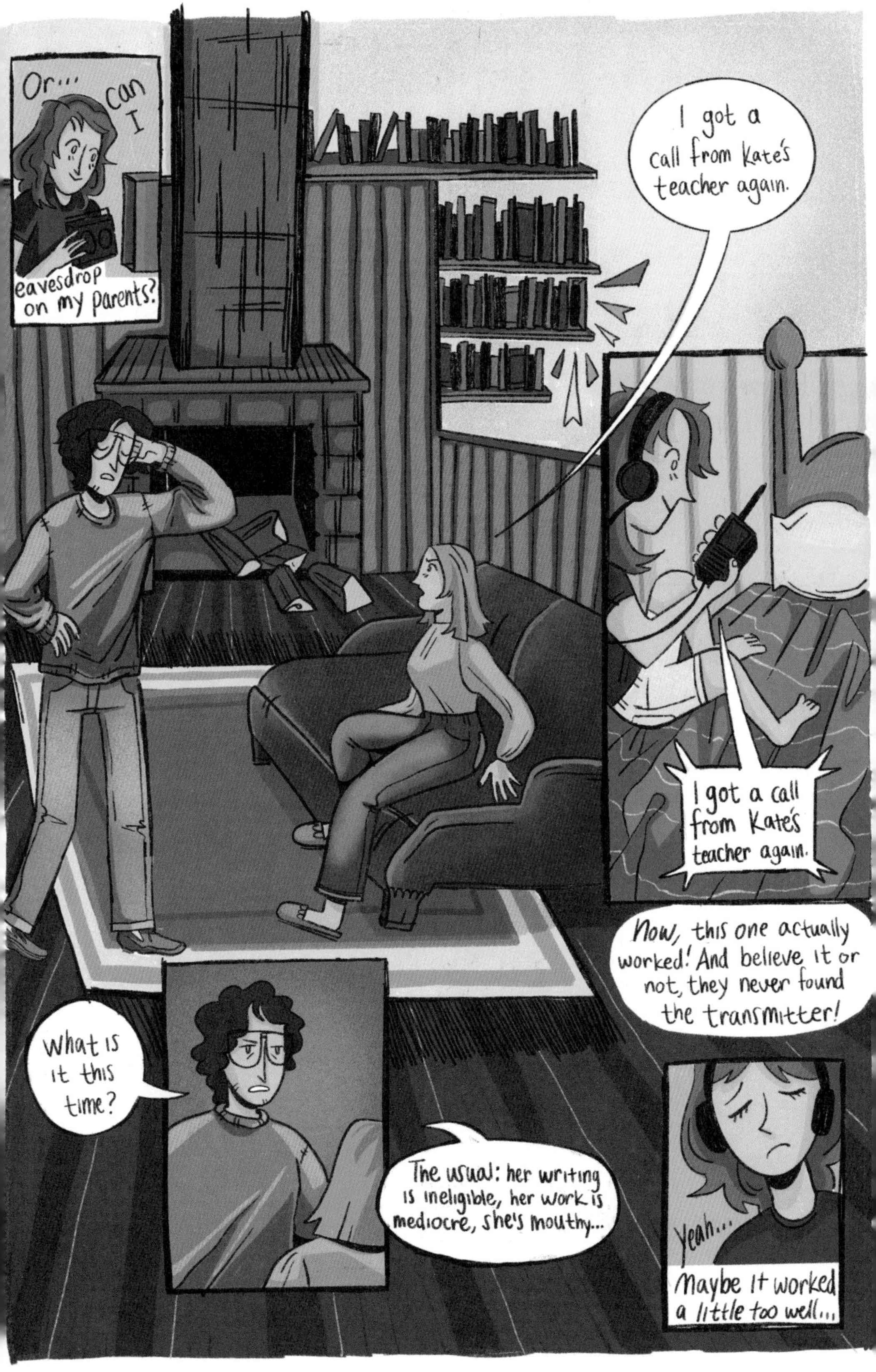
Or... can I eavesdrop on my parents?
I got a call from Kate's teacher again.
I got a call from Kate's teacher again.
Now, this one actually worked! And believe it or not, they never found the transmitter!
What is it this time?
The usual: her writing is ineligible, her work is mediocre, she's mouthy...
Yeah...
Maybe it worked a little too well...

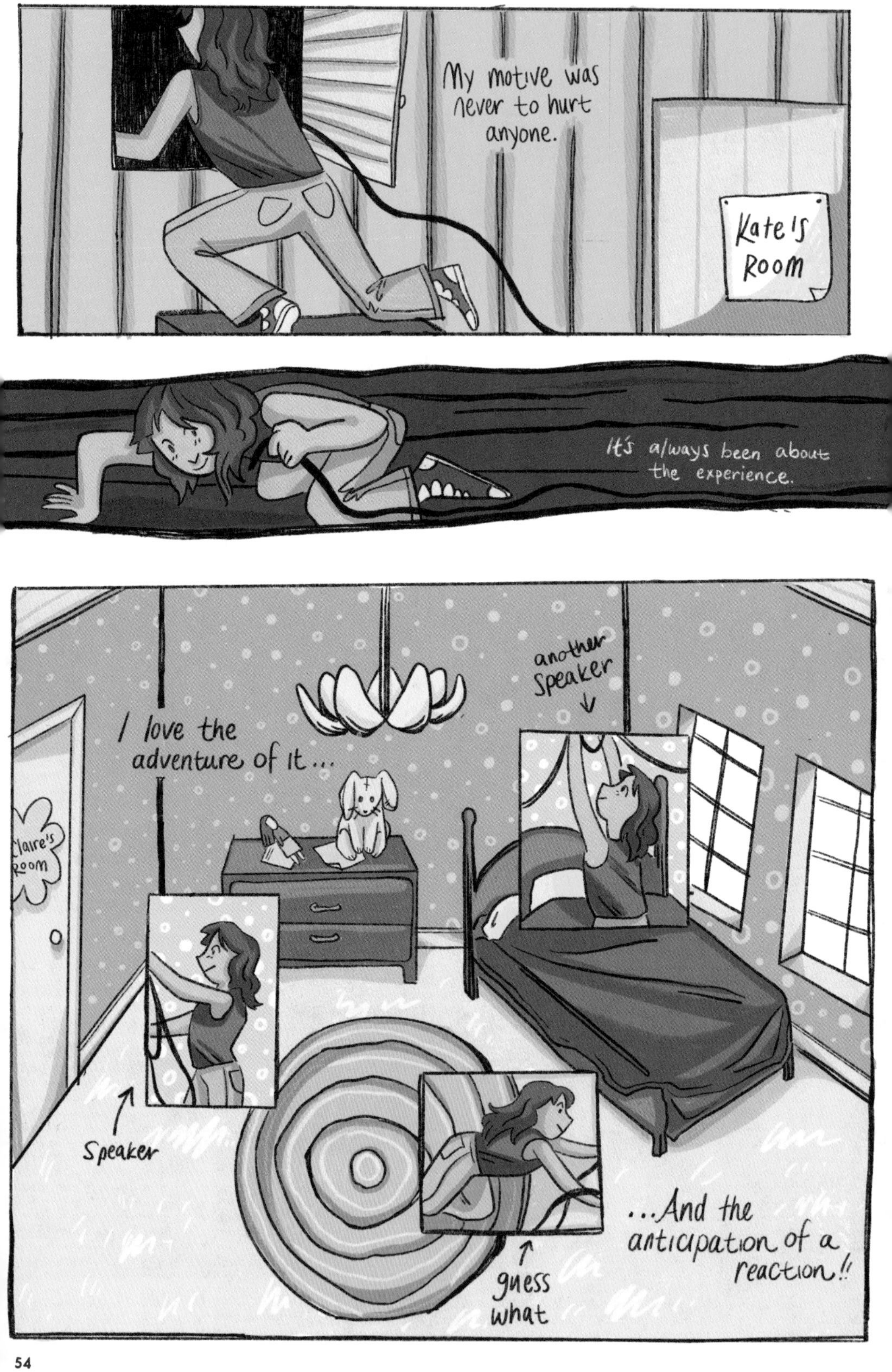
My motive was never to hurt anyone.
Kate's Room
It's always been about the experience.
I love the adventure of it...
another Speaker
Claire's Room
Speaker
...And the anticipation of a reaction!!
guess what

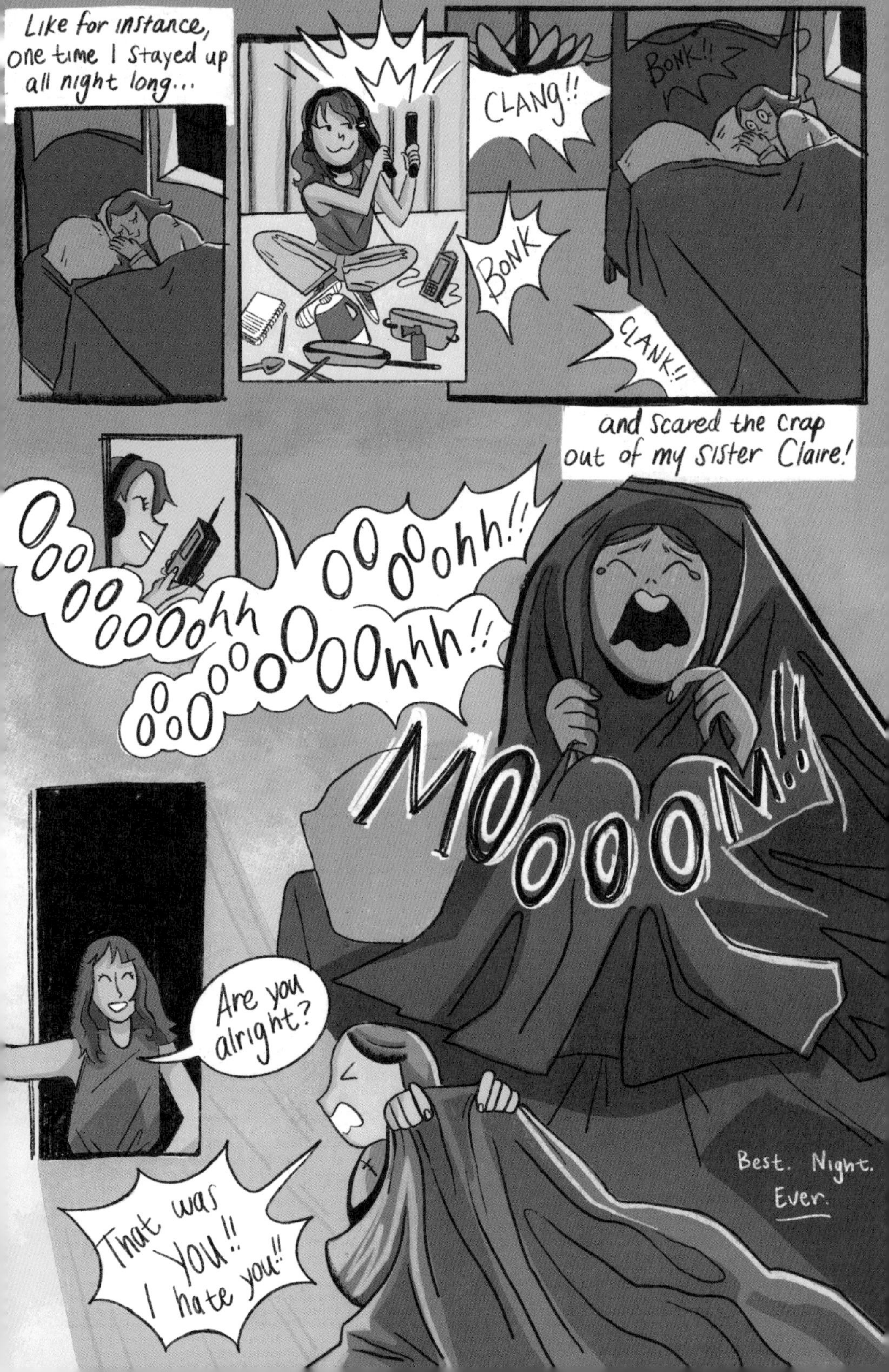

Like for instance, one time I stayed up all night long...
CLANG!!
BONK!!
BONK
CLANK!!
and scared the crap out of my sister Claire!
Oooooooooohh Oooohh!!
oooooooOOOOhhh!!
MOOOOOM!!
Are you alright?
That was YOU!! I hate you!!
Best. Night. Ever.

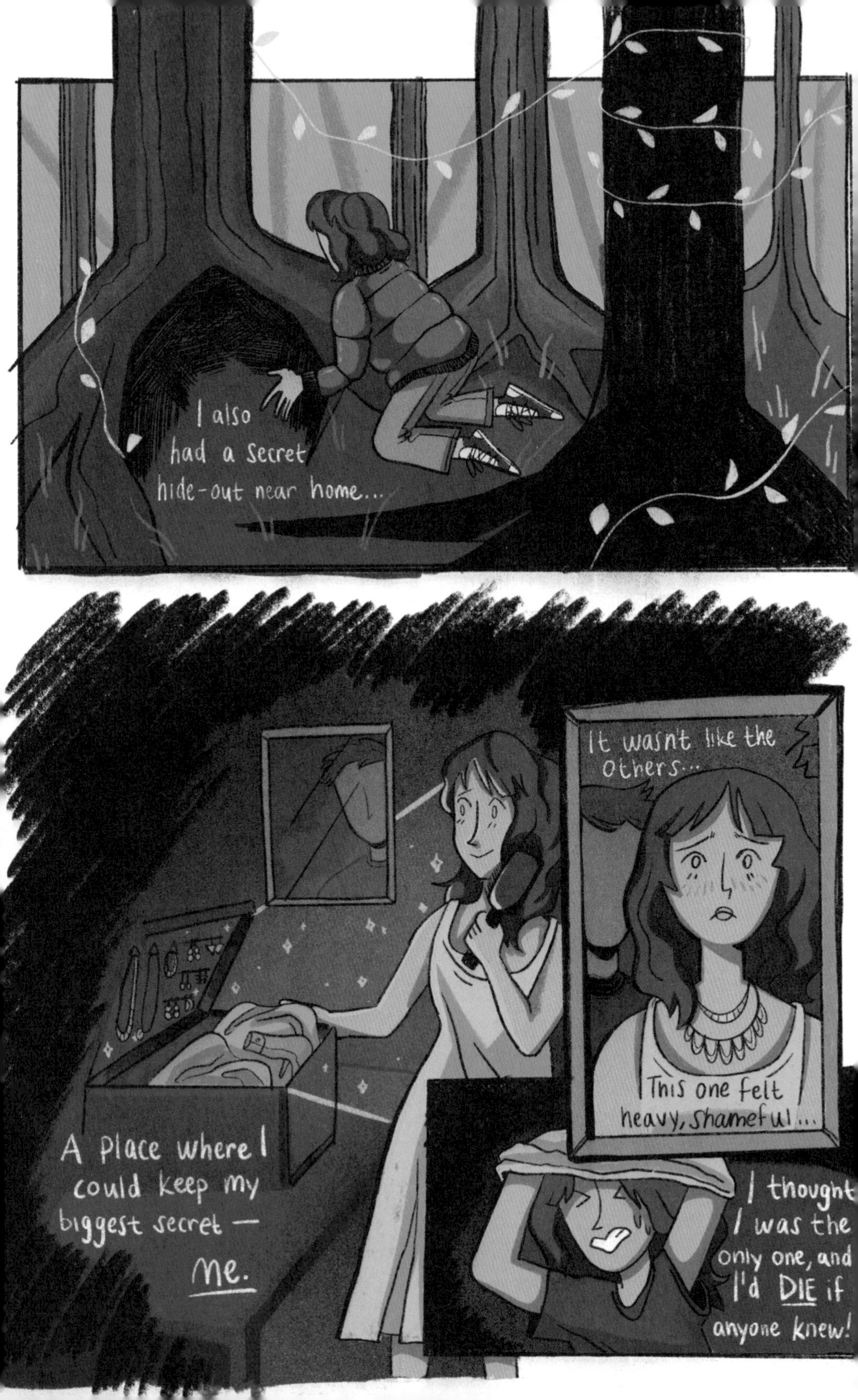
I also had a secret hide-out near home...
A place where I could keep my biggest secret — me.
It wasn't like the others...
This one felt heavy, shameful...
I thought I was the only one, and I'd DIE if anyone knew!

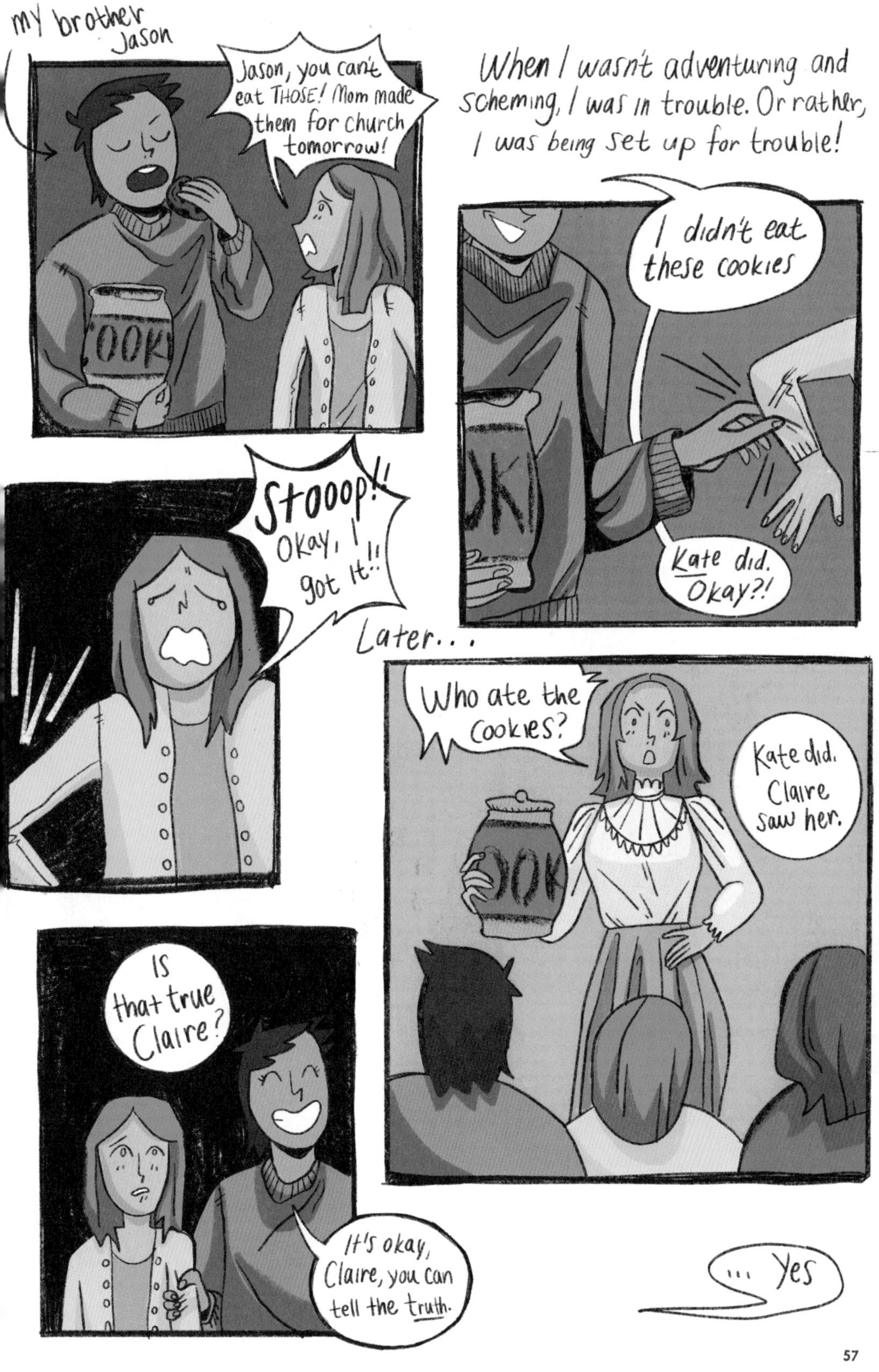
my brother Jason
Jason, you can't eat THOSE! Mom made them for church tomorrow!
When I wasn't adventuring and scheming, I was in trouble. Or rather, I was being set up for trouble!
I didn't eat these cookies
Kate did. Okay?!
OOK
Stooop!! Okay, I got it!!
Later...
Who ate the cookies?
Kate did. Claire saw her.
Is that true Claire?
It's okay, Claire, you can tell the truth.
... Yes

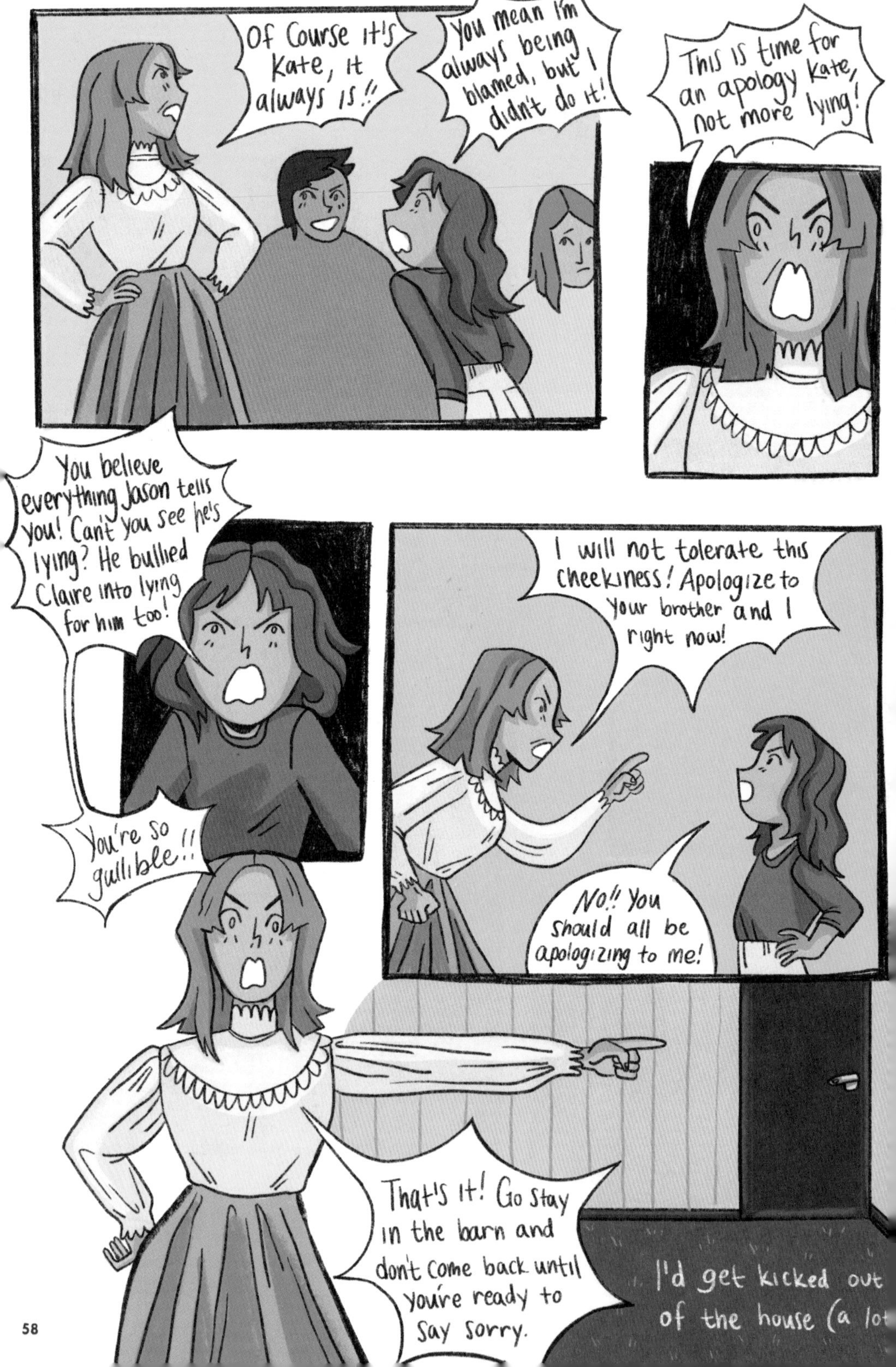
Of Course it's Kate, it always is!!
You mean I'm always being blamed, but I didn't do it!
This is time for an apology Kate, not more lying!
You believe everything Jason tells you! Can't you see he's lying? He bullied Claire into lying for him too!
You're so gullible!!
I will not tolerate this cheekiness! Apologize to your brother and I right now!
No!! You should all be apologizing to me!
That's it! Go stay in the barn and don't come back until you're ready to say sorry.
I'd get kicked out of the house (a lot

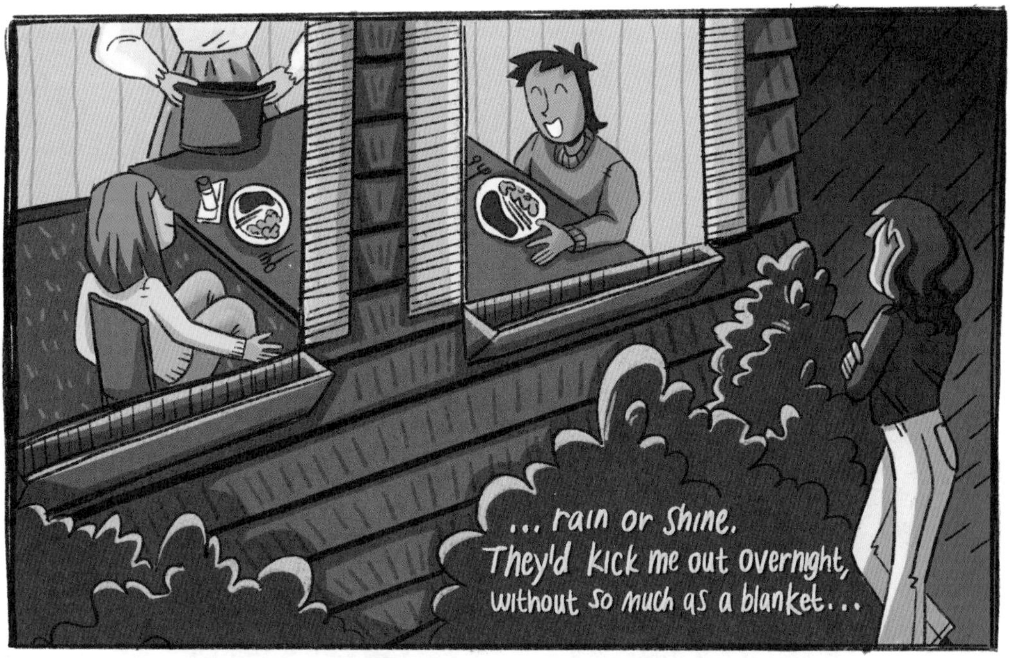
... rain or shine.
They'd kick me out overnight,
without so much as a blanket...

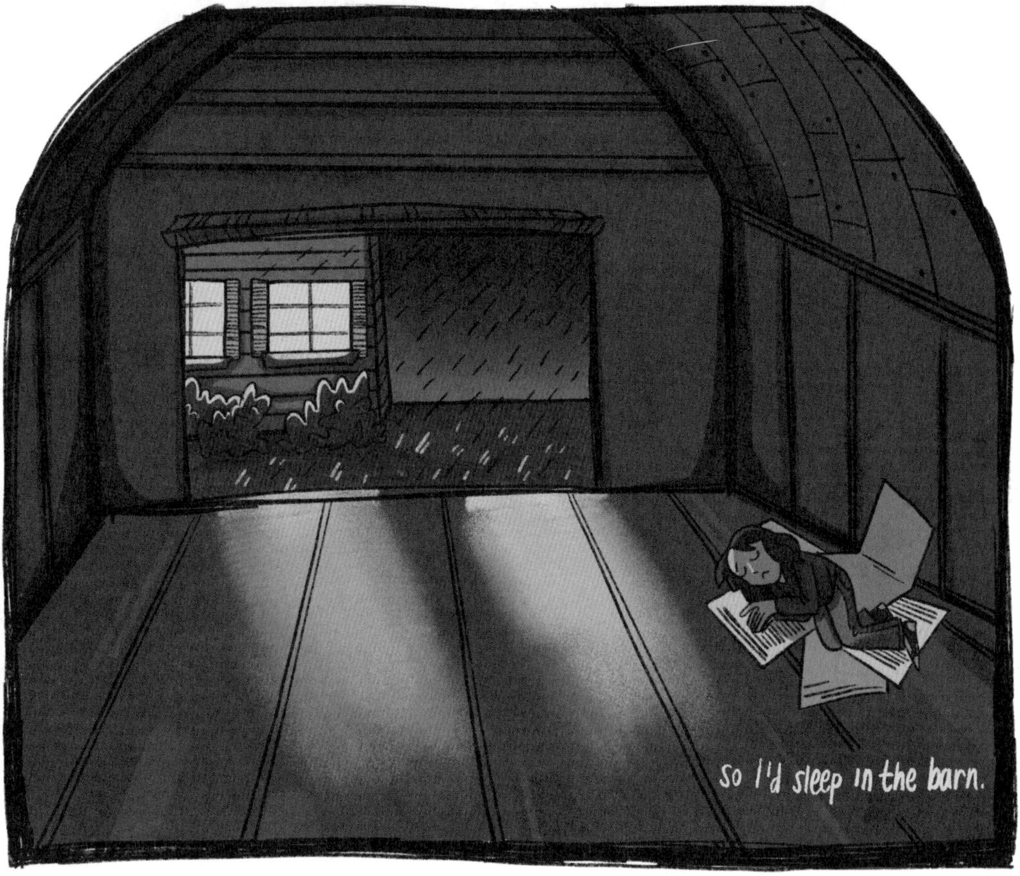
So I'd sleep in the barn.

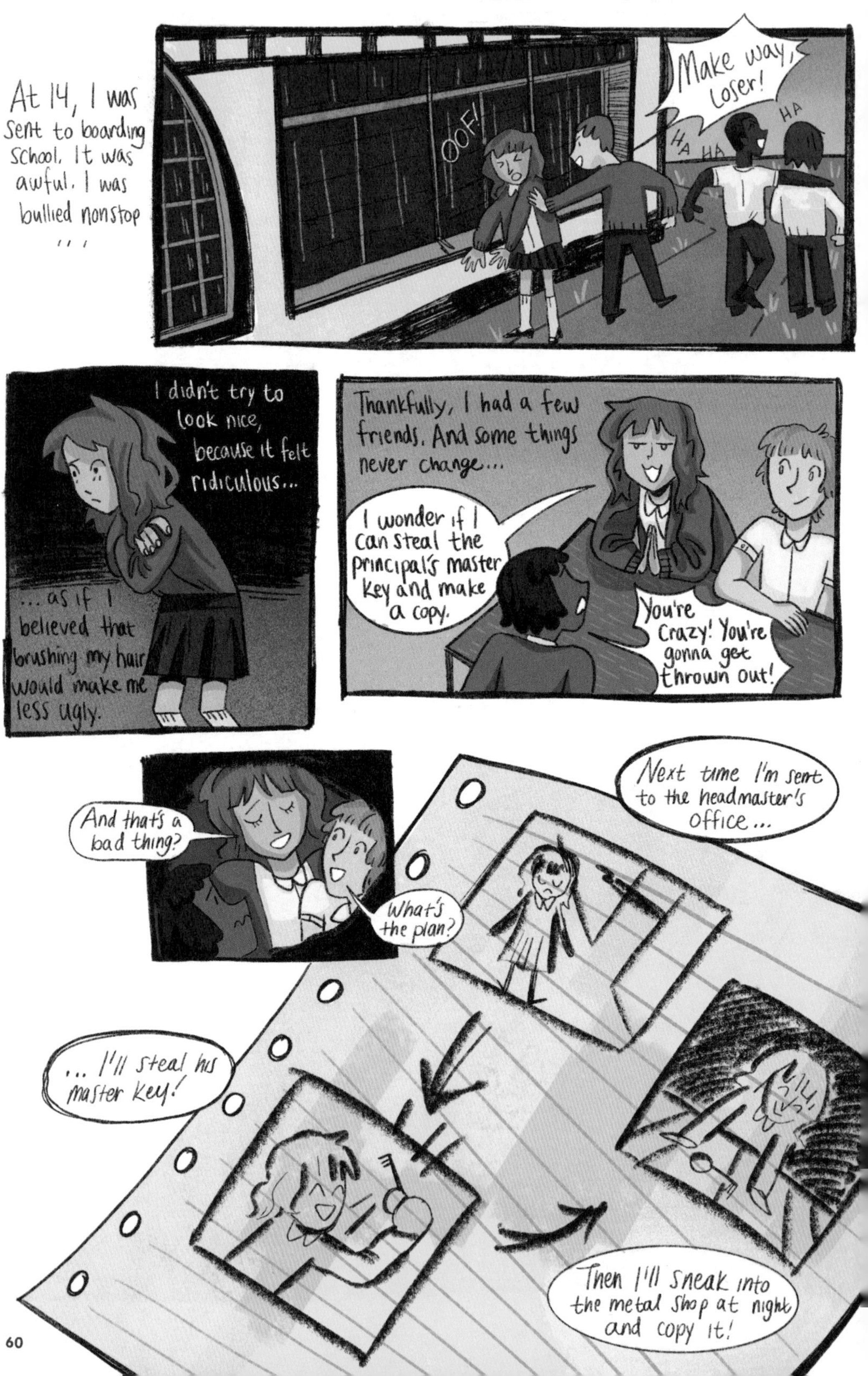
At 14, I was sent to boarding school. It was awful. I was bullied nonstop . . .
OOF!
Make way, loser!
HA
HA
HA
I didn't try to look nice, because it felt ridiculous...
...as if I believed that brushing my hair would make me less ugly.
Thankfully, I had a few friends. And some things never change...
I wonder if I can steal the principal's master key and make a copy.
You're crazy! You're gonna get thrown out!
And that's a bad thing?
What's the plan?
Next time I'm sent to the headmaster's office...
...I'll steal his master key!
Then I'll sneak into the metal shop at night and copy it!

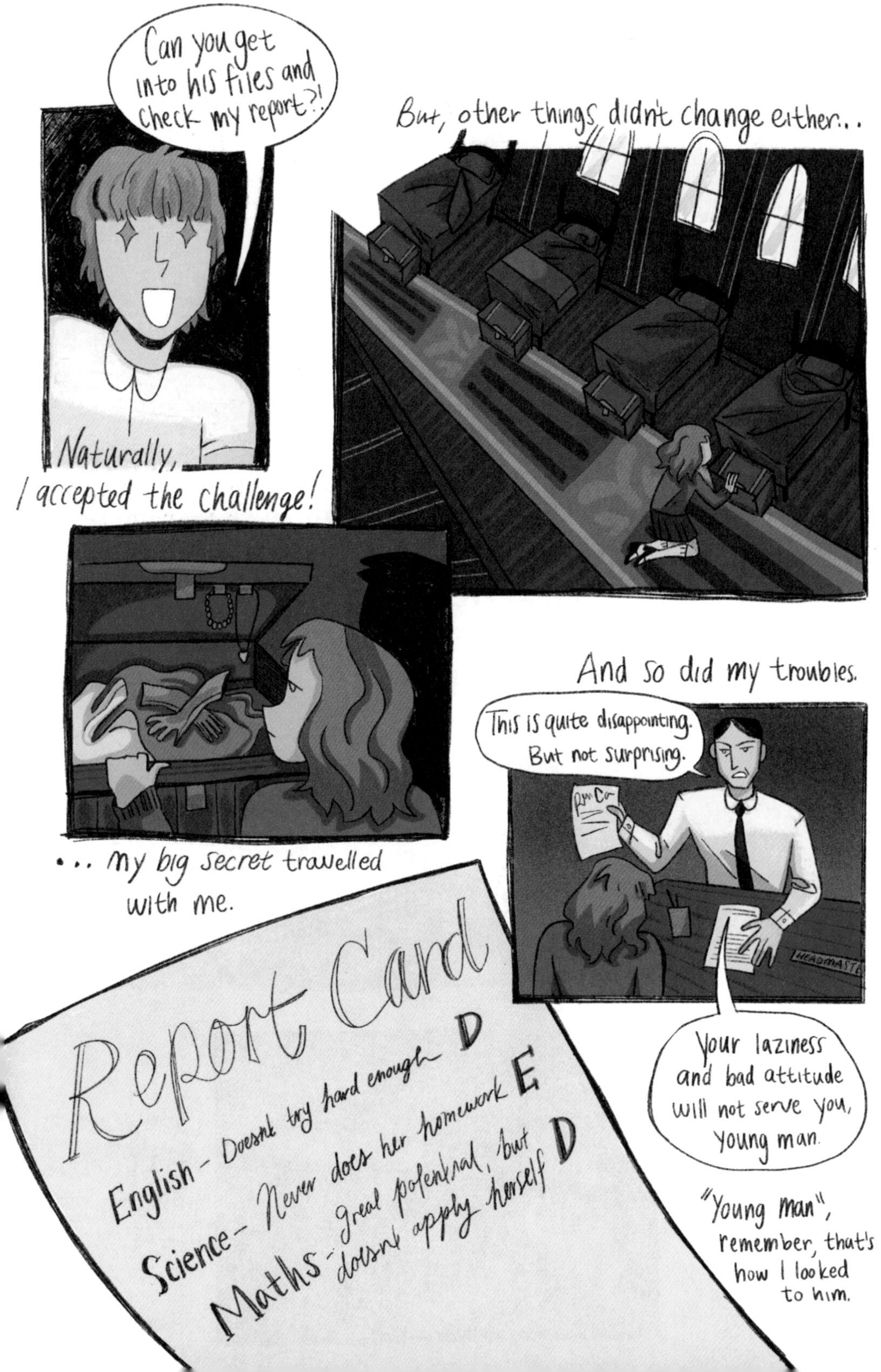
Can you get into his files and check my report?!
Naturally, I accepted the challenge!
But, other things didn't change either...
... my big secret travelled with me.
And so did my troubles.
This is quite disappointing. But not surprising.
HEADMASTE
Your laziness and bad attitude will not serve you, young man.
"Young man", remember, that's how I looked to him.
Report Card
English - Doesn't try hard enough D
Science - Never does her homework E
Maths - Great potential, but doesn't apply herself D

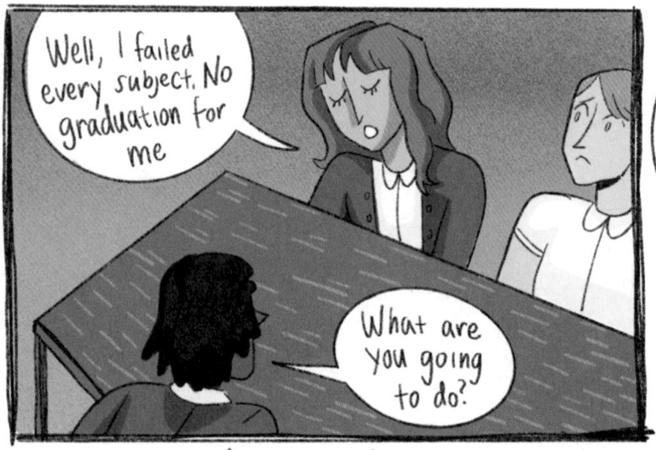
Well, I failed every subject. No graduation for me
What are you going to do?

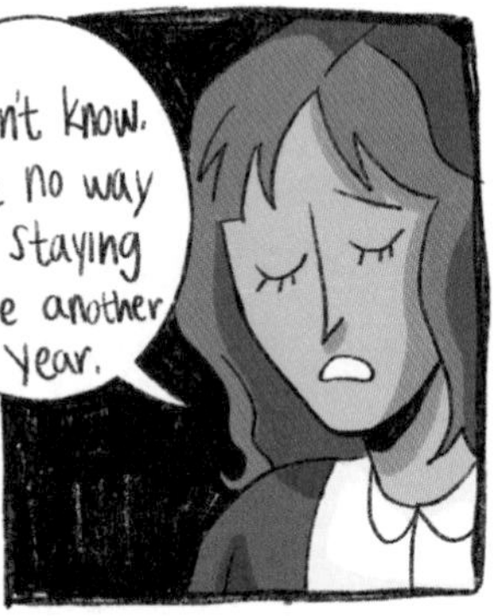
I don't know. But no way I'm staying here another year.

I went home and made up my mind to get a job, save money, and move as far away as I could think of...

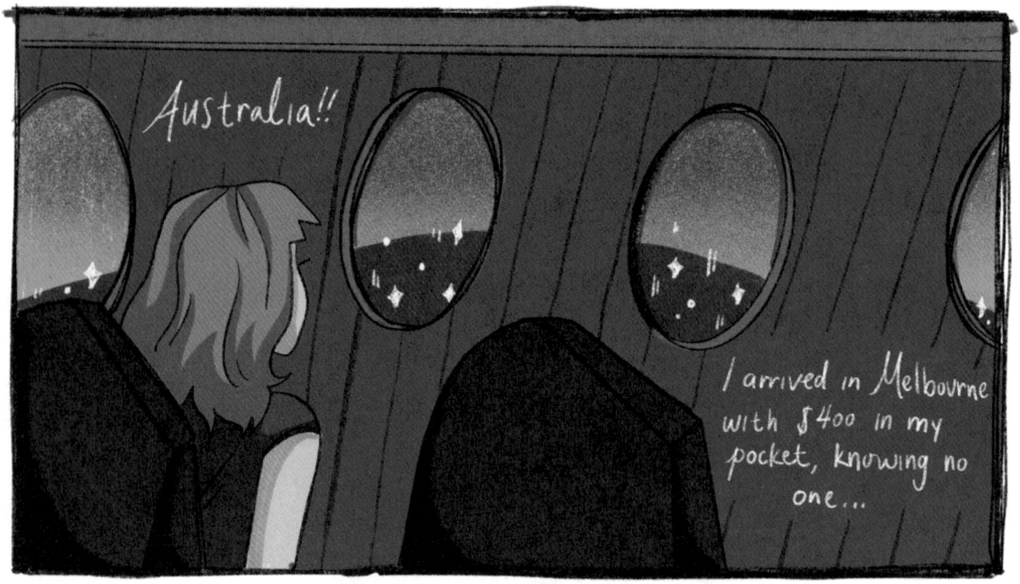
Australia!!
I arrived in Melbourne with $400 in my pocket, knowing no one...

I traveled around, doing odd jobs.

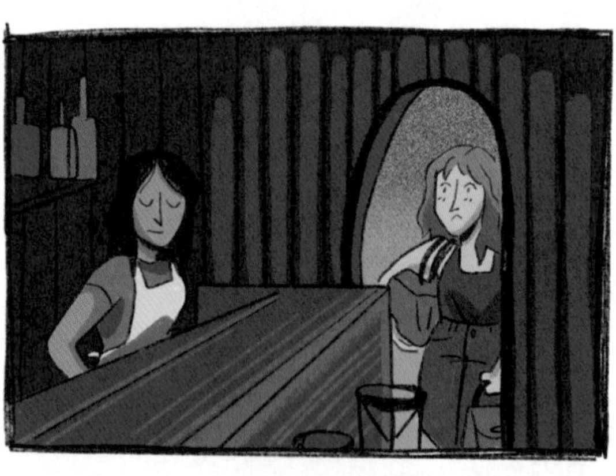

Luckily, one day, at a pub in a ghost town, someone offered me work . . .

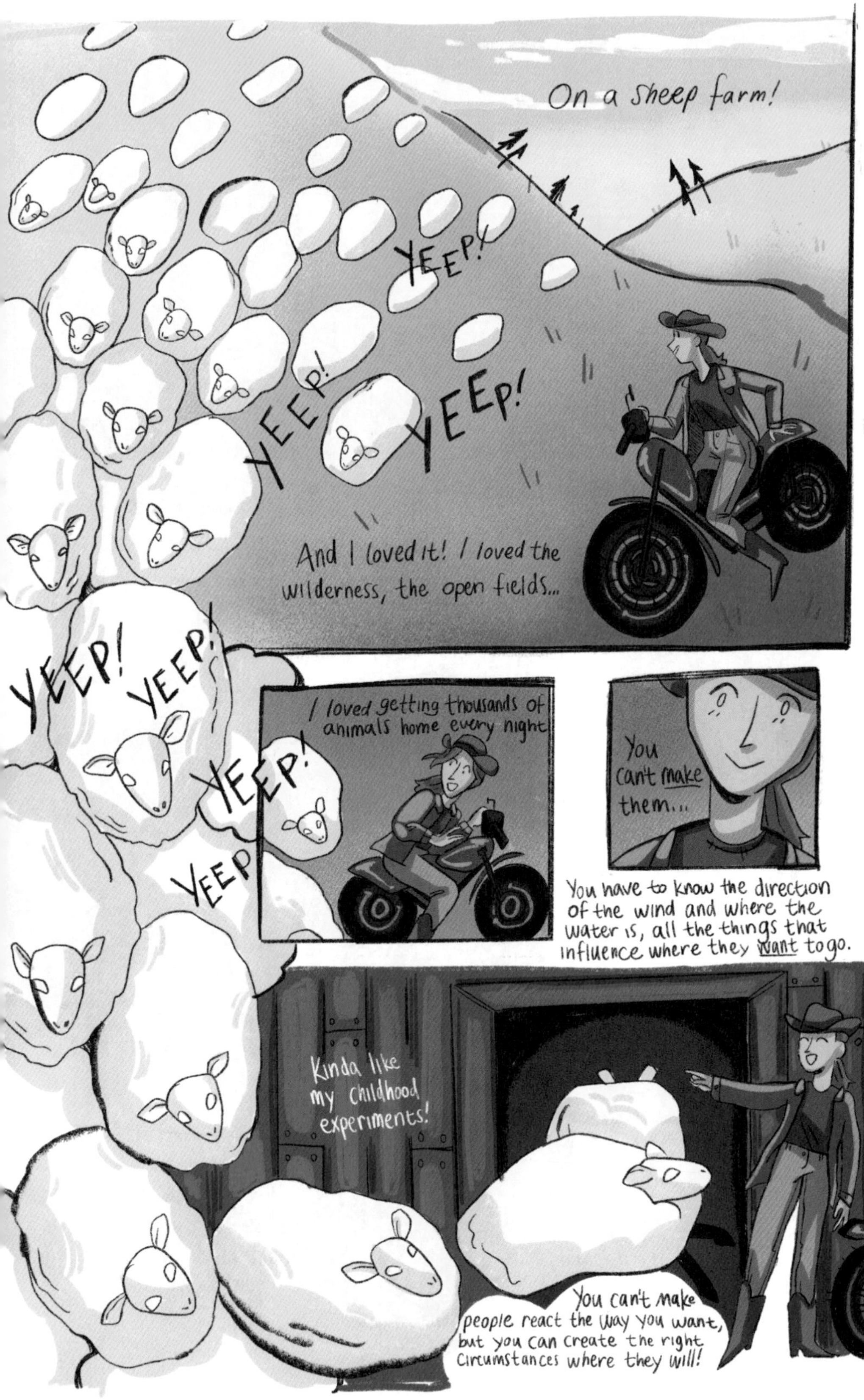
On a sheep farm!
YEEP!
YEEP!
YEEP!
And I loved it! I loved the wilderness, the open fields...
YEEP!
YEEP!
I loved getting thousands of animals home every night
YEEP!
YEEP
You can't make them...
You have to know the direction of the wind and where the water is, all the things that influence where they want to go.
Kinda like my childhood experiments!
You can't make people react the way you want, but you can create the right circumstances where they will!

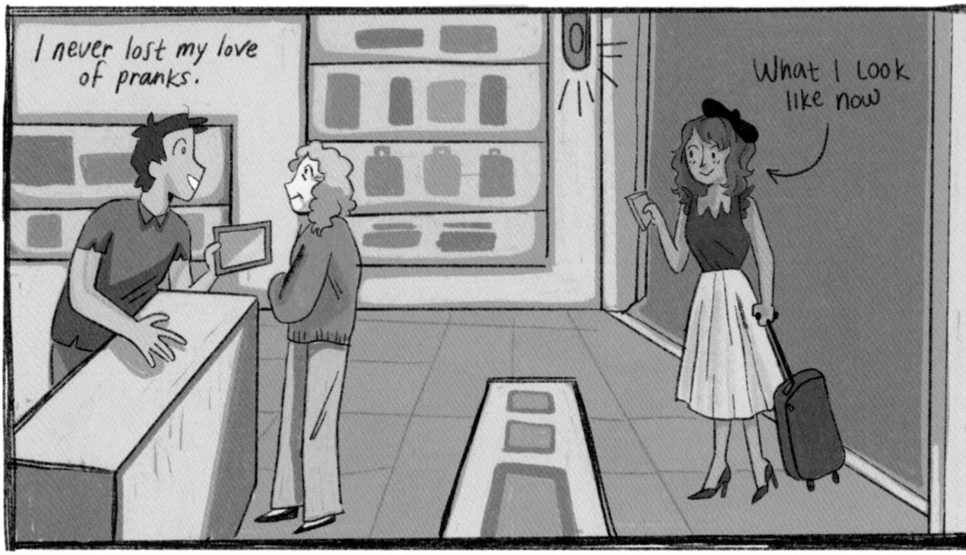
I never lost my love of pranks.
What I look like now

Or my fascination for electronics.

Eventually I decided to go back to University to study it!

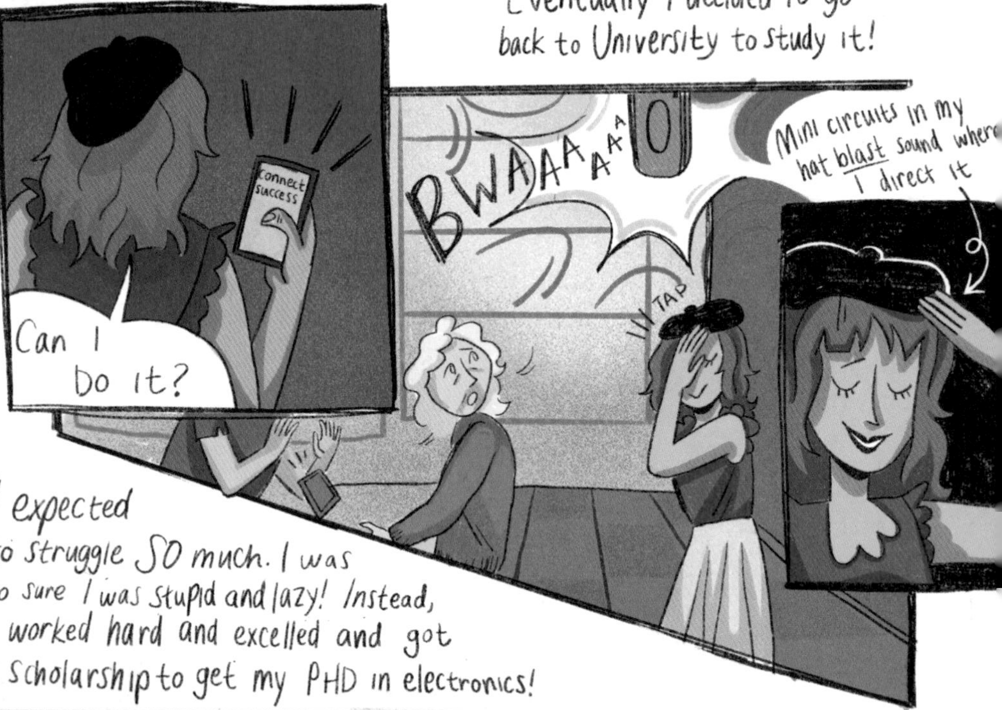
Connect success
Can I Do it?
BWAAAAA
TAP
Mini circuits in my hat blast sound where I direct it

I expected to struggle SO much. I was so sure I was stupid and lazy! Instead, I worked hard and excelled and got a scholarship to get my PHD in electronics!

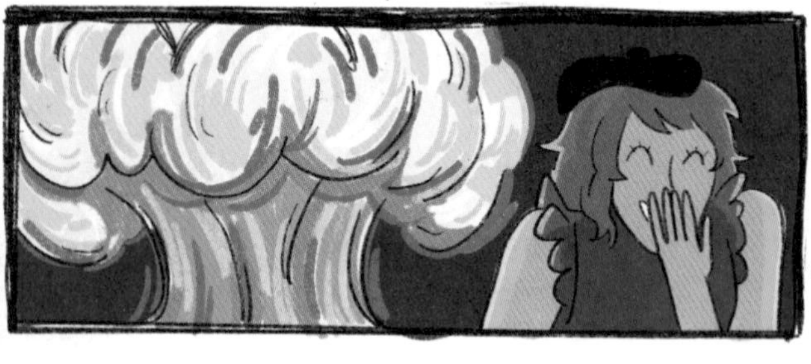

And guess what?

Electrons are like sheep! You have to manipulate the environment to get them to do what you want!

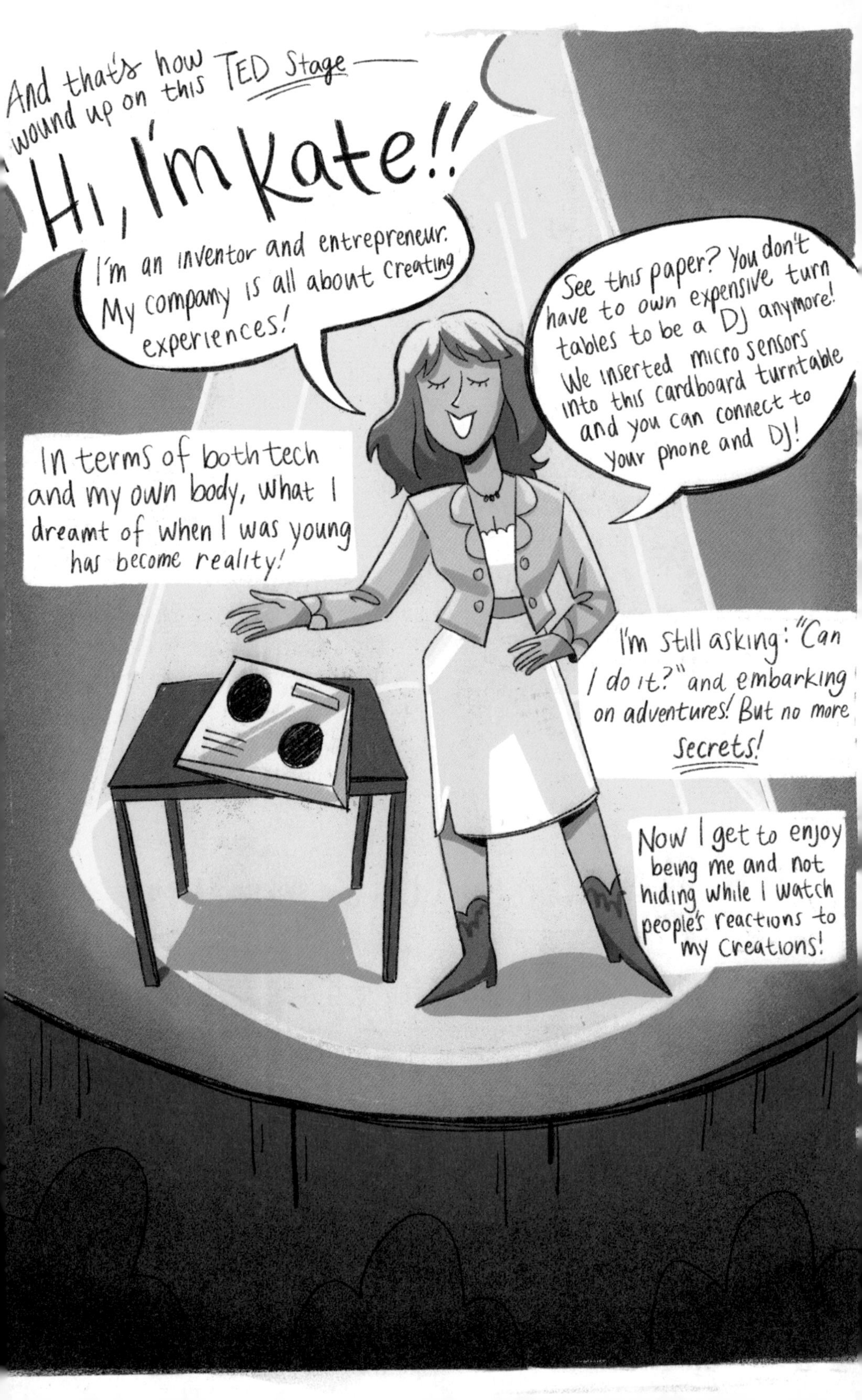

And that's how I wound up on this TED Stage—
Hi, I'm Kate!!
I'm an inventor and entrepreneur. My company is all about creating experiences!
See this paper? You don't have to own expensive turn tables to be a DJ anymore! We inserted micro sensors into this cardboard turntable and you can connect to your phone and DJ!
In terms of both tech and my own body, what I dreamt of when I was young has become reality!
I'm still asking: "Can I do it?" and embarking on adventures! But no more secrets!
Now I get to enjoy being me and not hiding while I watch people's reactions to my creations!

BECOMING ROBBIE AHMED

Robbie Ahmed (he/him) is a singer-songwriter, writer and educator. Growing up in 4 countries; Russia, Saudi Arabia, Bangladesh and now Canada; he writes & sings on intersections of self-love, immigrations, mental health, spirituality, and trans representation in the media. He also spent 10 years working on advocacy projects for inclusion of trans people in the HIV sector, racialized mental health, and immigrant queer rights.

Written by Sammy Lisel
Illustrated by Victor Martins

Victor Martins (they/them) is a cartoonist and illustrator. They are enthusiastic about trees to the point where they are frequently late because they got distracted by a tree.

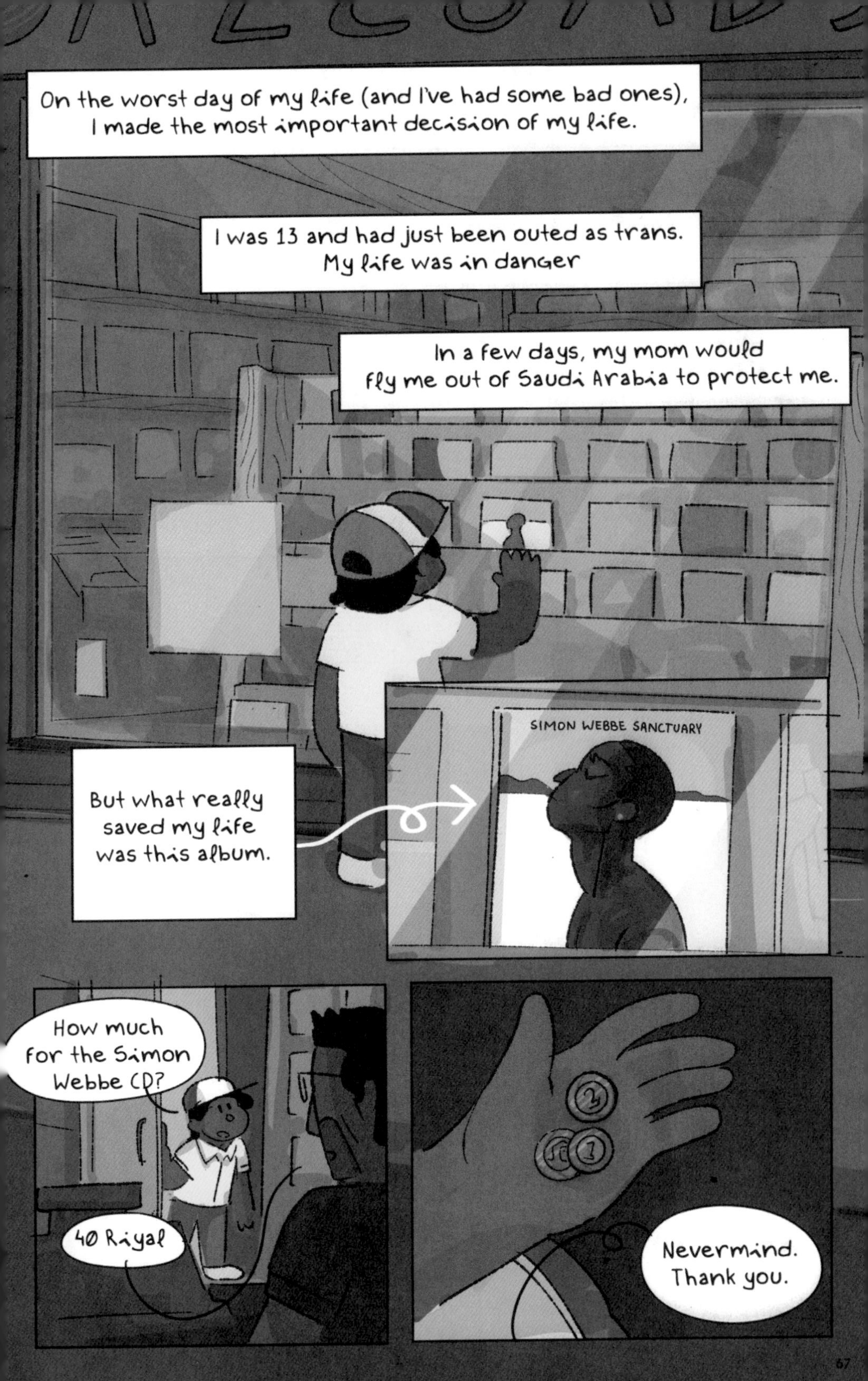
On the worst day of my life (and I've had some bad ones), I made the most important decision of my life.
I was 13 and had just been outed as trans. My life was in danger
In a few days, my mom would fly me out of Saudi Arabia to protect me.
SIMON WEBBE SANCTUARY
But what really saved my life was this album.
How much for the Simon Webbe CD?
40 Riyal
Nevermind. Thank you.

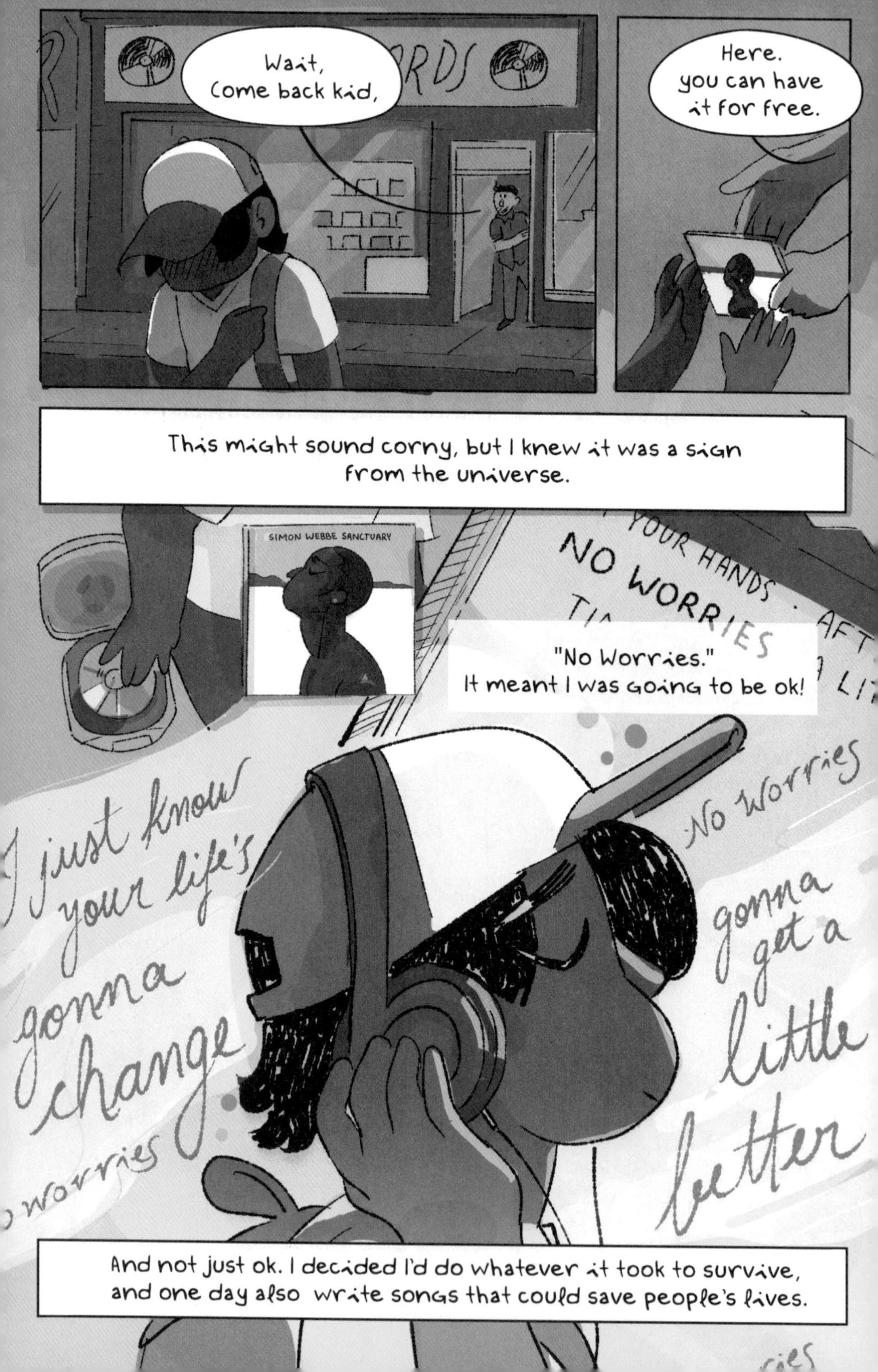

Wait, Come back kid,
Here. you can have it for free.
This might sound corny, but I knew it was a sign from the universe.
SIMON WEBBE SANCTUARY
NO WORRIES
"No Worries." It meant I was going to be ok!
I just know your life's gonna change
No worries
gonna get a little better
And not just ok. I decided I'd do whatever it took to survive, and one day also write songs that could save people's lives.

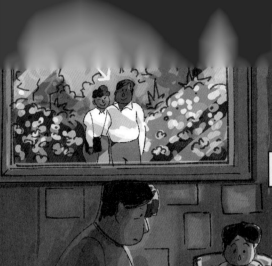

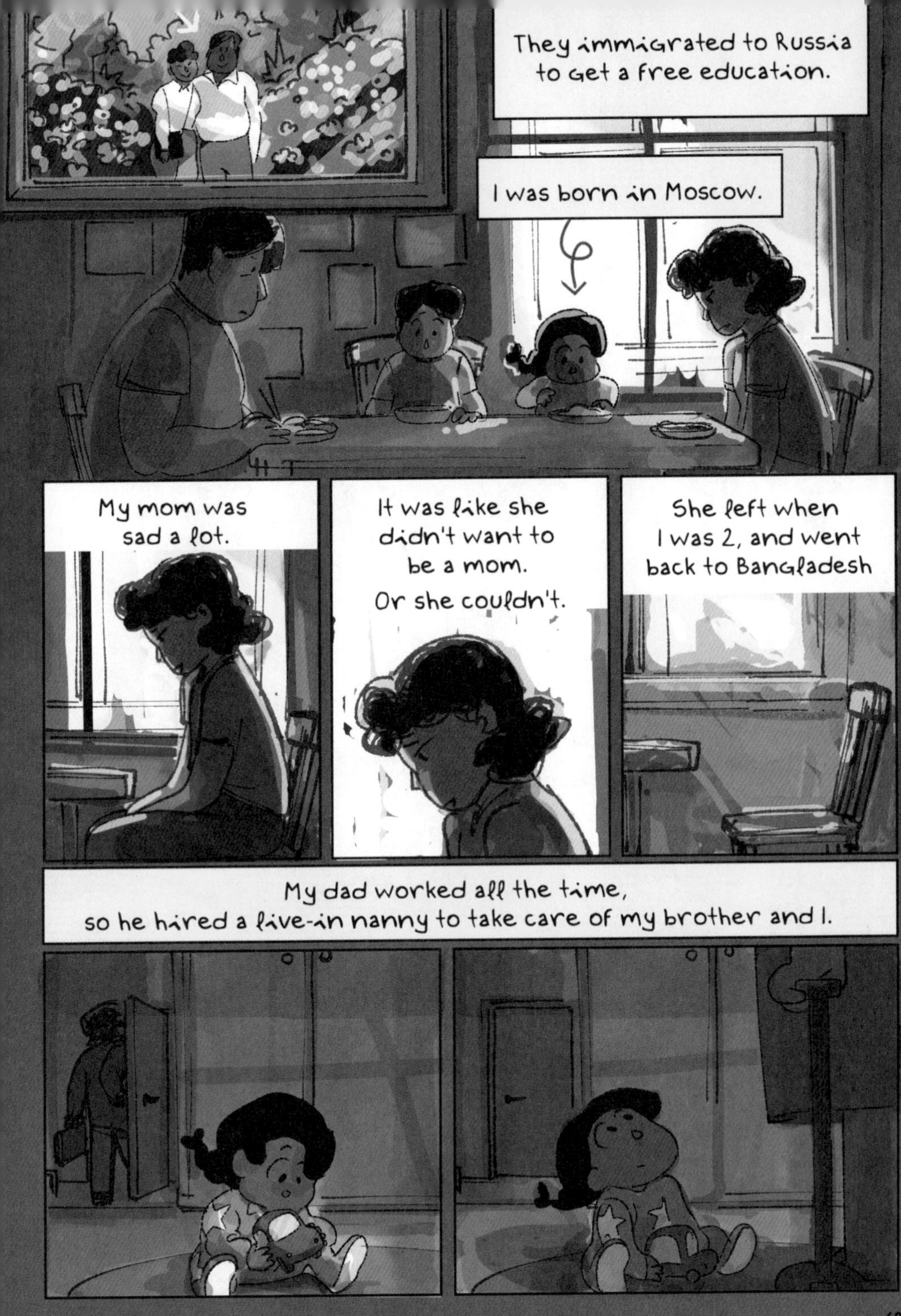
They immigrated to Russia to get a free education.
I was born in Moscow.
My mom was sad a lot.
It was like she didn't want to be a mom.
Or she couldn't.
She left when I was 2, and went back to Bangladesh
My dad worked all the time, so he hired a live-in nanny to take care of my brother and I.

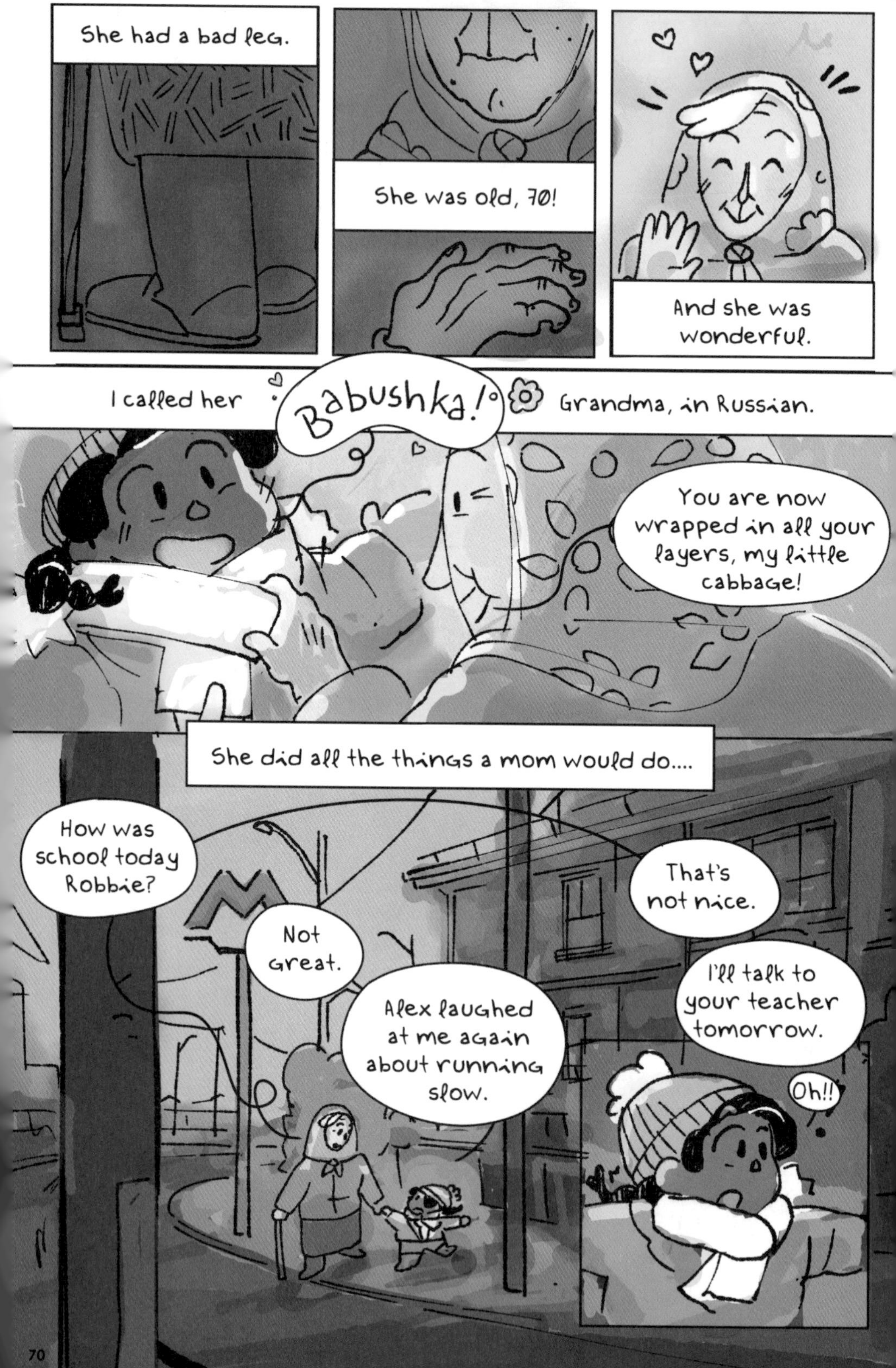
She had a bad leg.
She was old, 70!
And she was wonderful.
I called her
Babushka!
Grandma, in Russian.
You are now wrapped in all your layers, my little cabbage!
She did all the things a mom would do....
How was school today Robbie?
Not great.
Alex laughed at me again about running slow.
That's not nice.
I'll talk to your teacher tomorrow.
Oh!!

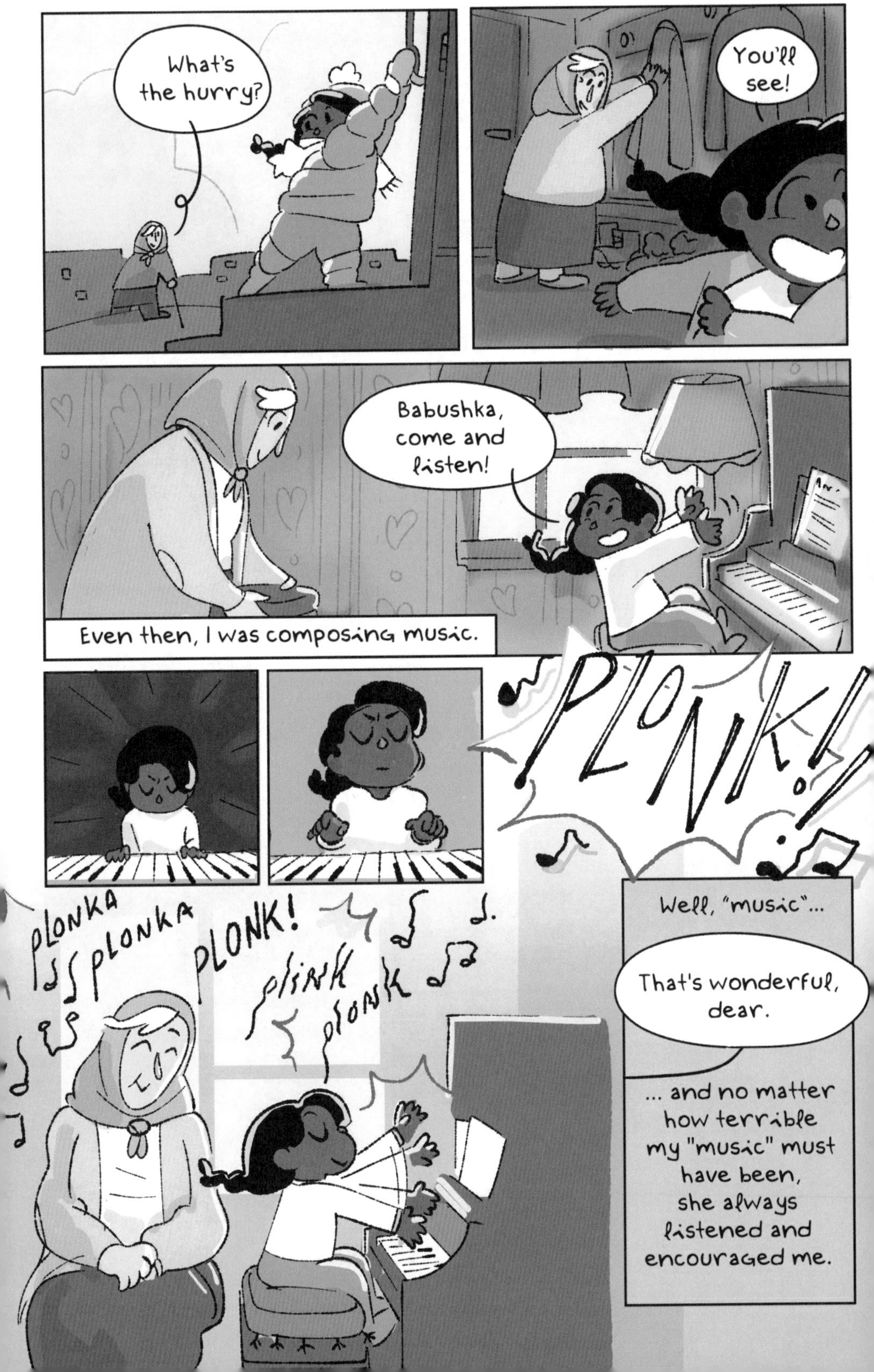
What's the hurry?
You'll see!
Babushka, come and listen!
Even then, I was composing music.
PLONK!!
Well, "music"...
PLONKA PLONKA PLONK!
plink plonk
That's wonderful, dear.
... and no matter how terrible my "music" must have been, she always listened and encouraged me.

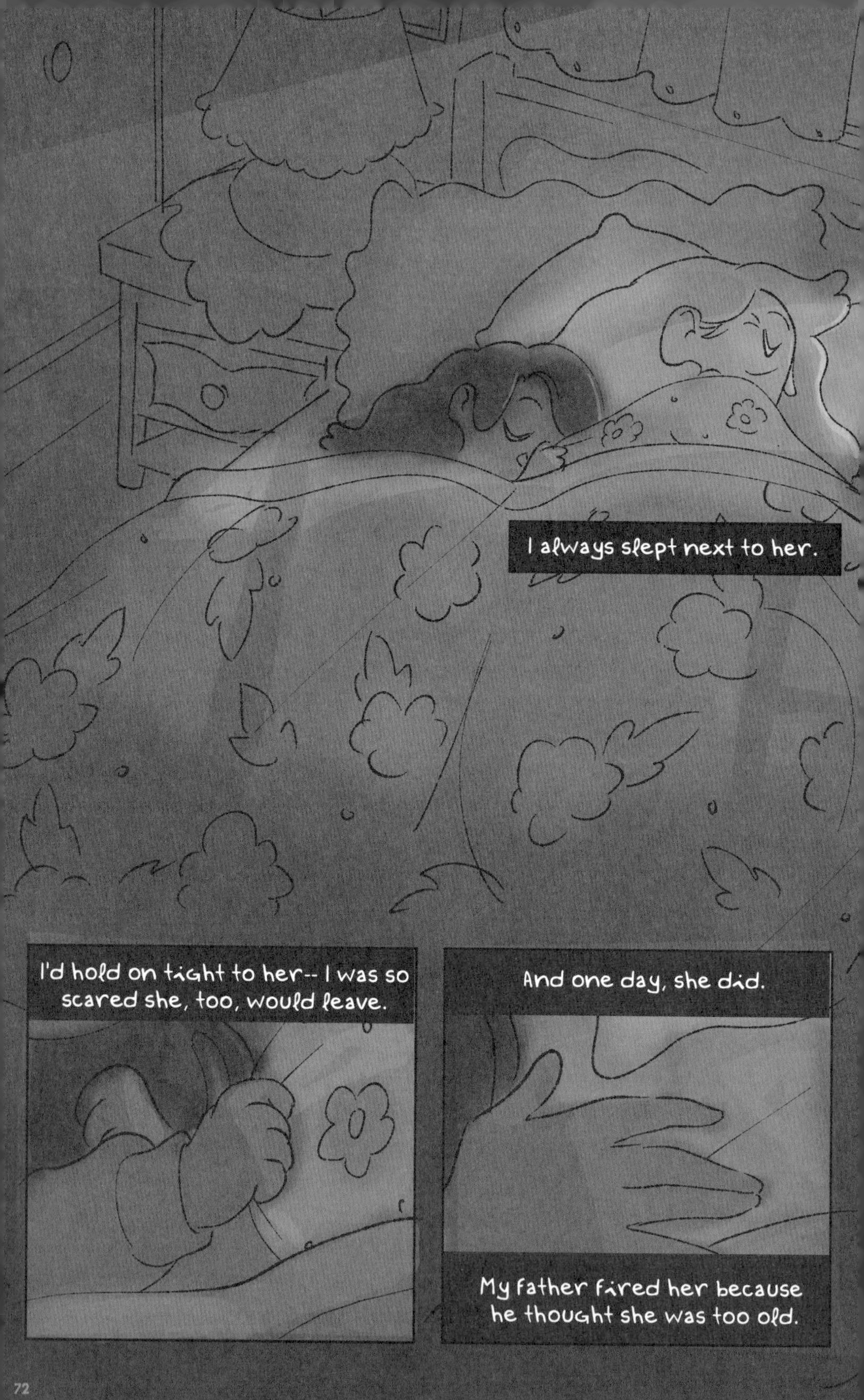
I always slept next to her.
I'd hold on tight to her-- I was so scared she, too, would leave.
And one day, she did.
My father fired her because he thought she was too old.

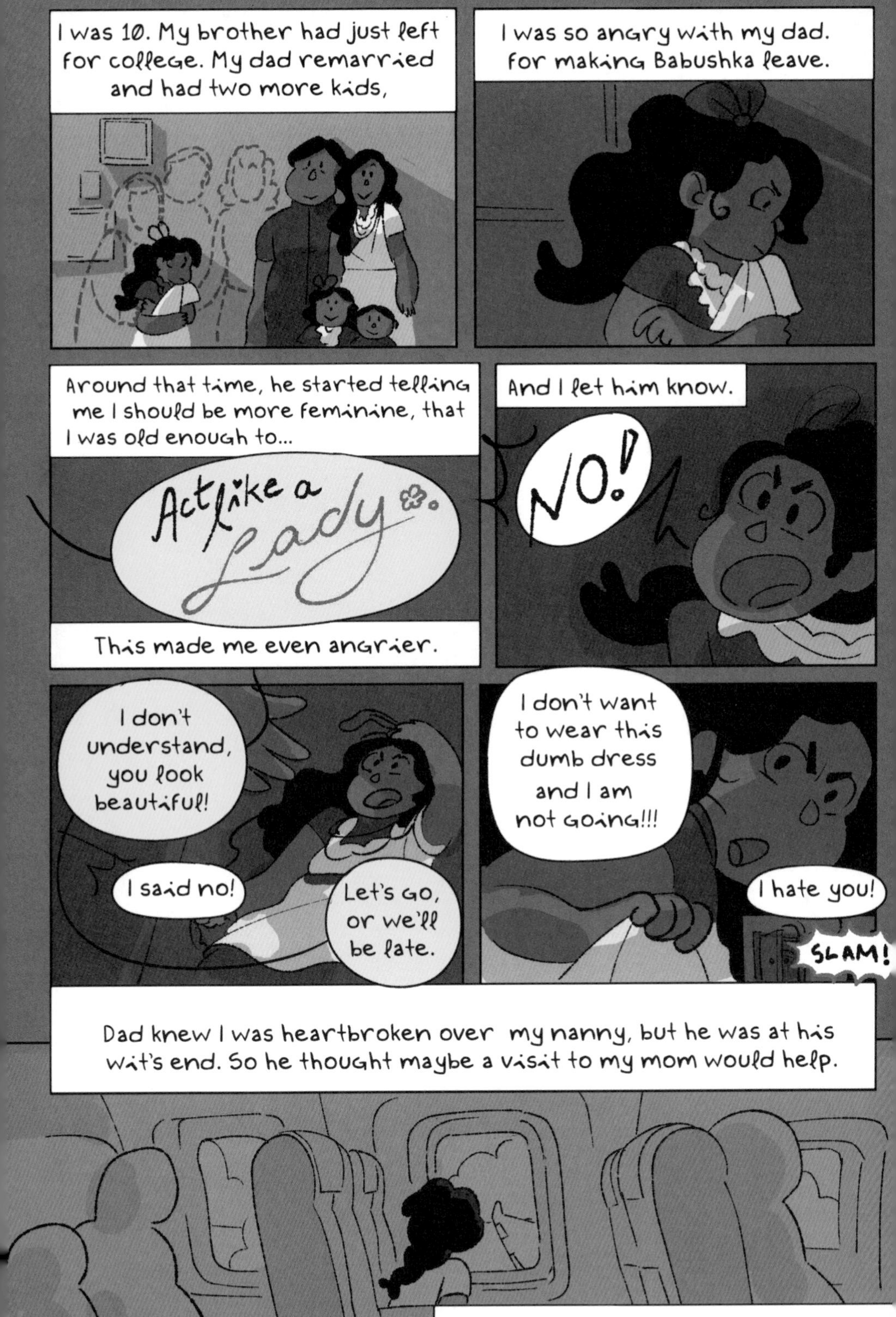
I was 10. My brother had just left for college. My dad remarried and had two more kids,
I was so angry with my dad. for making Babushka leave.
Around that time, he started telling me I should be more feminine, that I was old enough to...
Act like a Lady
This made me even angrier.
And I let him know.
NO!
I don't understand, you look beautiful!
I said no!
Let's go, or we'll be late.
I don't want to wear this dumb dress and I am not going!!!
I hate you!
SLAM!
Dad knew I was heartbroken over my nanny, but he was at his wit's end. So he thought maybe a visit to my mom would help.
... I hadn't seen her in over 8 years!

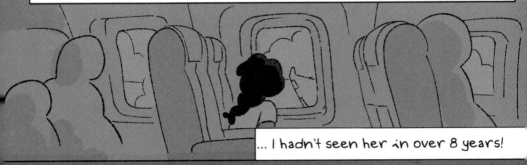

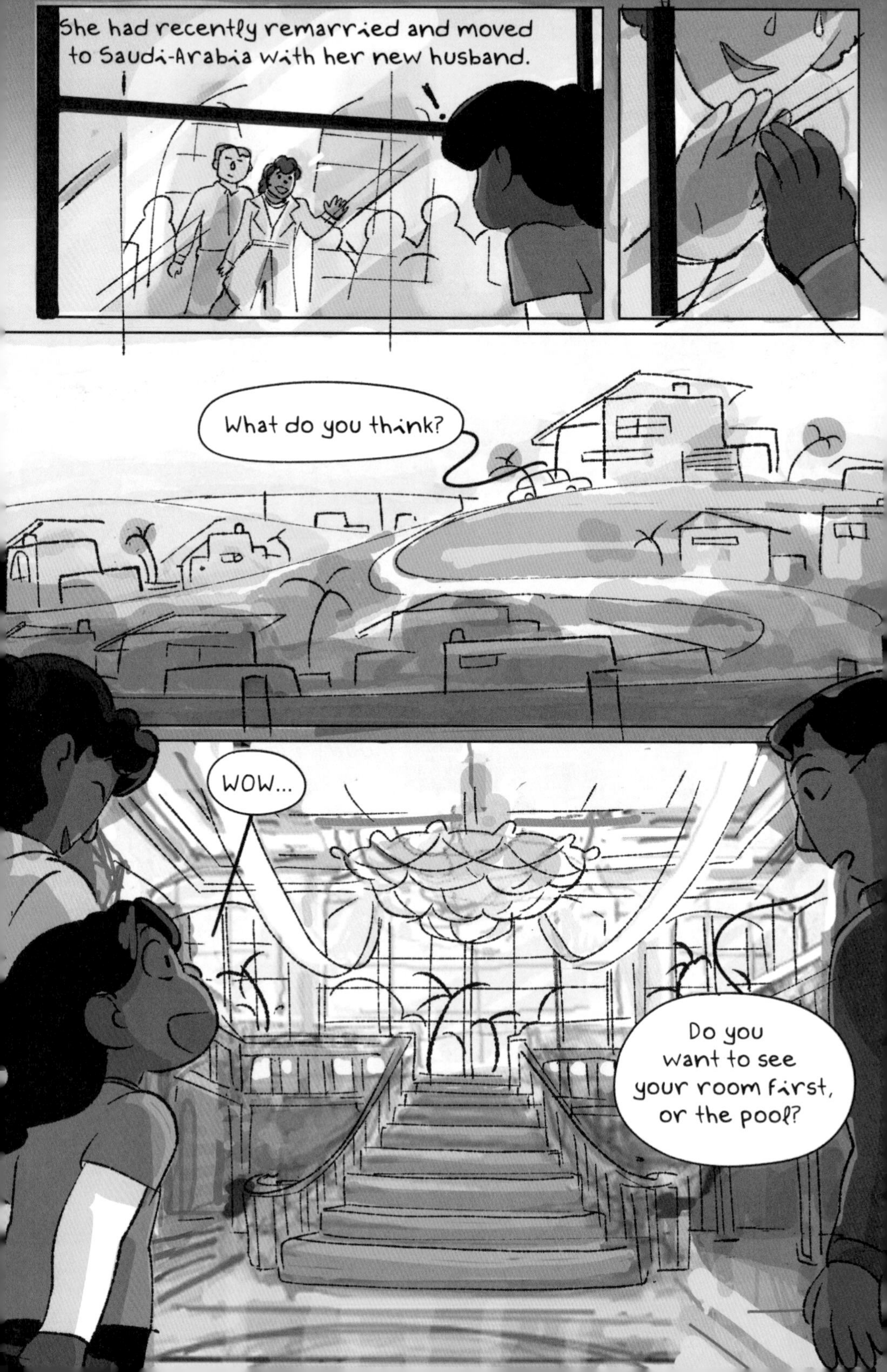
She had recently remarried and moved to Saudi-Arabia with her new husband.
!
What do you think?
WOW...
Do you want to see your room first, or the pool?

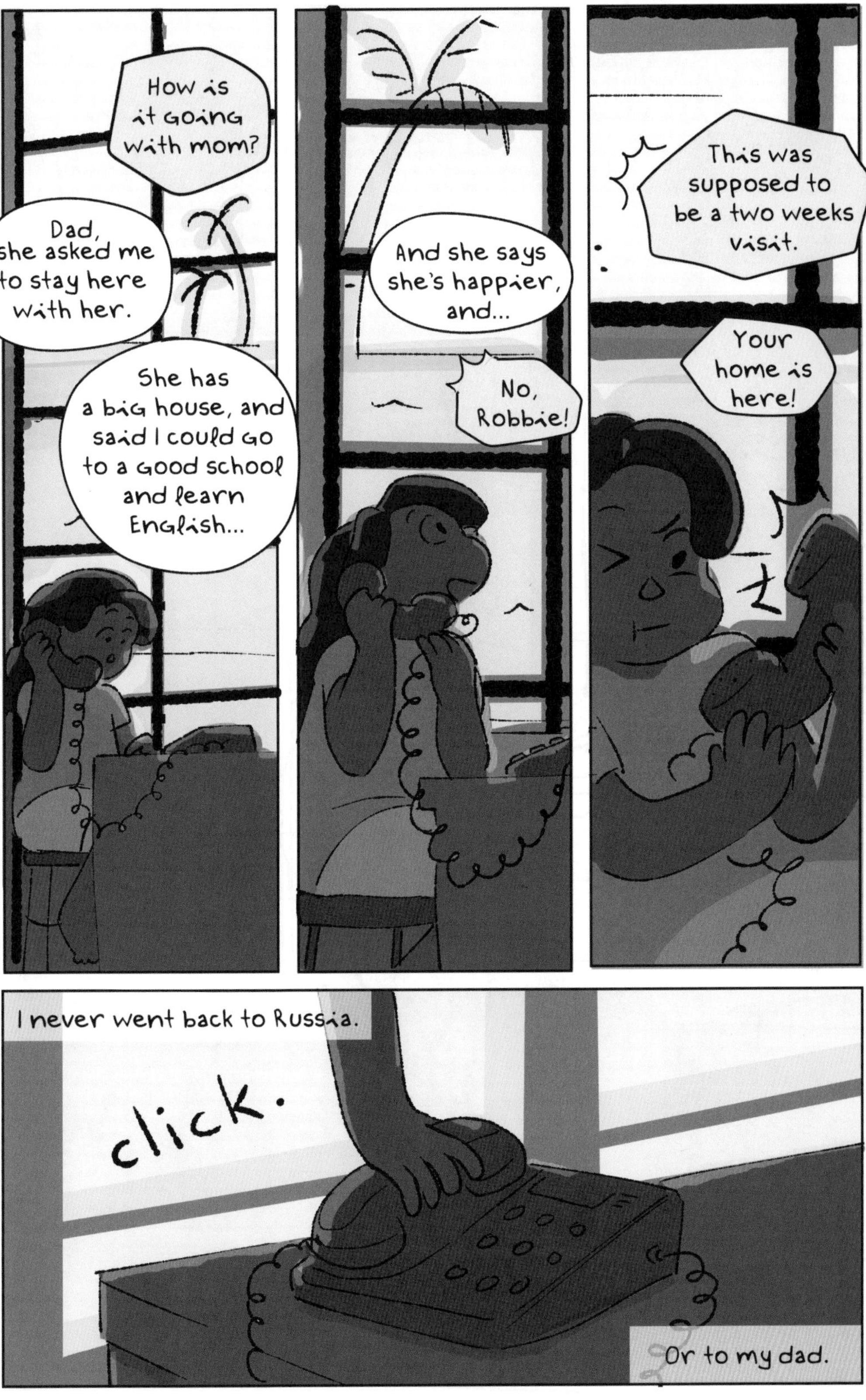
How is it going with mom?
Dad, she asked me to stay here with her.
She has a big house, and said I could go to a good school and learn English...
And she says she's happier, and...
No, Robbie!
This was supposed to be a two weeks visit.
Your home is here!
I never went back to Russia.
click.
Or to my dad.

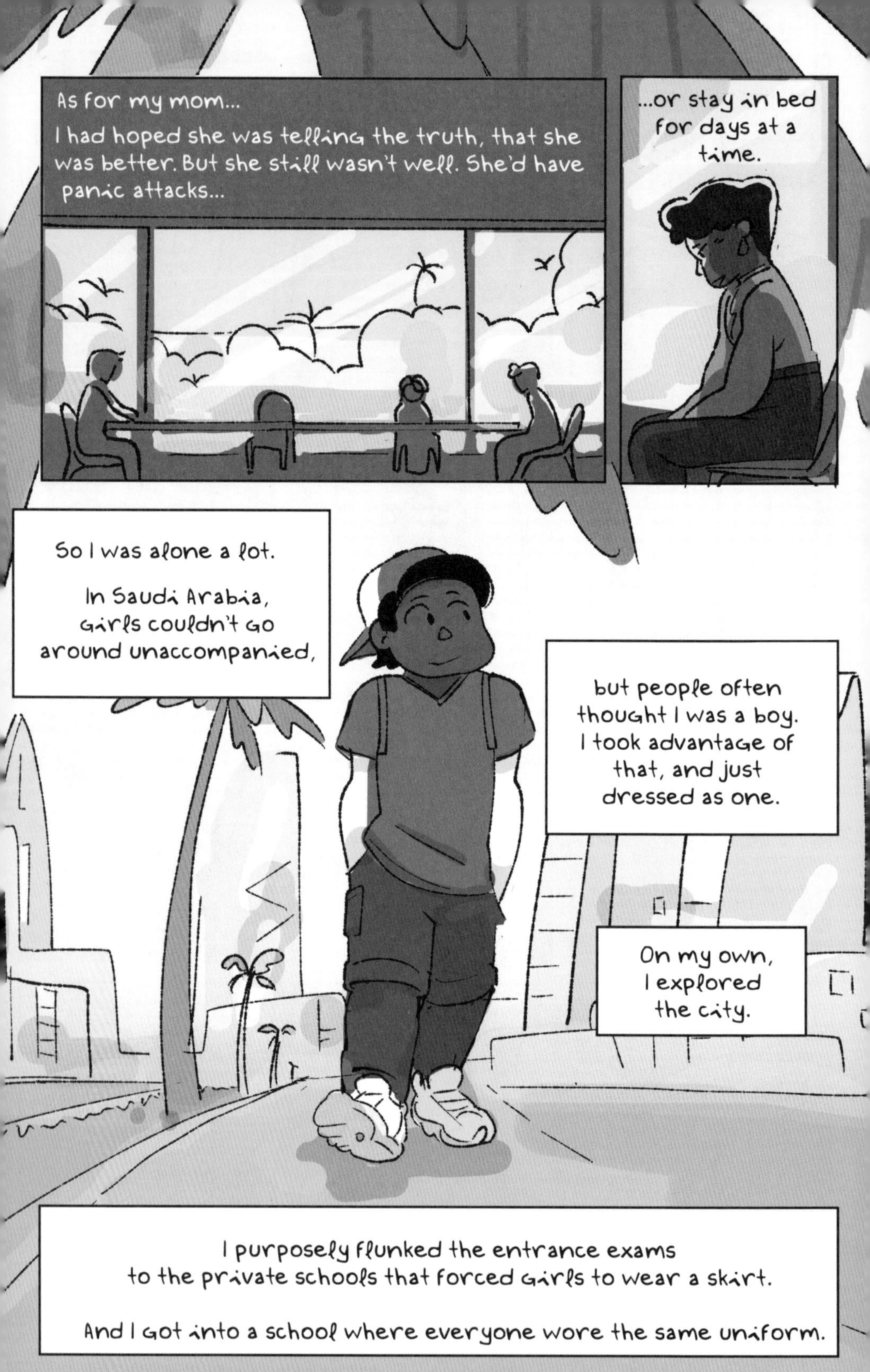
As for my mom...
I had hoped she was telling the truth, that she was better. But she still wasn't well. She'd have panic attacks...
...or stay in bed for days at a time.
So I was alone a lot.
In Saudi Arabia, girls couldn't go around unaccompanied,
but people often thought I was a boy. I took advantage of that, and just dressed as one.
On my own, I explored the city.
I purposely flunked the entrance exams to the private schools that forced girls to wear a skirt.
And I got into a school where everyone wore the same uniform.

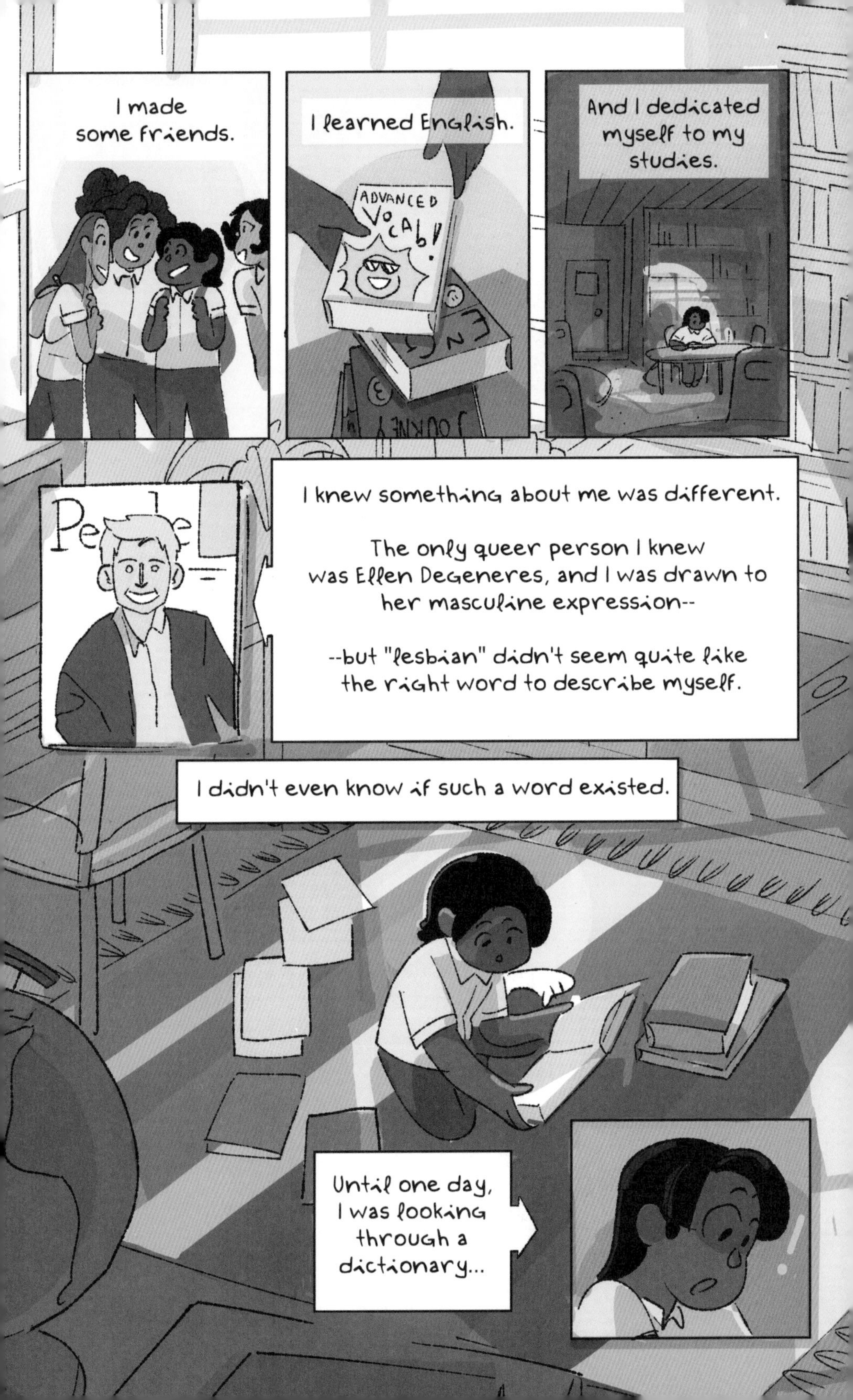
I made some friends.
I learned English.
ADVANCED VOCAB!
And I dedicated myself to my studies.
I knew something about me was different.
The only queer person I knew was Ellen Degeneres, and I was drawn to her masculine expression--
--but "lesbian" didn't seem quite like the right word to describe myself.
I didn't even know if such a word existed.
Until one day, I was looking through a dictionary...

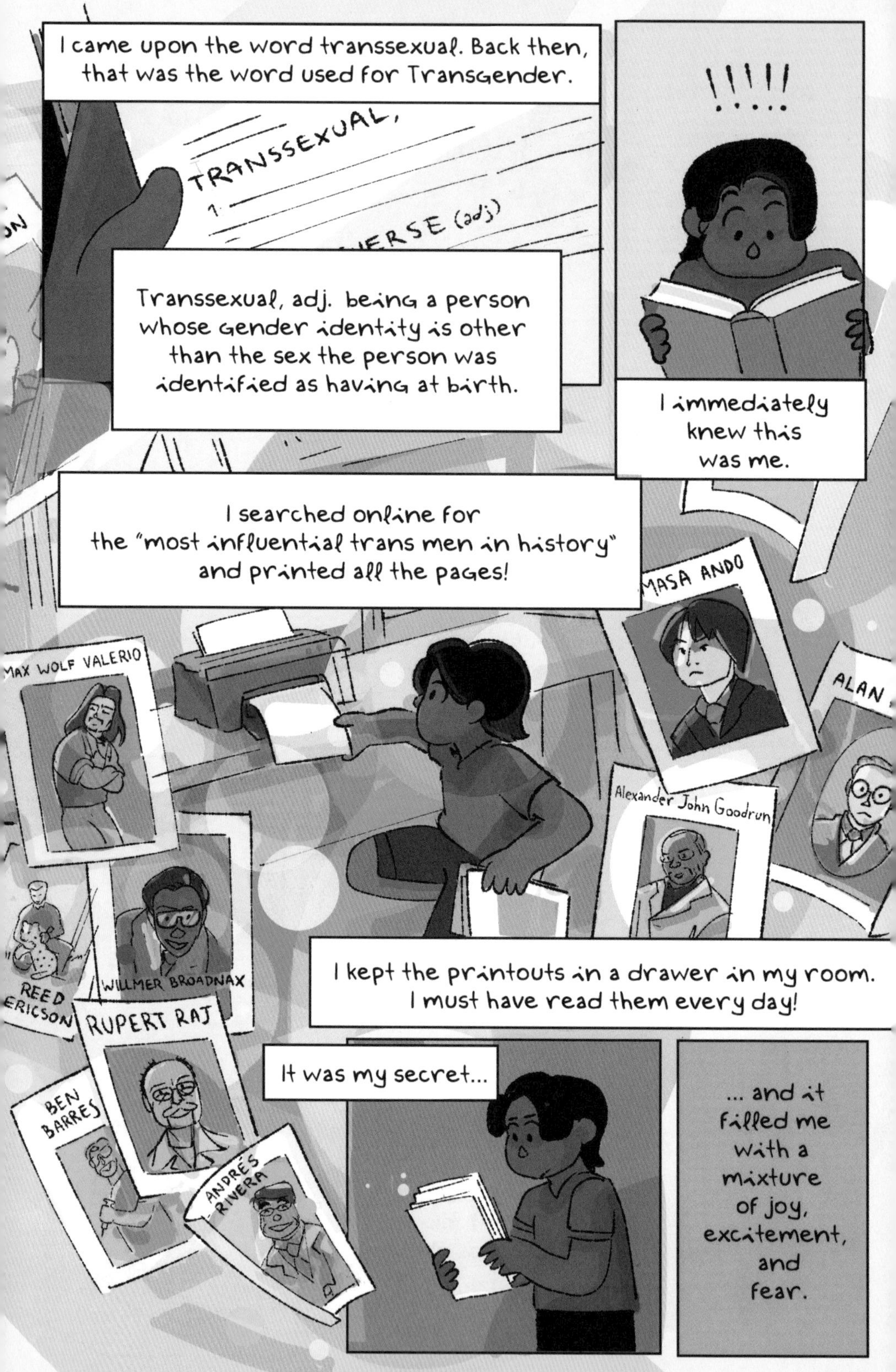
I came upon the word transsexual. Back then, that was the word used for Transgender.
TRANSSEXUAL,
Transsexual, adj. being a person whose gender identity is other than the sex the person was identified as having at birth.
!!!!!
I immediately knew this was me.
I searched online for the "most influential trans men in history" and printed all the pages!
MASA ANDO
MAX WOLF VALERIO
ALAN
Alexander John Goodrun
REED ERICSON
WILLMER BROADNAX
I kept the printouts in a drawer in my room. I must have read them every day!
RUPERT RAJ
BEN BARRES
ANDRÉS RIVERA
It was my secret...
... and it filled me with a mixture of joy, excitement, and fear.

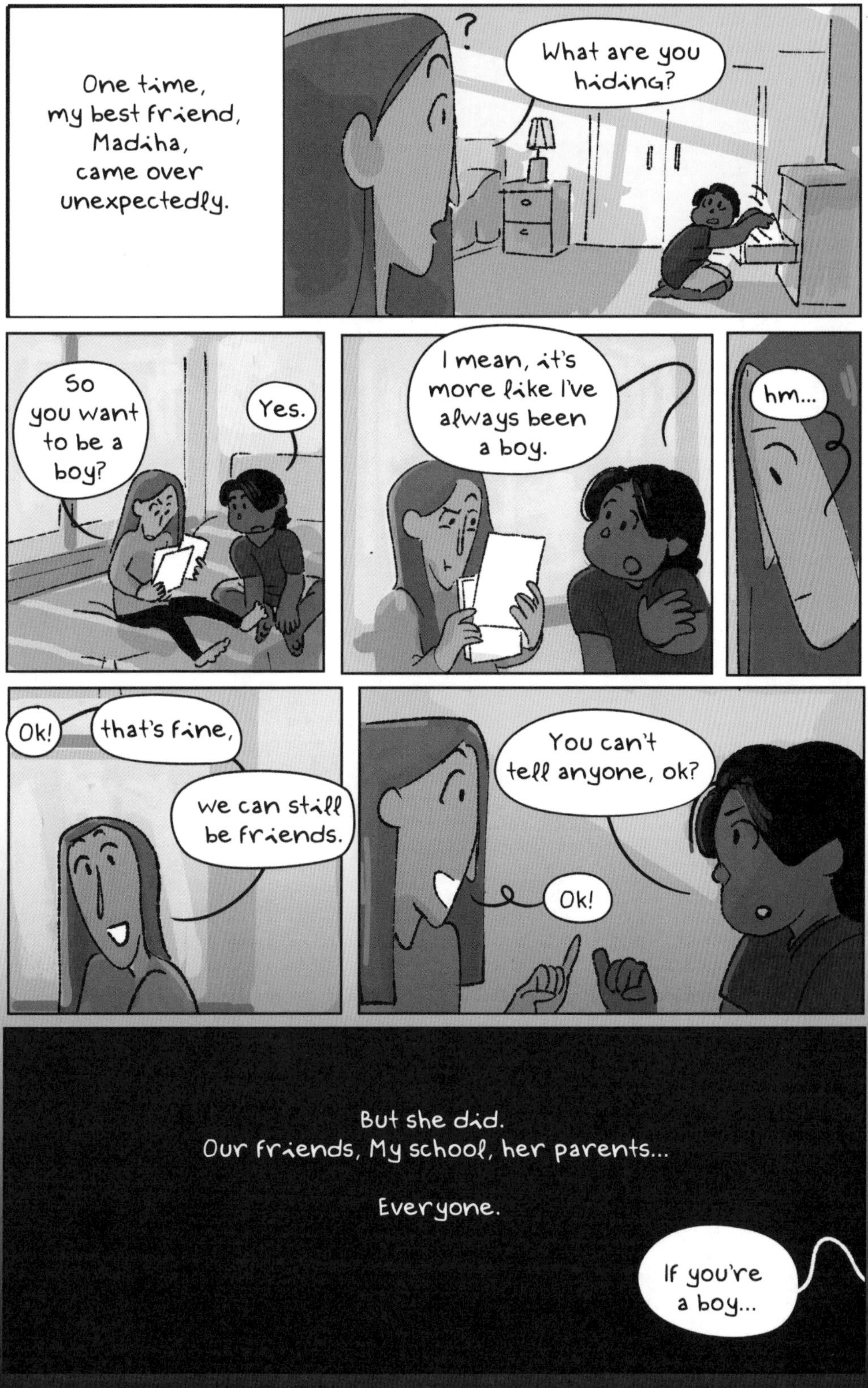

One time,
my best friend,
Madiha,
came over
unexpectedly.
?
What are you hiding?
So you want to be a boy?
Yes.
I mean, it's more like I've always been a boy.
hm...
Ok!
that's fine,
we can still be friends.
You can't tell anyone, ok?
Ok!
But she did.
Our friends, My school, her parents...
Everyone.
If you're a boy...

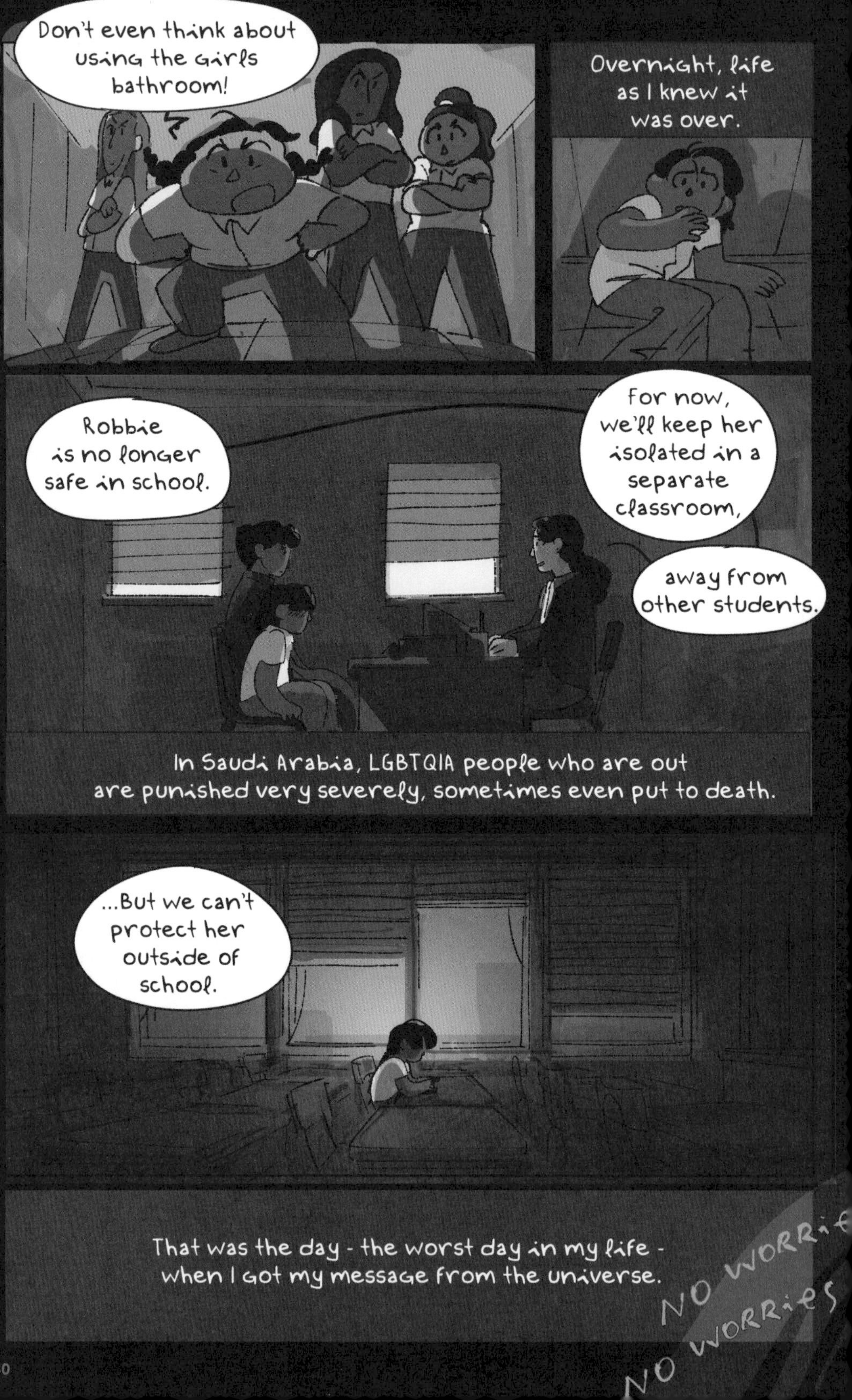
Don't even think about using the Girls bathroom!
Overnight, life as I knew it was over.
Robbie is no longer safe in school.
For now, we'll keep her isolated in a separate classroom,
away from other students.
In Saudi Arabia, LGBTQIA people who are out are punished very severely, sometimes even put to death.
...But we can't protect her outside of school.
That was the day - the worst day in my life - when I got my message from the universe.
NO WORRIES

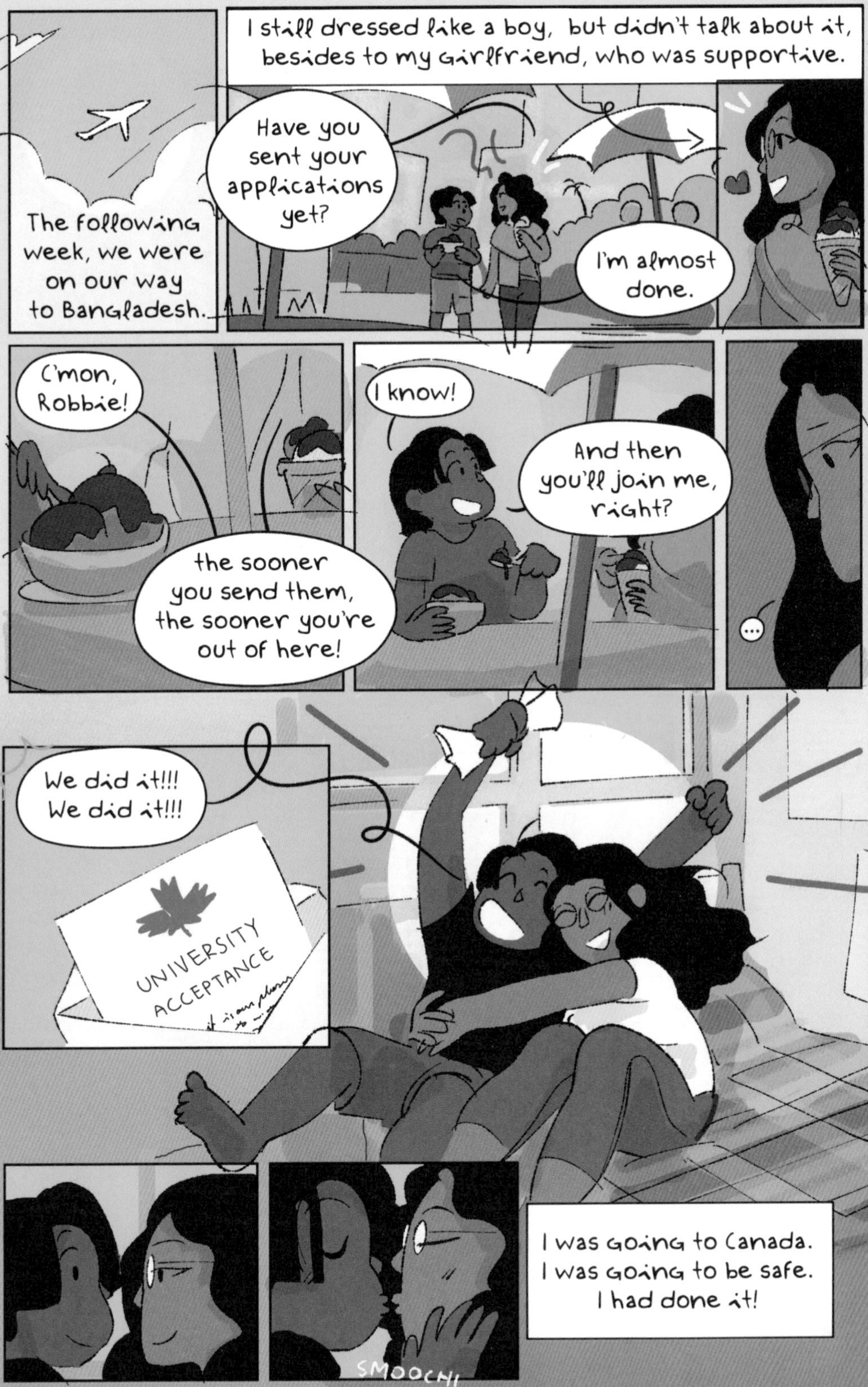

The following week, we were on our way to Bangladesh.
I still dressed like a boy, but didn't talk about it, besides to my girlfriend, who was supportive.
Have you sent your applications yet?
I'm almost done.
C'mon, Robbie!
the sooner you send them, the sooner you're out of here!
I know!
And then you'll join me, right?
...
We did it!!! We did it!!!
UNIVERSITY ACCEPTANCE
SMOOCH!
I was going to Canada. I was going to be safe. I had done it!

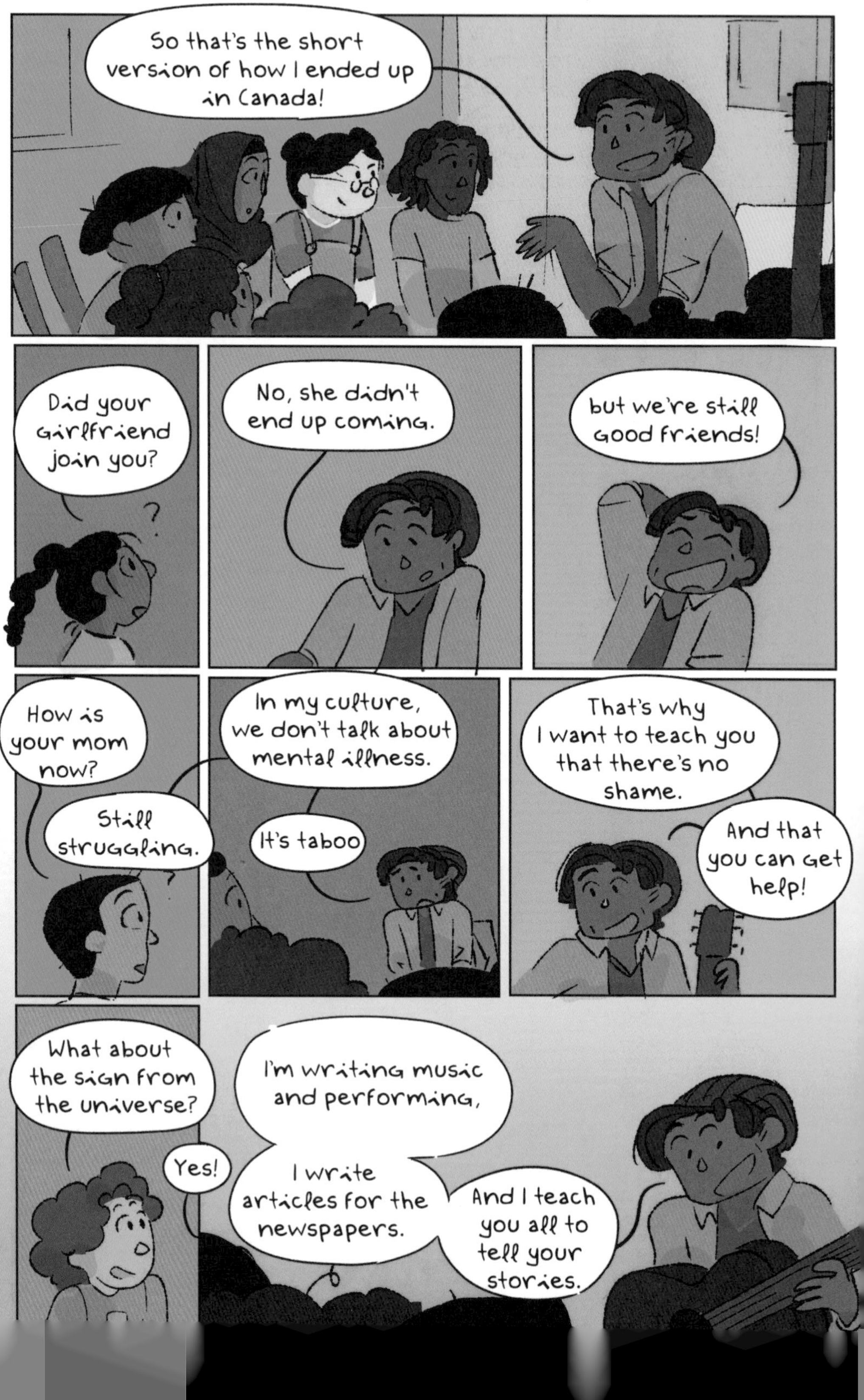
So that's the short version of how I ended up in Canada!
Did your girlfriend join you?
No, she didn't end up coming.
but we're still good friends!
How is your mom now?
Still struggling.
In my culture, we don't talk about mental illness.
It's taboo
That's why I want to teach you that there's no shame.
And that you can get help!
What about the sign from the universe?
Yes!
I'm writing music and performing,
I write articles for the newspapers.
And I teach you all to tell your stories.

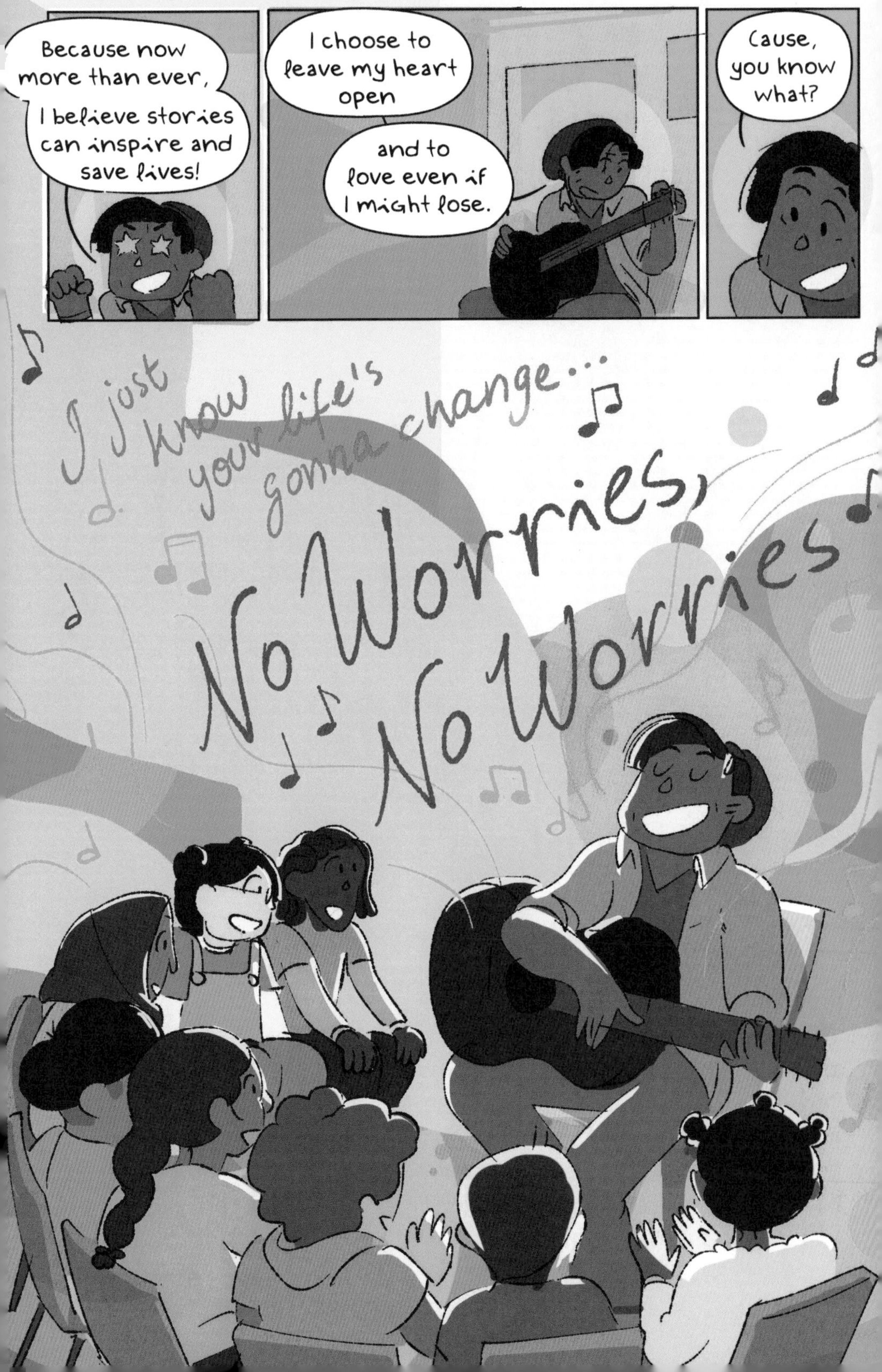
Because now more than ever,
I believe stories can inspire and save lives!
I choose to leave my heart open
and to love even if I might lose.
Cause, you know what?
I just know your life's gonna change...
No Worries, No Worries

BECOMING DIAMOND STYLZ

When not playing *Zelda* or watching old reruns of her favorite TV shows, Diamond is the Executive director of Black Trans Women Inc, an advocacy group focused on building strong and effective Black trans leadership and socioeconomic power. Diamond is the host and creator of the award-winning LGBTQ podcast, *Marsha's Plate.*

Written by Sammy Lisel
Illustrated by Kameron White

Kameron White is a comic artist, illustrator, and designer residing in Minneapolis, MN. With his work, he aims to display diverse groups so that everyone can see themselves represented positively. When not drawing, Kameron likes to watch horror movies, cook, collect dolls, and hang out with his partner and three cats.

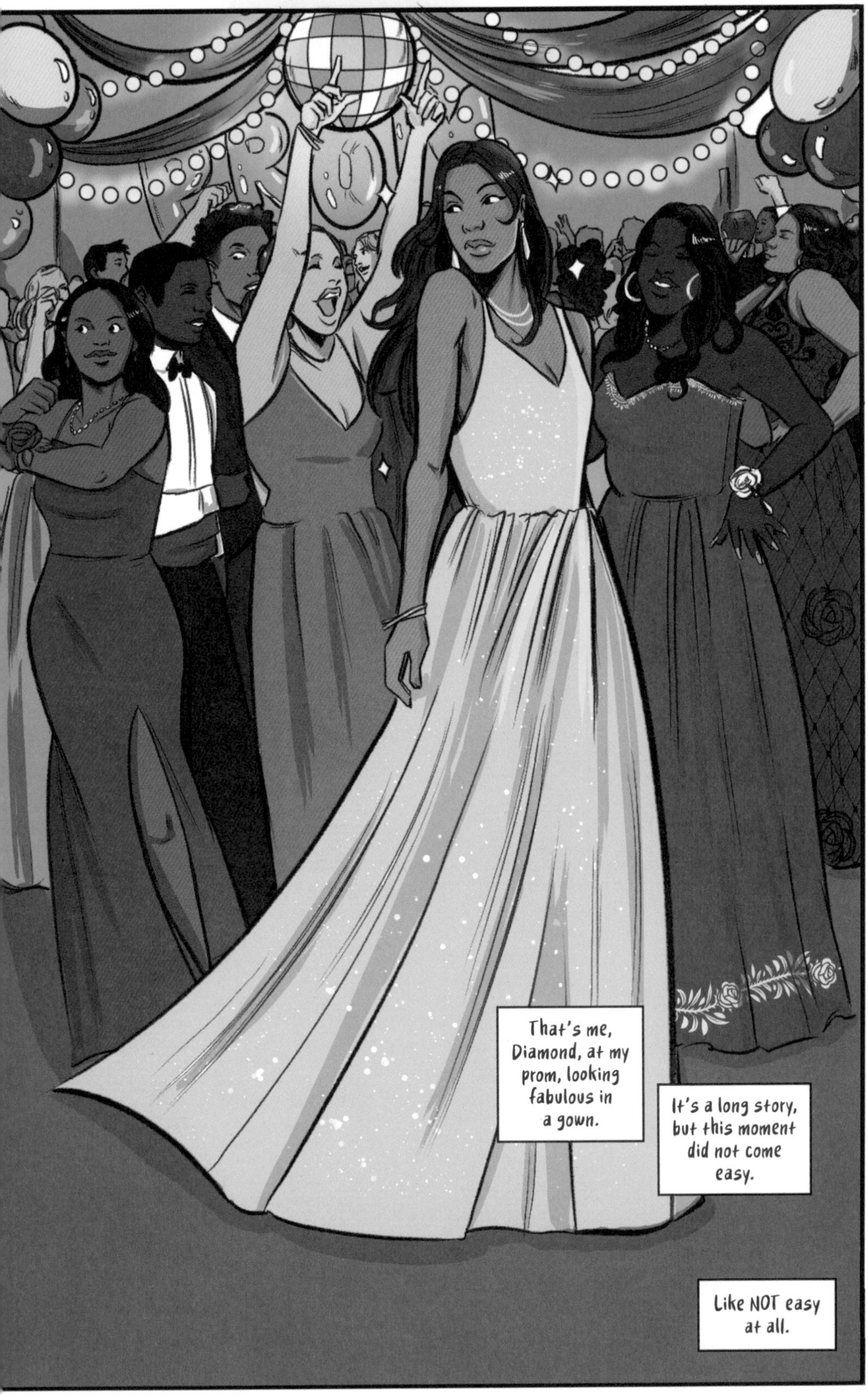

That's me, Diamond, at my prom, looking fabulous in a gown.
It's a long story, but this moment did not come easy.
Like NOT easy at all.

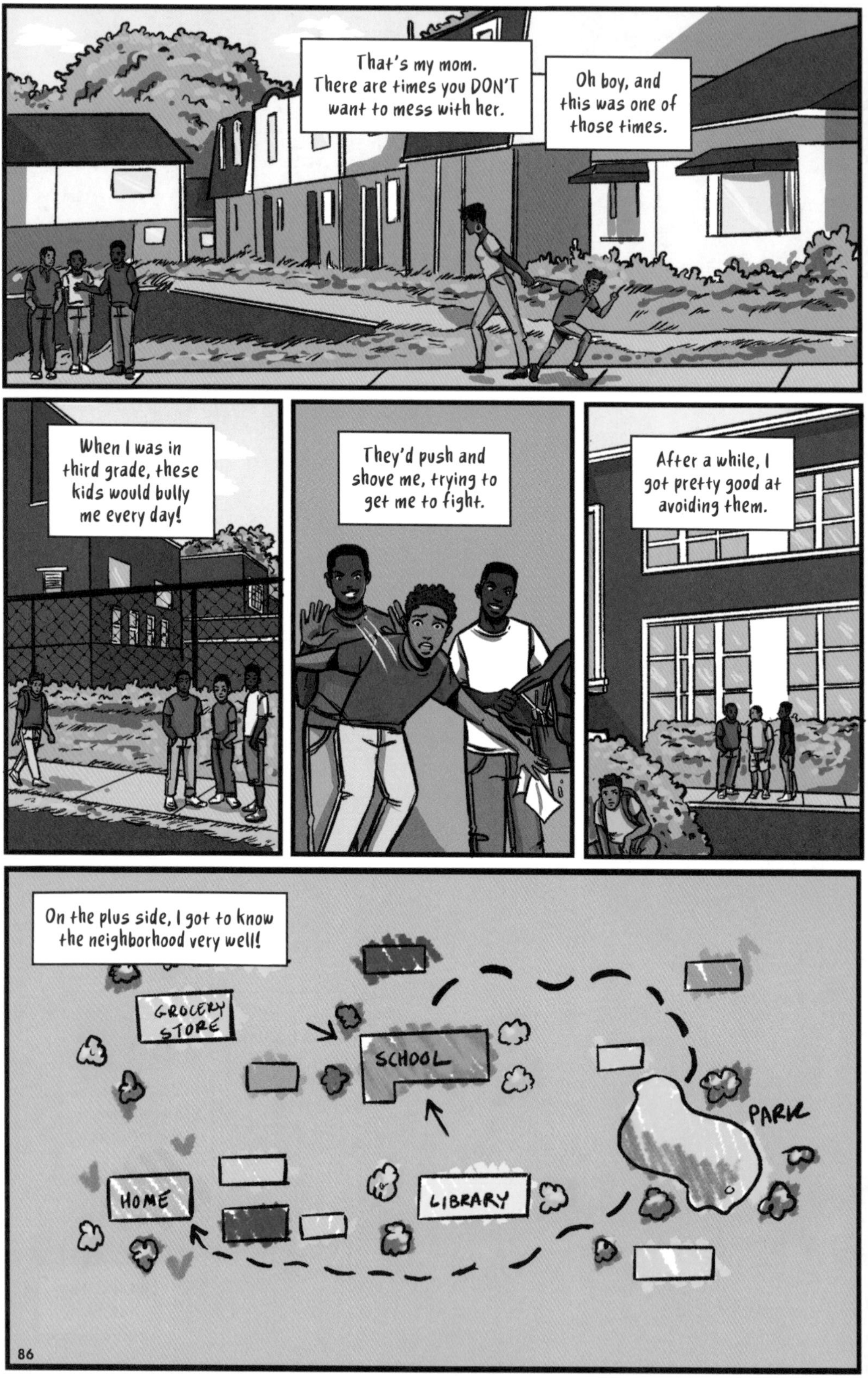
That's my mom.
There are times you DON'T want to mess with her.
Oh boy, and this was one of those times.
When I was in third grade, these kids would bully me every day!
They'd push and shove me, trying to get me to fight.
After a while, I got pretty good at avoiding them.
On the plus side, I got to know the neighborhood very well!
GROCERY STORE
SCHOOL
PARK
LIBRARY
HOME

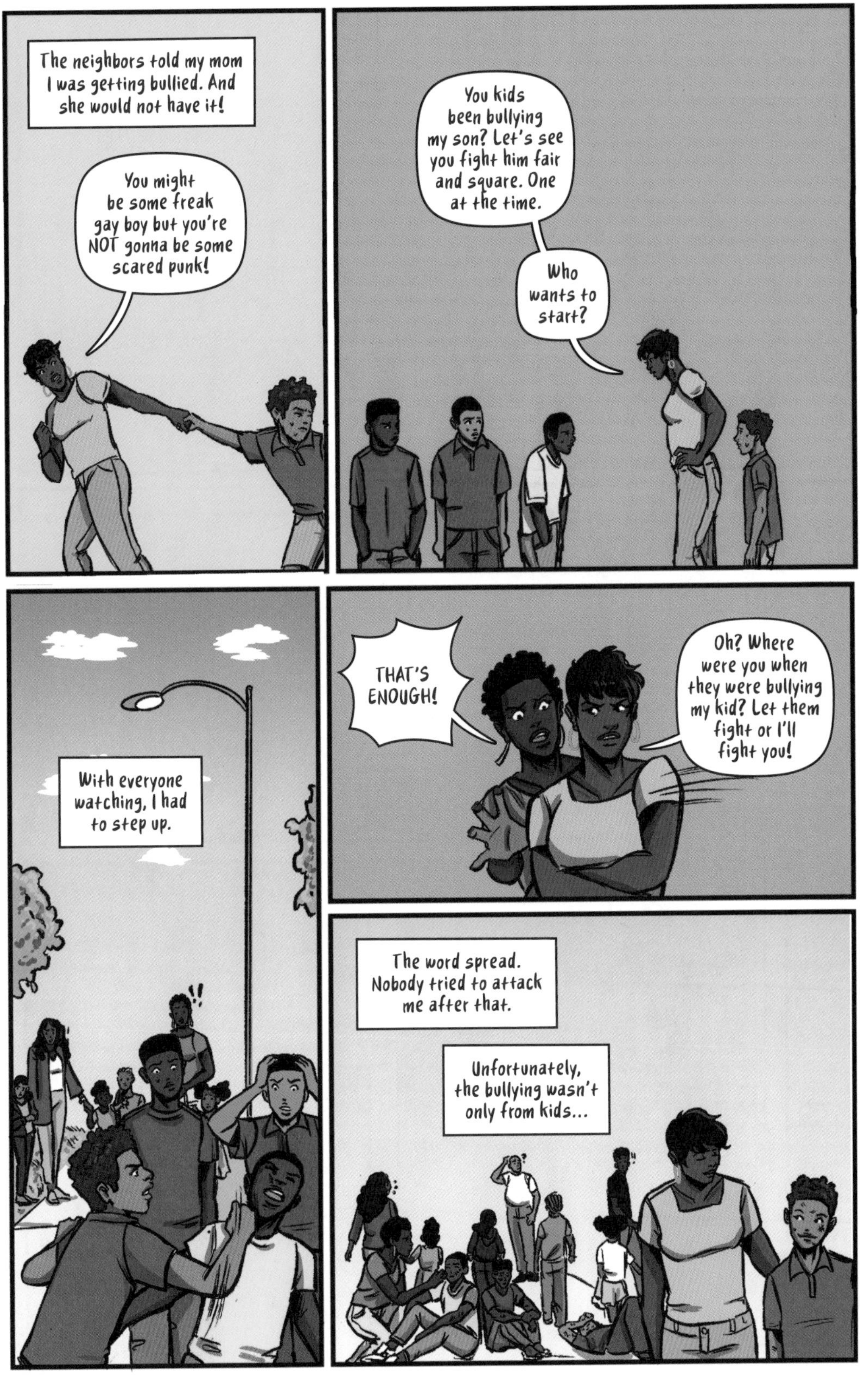

The neighbors told my mom I was getting bullied. And she would not have it!
You might be some freak gay boy but you're NOT gonna be some scared punk!
You kids been bullying my son? Let's see you fight him fair and square. One at the time.
Who wants to start?
With everyone watching, I had to step up.
THAT'S ENOUGH!
Oh? Where were you when they were bullying my kid? Let them fight or I'll fight you!
The word spread. Nobody tried to attack me after that.
Unfortunately, the bullying wasn't only from kids...

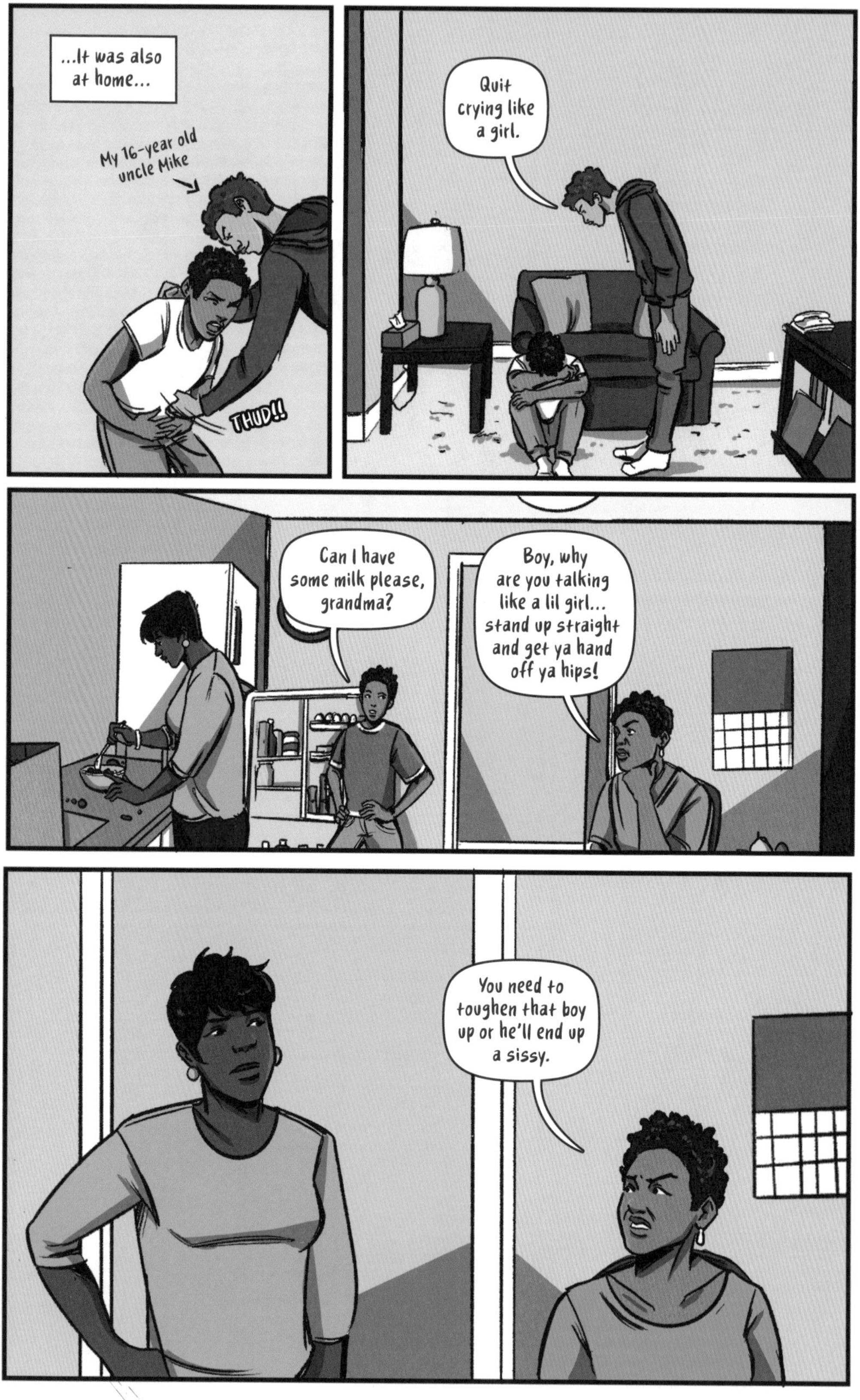
...It was also at home...
My 16-year old uncle Mike
THUD!!
Quit crying like a girl.
Can I have some milk please, grandma?
Boy, why are you talking like a lil girl... stand up straight and get ya hand off ya hips!
You need to toughen that boy up or he'll end up a sissy.

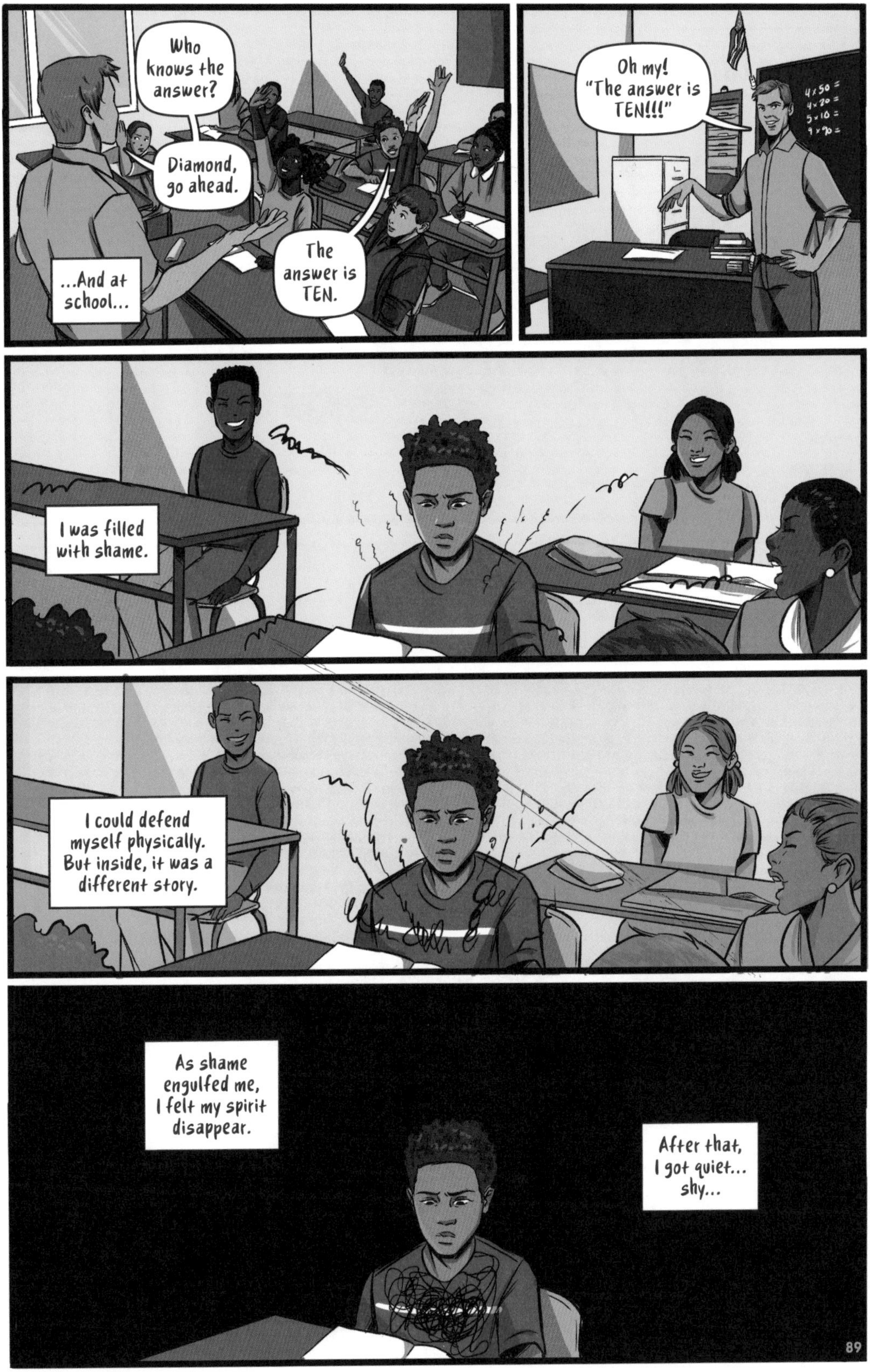
Who knows the answer?
Diamond, go ahead.
The answer is TEN.
...And at school...
Oh my! "The answer is TEN!!!"
4×50 =
4×20 =
5×10 =
9×90 =
I was filled with shame.
I could defend myself physically. But inside, it was a different story.
As shame engulfed me, I felt my spirit disappear.
After that, I got quiet... shy...

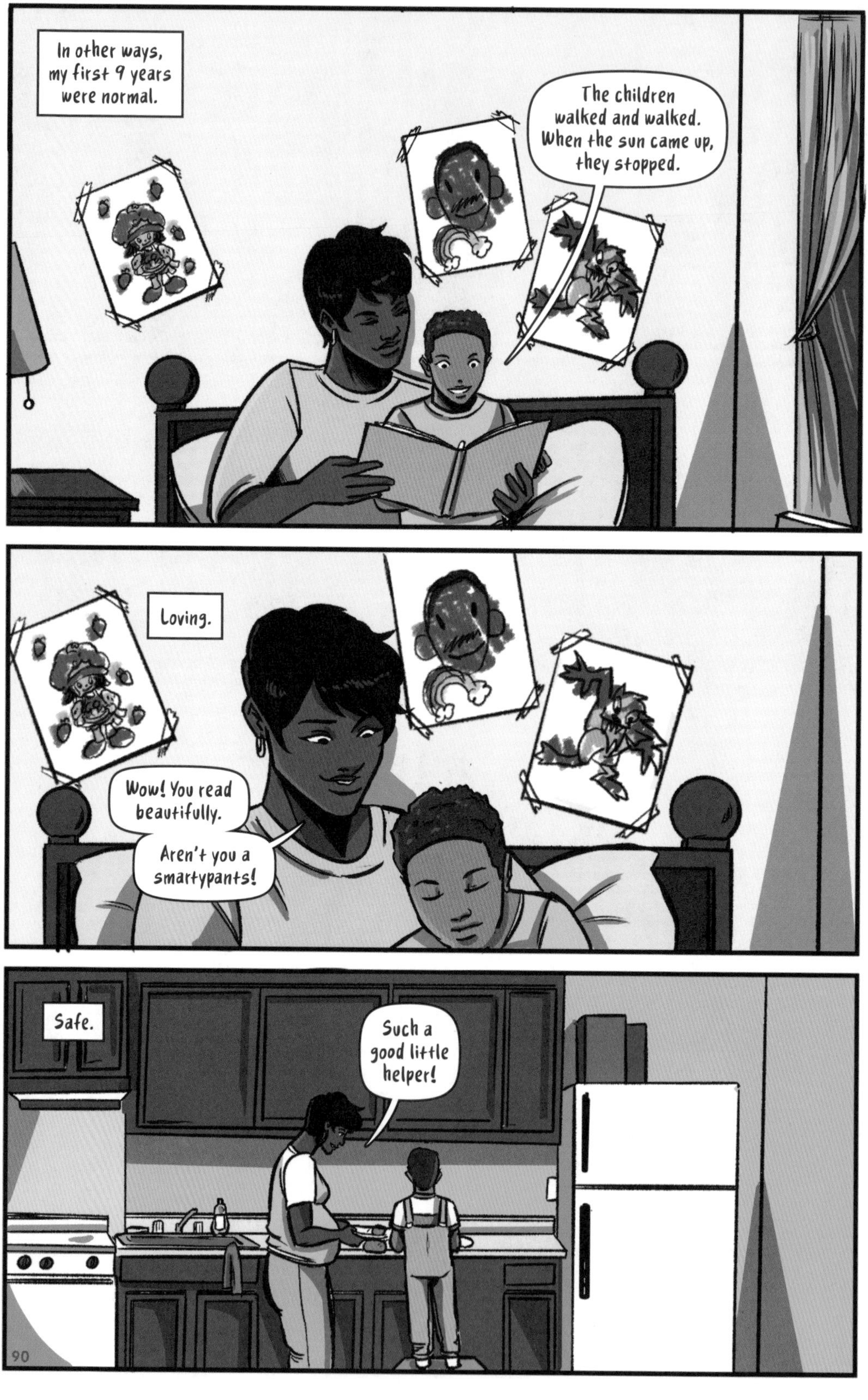
In other ways, my first 9 years were normal.
The children walked and walked. When the sun came up, they stopped.
Loving.
Wow! You read beautifully.
Aren't you a smartypants!
Safe.
Such a good little helper!

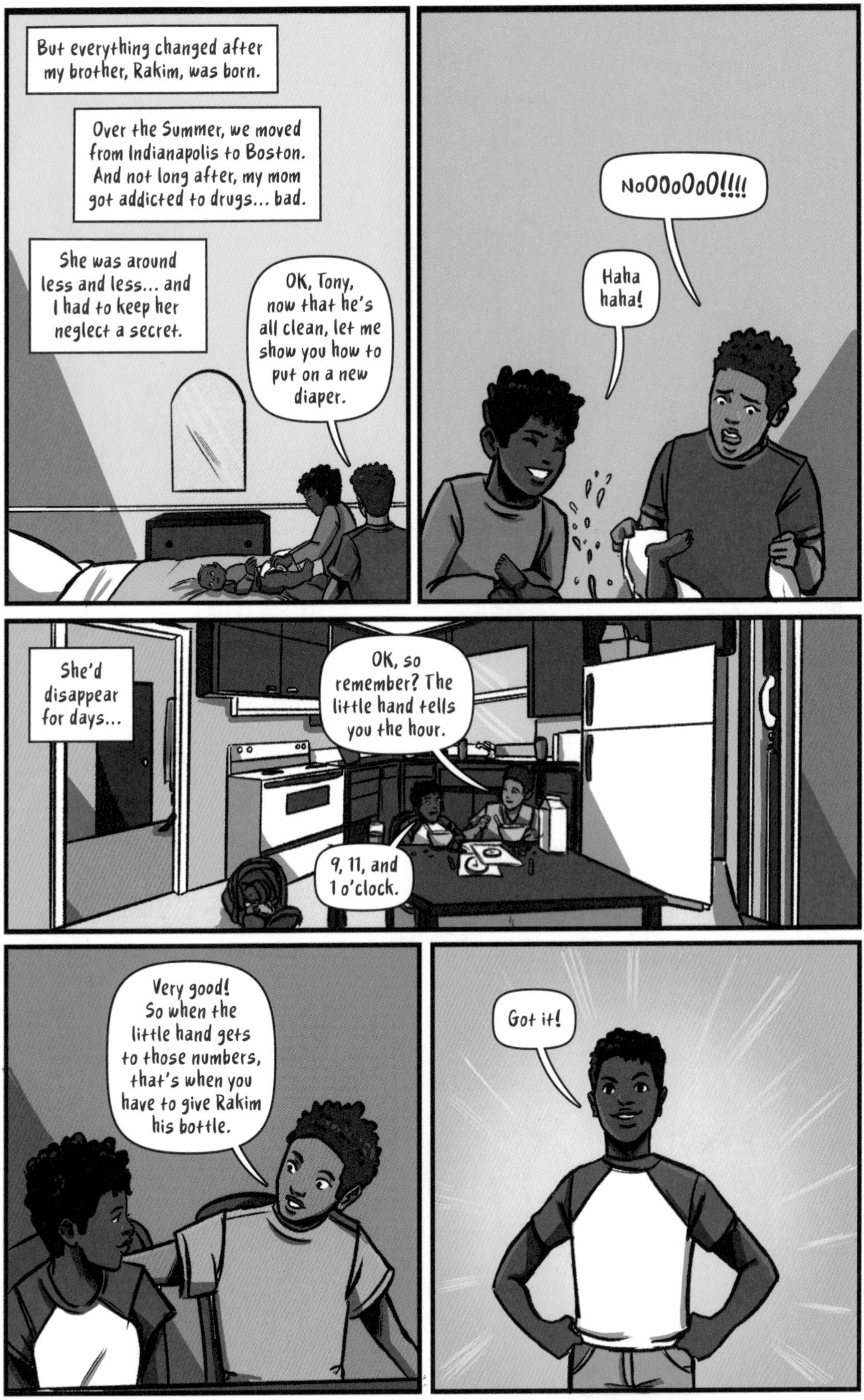
But everything changed after my brother, Rakim, was born.
Over the Summer, we moved from Indianapolis to Boston. And not long after, my mom got addicted to drugs... bad.
She was around less and less... and I had to keep her neglect a secret.
OK, Tony, now that he's all clean, let me show you how to put on a new diaper.
NoOOoOoO!!!!
Haha haha!
She'd disappear for days...
OK, so remember? The little hand tells you the hour.
9, 11, and 1 o'clock.
Very good! So when the little hand gets to those numbers, that's when you have to give Rakim his bottle.
Got it!

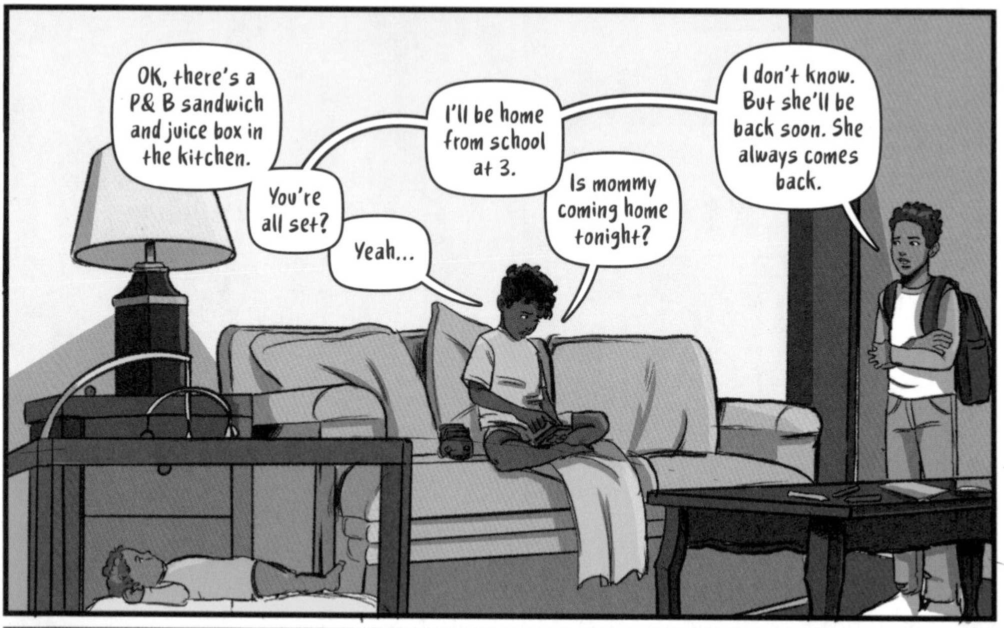
OK, there's a P& B sandwich and juice box in the kitchen.
You're all set?
Yeah...
I'll be home from school at 3.
Is mommy coming home tonight?
I don't know. But she'll be back soon. She always comes back.

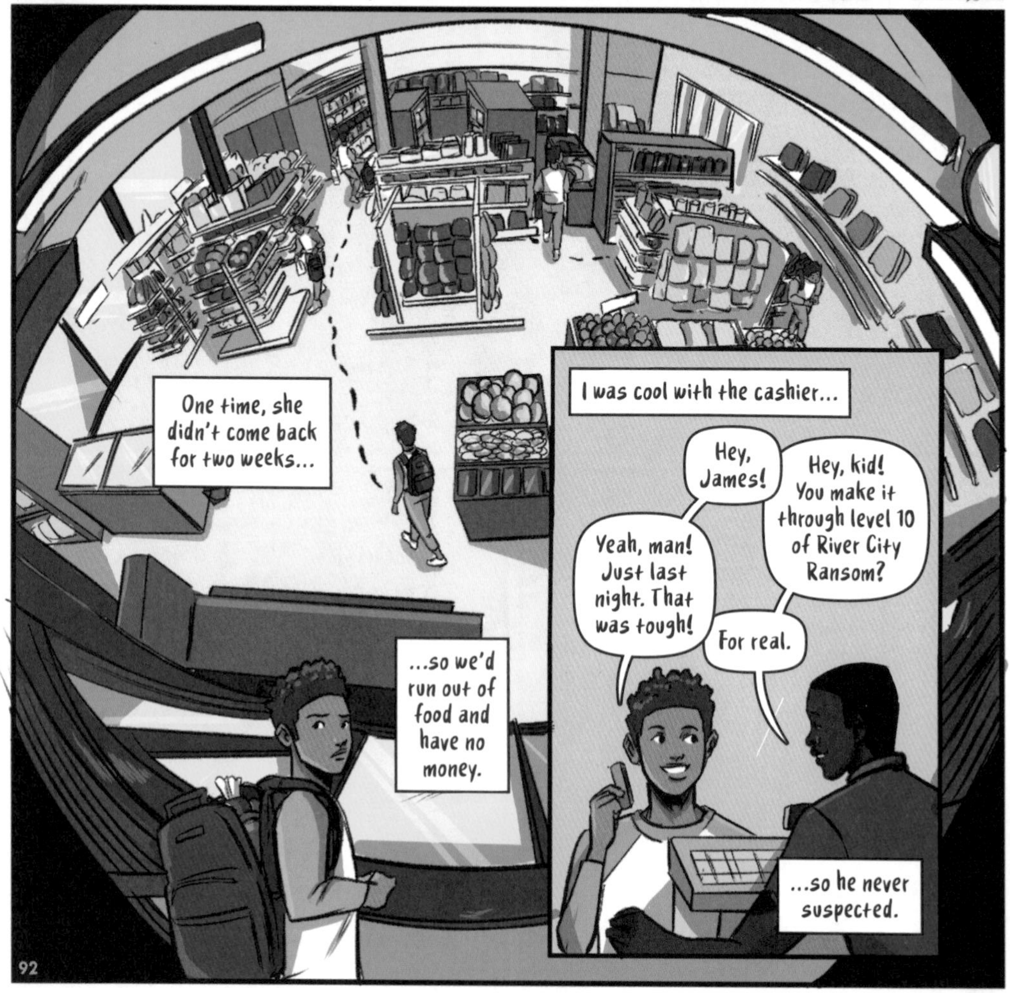
One time, she didn't come back for two weeks...
...so we'd run out of food and have no money.
I was cool with the cashier...
Hey, James!
Hey, kid! You make it through level 10 of River City Ransom?
Yeah, man! Just last night. That was tough!
For real.
...so he never suspected.

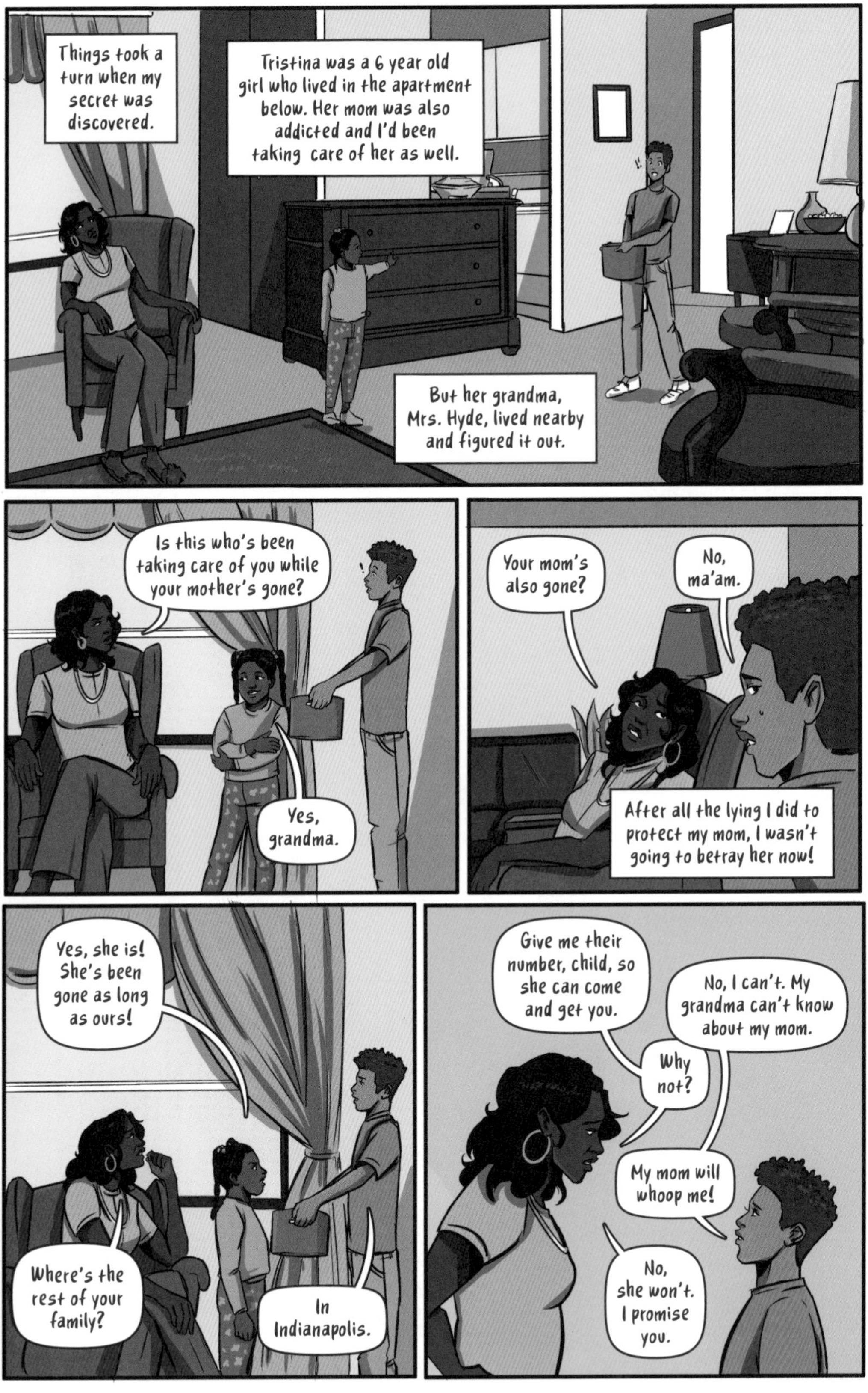
Things took a turn when my secret was discovered.
Tristina was a 6 year old girl who lived in the apartment below. Her mom was also addicted and I'd been taking care of her as well.
But her grandma, Mrs. Hyde, lived nearby and figured it out.
!!
Is this who's been taking care of you while your mother's gone?
!
Yes, grandma.
Your mom's also gone?
No, ma'am.
After all the lying I did to protect my mom, I wasn't going to betray her now!
Yes, she is! She's been gone as long as ours!
Where's the rest of your family?
In Indianapolis.
Give me their number, child, so she can come and get you.
No, I can't. My grandma can't know about my mom.
Why not?
My mom will whoop me!
No, she won't. I promise you.

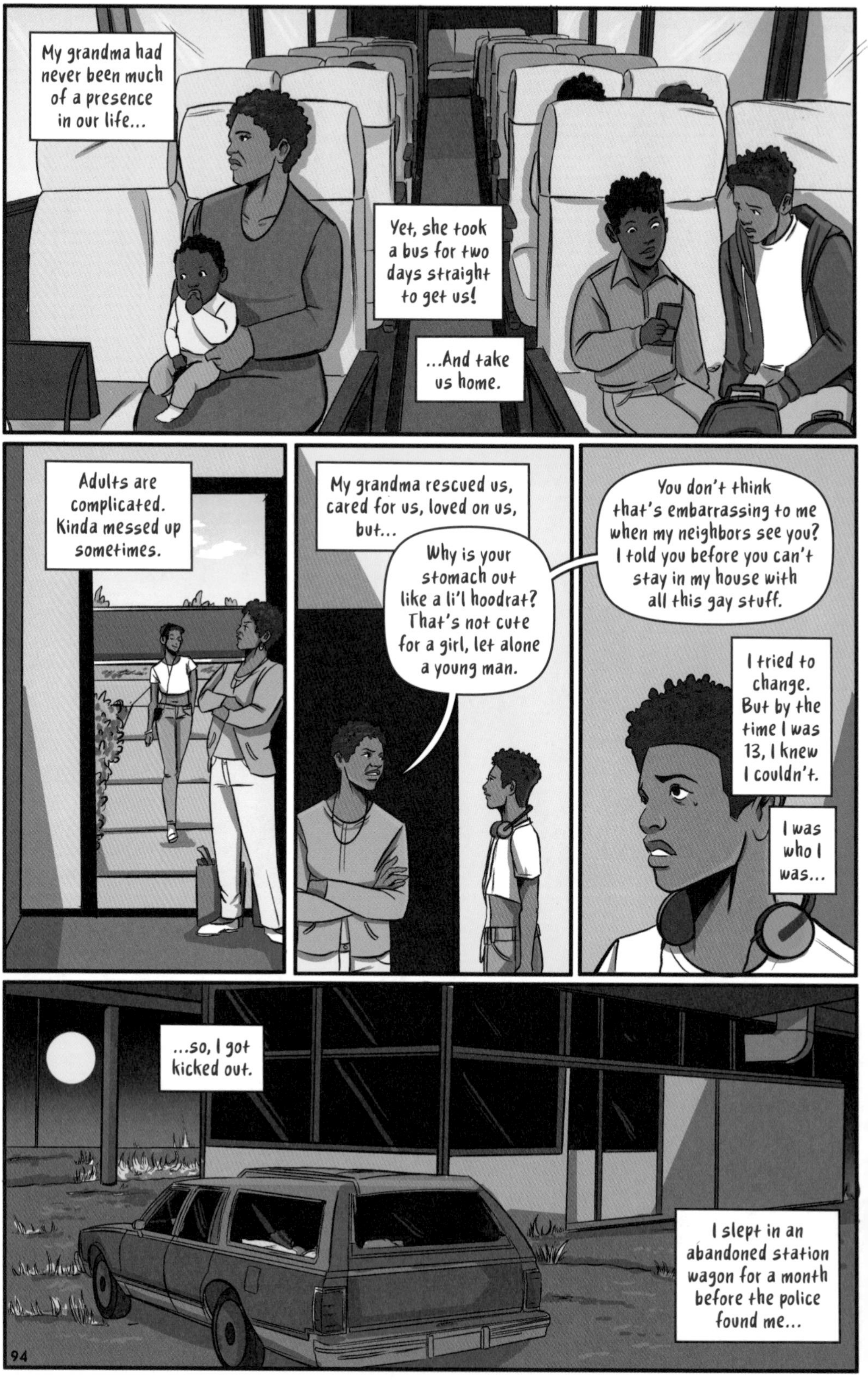

My grandma had never been much of a presence in our life...
Yet, she took a bus for two days straight to get us!
...And take us home.
Adults are complicated. Kinda messed up sometimes.
My grandma rescued us, cared for us, loved on us, but...
Why is your stomach out like a li'l hoodrat? That's not cute for a girl, let alone a young man.
You don't think that's embarrassing to me when my neighbors see you? I told you before you can't stay in my house with all this gay stuff.
I tried to change. But by the time I was 13, I knew I couldn't.
I was who I was...
...so, I got kicked out.
I slept in an abandoned station wagon for a month before the police found me...

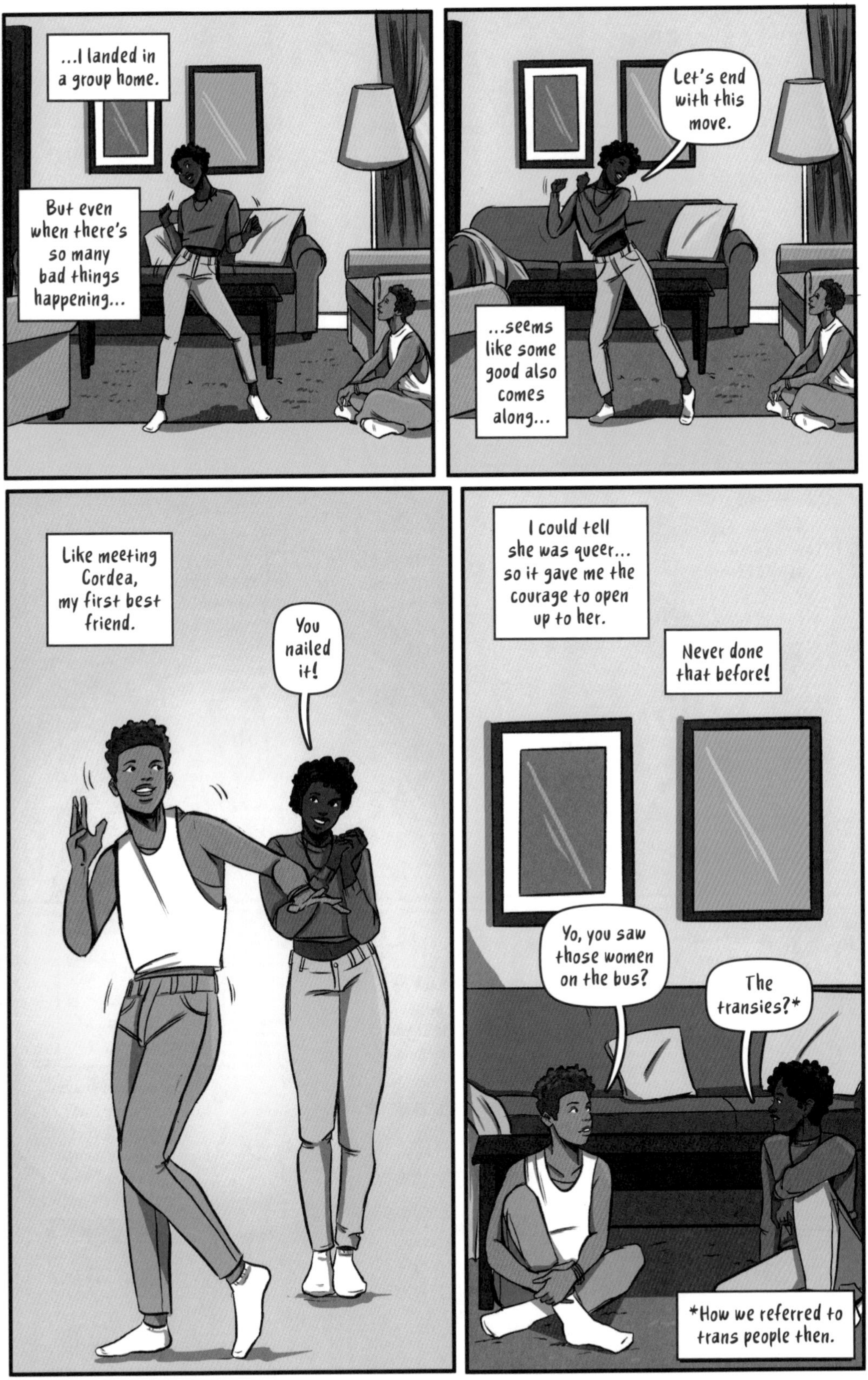
...I landed in a group home.
But even when there's so many bad things happening...
Let's end with this move.
...seems like some good also comes along...
Like meeting Cordea, my first best friend.
You nailed it!
I could tell she was queer... so it gave me the courage to open up to her.
Never done that before!
Yo, you saw those women on the bus?
The transies?*
*How we referred to trans people then.

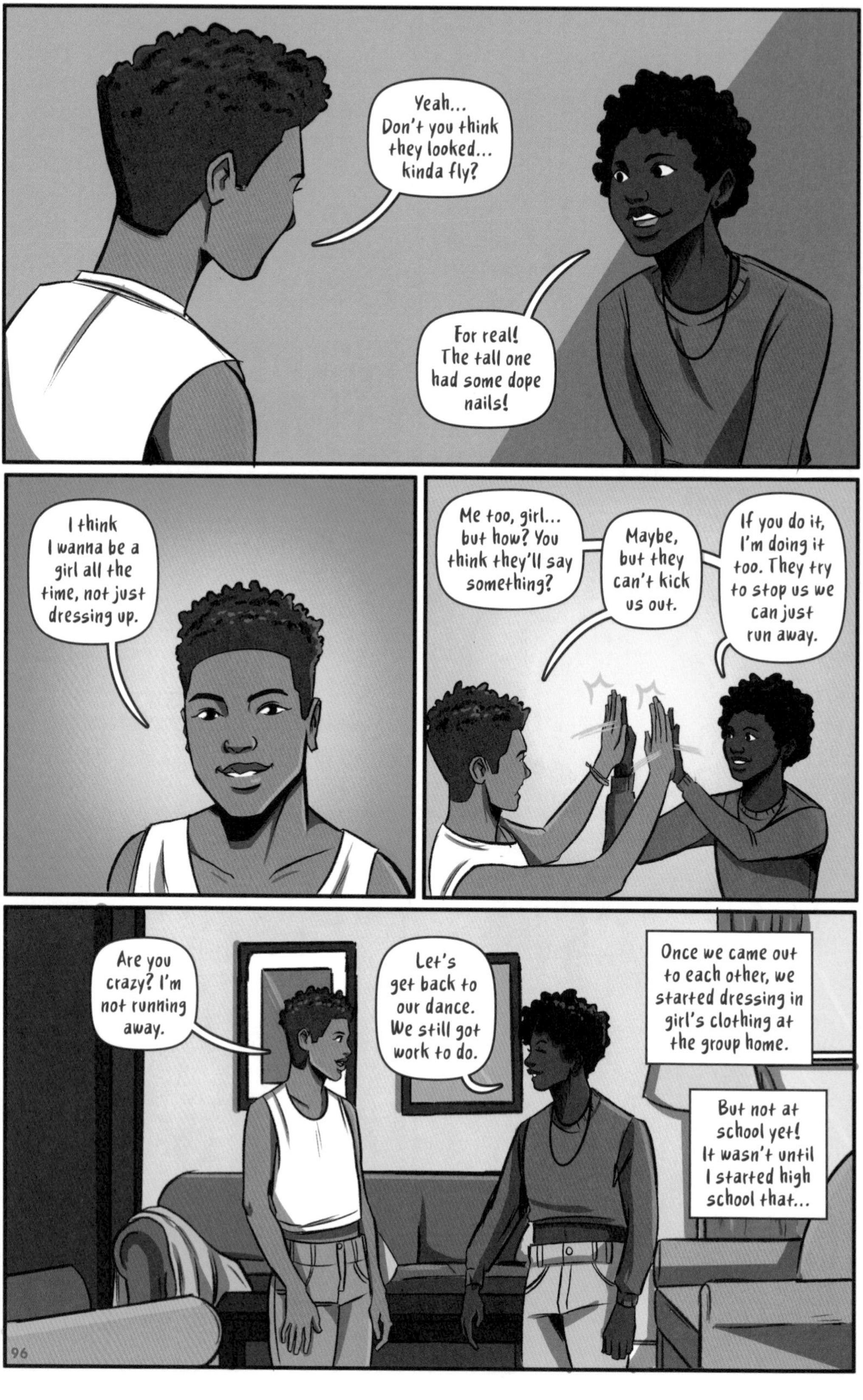

Yeah... Don't you think they looked... kinda fly?
For real! The tall one had some dope nails!
I think I wanna be a girl all the time, not just dressing up.
Me too, girl... but how? You think they'll say something?
Maybe, but they can't kick us out.
If you do it, I'm doing it too. They try to stop us we can just run away.
Are you crazy? I'm not running away.
Let's get back to our dance. We still got work to do.
Once we came out to each other, we started dressing in girl's clothing at the group home.
But not at school yet! It wasn't until I started high school that...

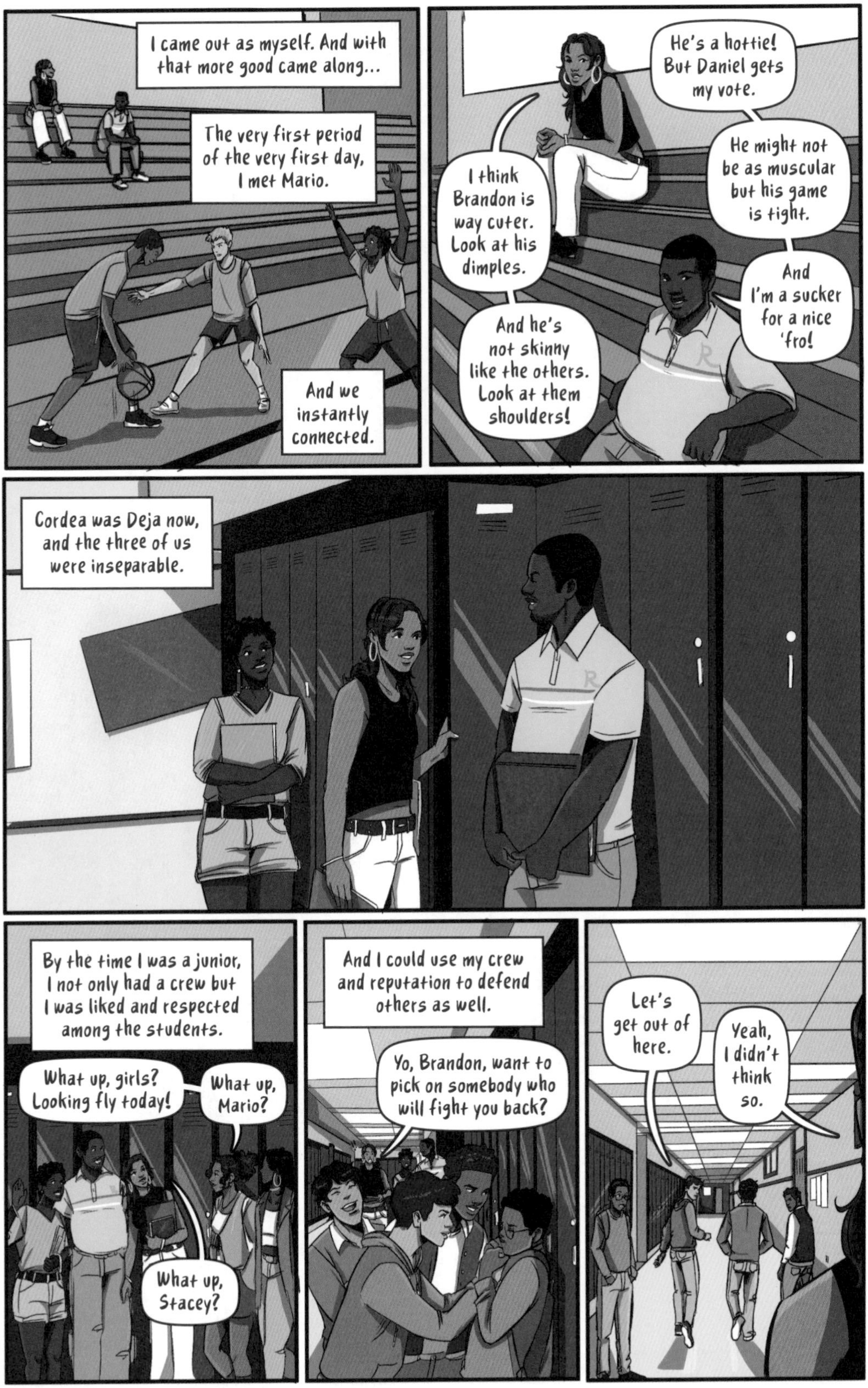
I came out as myself. And with that more good came along...
The very first period of the very first day, I met Mario.
And we instantly connected.
I think Brandon is way cuter. Look at his dimples.
He's a hottie! But Daniel gets my vote.
He might not be as muscular but his game is tight.
And he's not skinny like the others. Look at them shoulders!
And I'm a sucker for a nice 'fro!
Cordea was Deja now, and the three of us were inseparable.
By the time I was a junior, I not only had a crew but I was liked and respected among the students.
What up, girls? Looking fly today!
What up, Mario?
What up, Stacey?
And I could use my crew and reputation to defend others as well.
Yo, Brandon, want to pick on somebody who will fight you back?
Let's get out of here.
Yeah, I didn't think so.

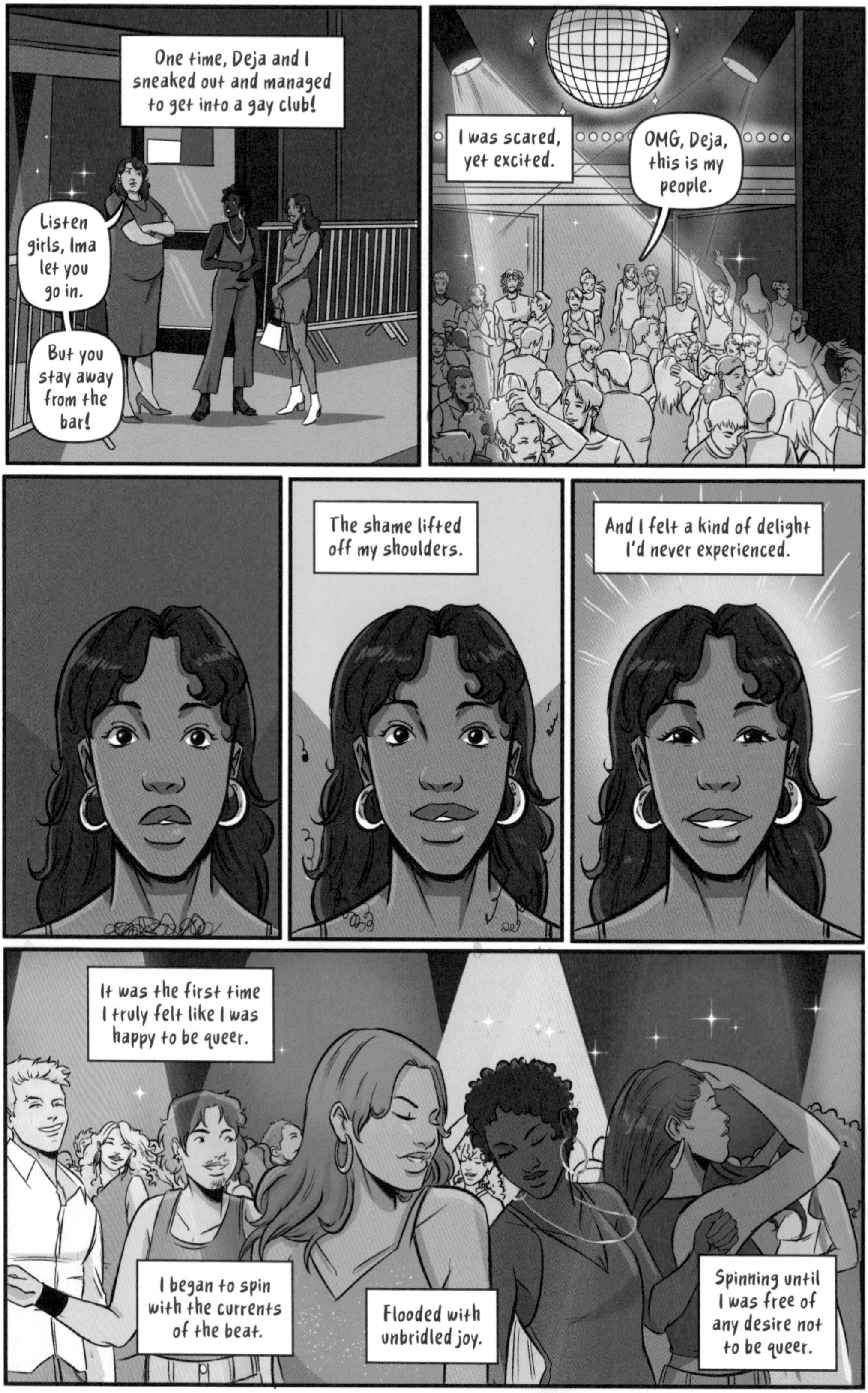
One time, Deja and I sneaked out and managed to get into a gay club!
Listen girls, Ima let you go in.
But you stay away from the bar!
I was scared, yet excited.
OMG, Deja, this is my people.
The shame lifted off my shoulders.
And I felt a kind of delight I'd never experienced.
It was the first time I truly felt like I was happy to be queer.
I began to spin with the currents of the beat.
Flooded with unbridled joy.
Spinning until I was free of any desire not to be queer.

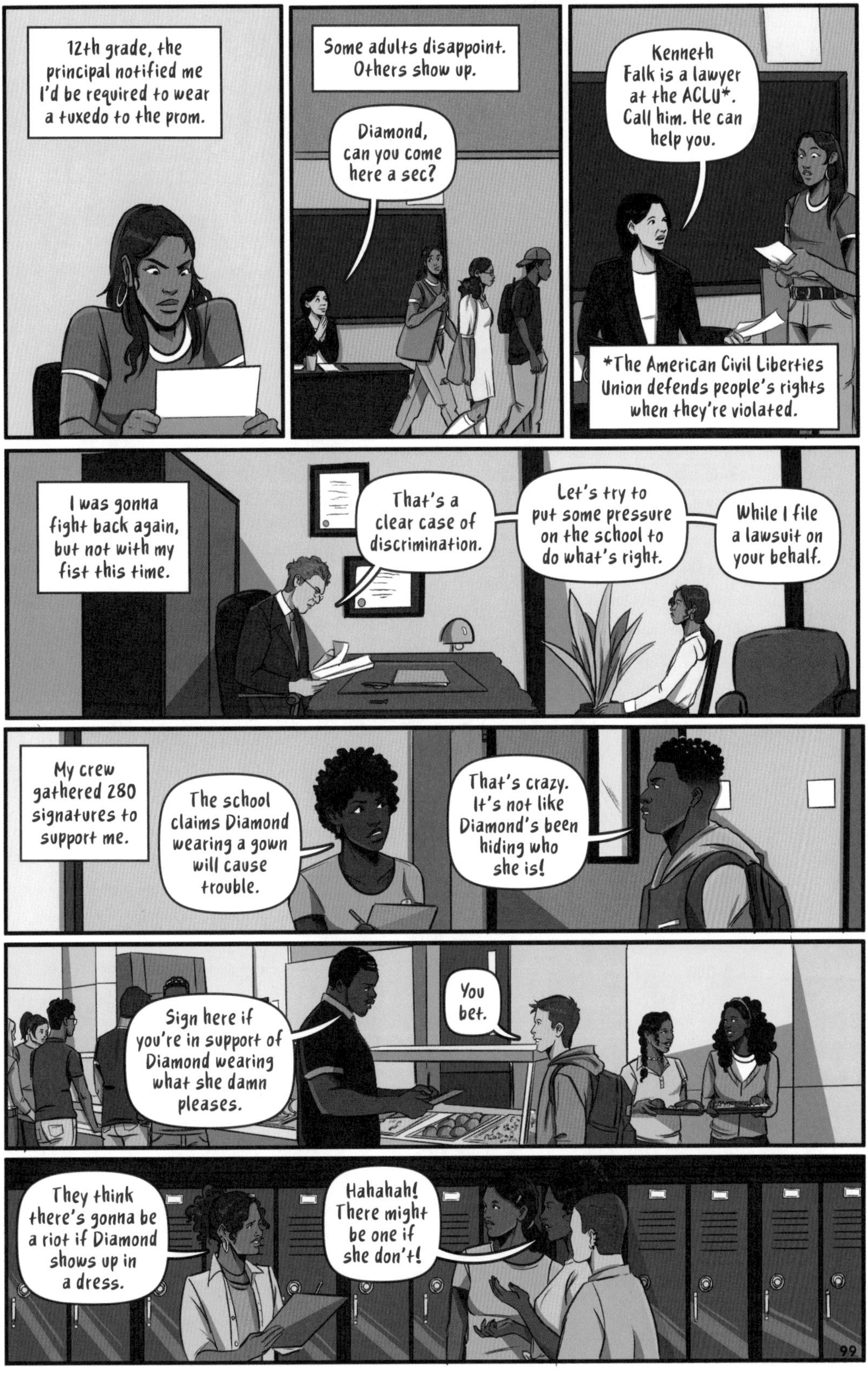
12th grade, the principal notified me I'd be required to wear a tuxedo to the prom.
Some adults disappoint. Others show up.
Diamond, can you come here a sec?
Kenneth Falk is a lawyer at the ACLU*. Call him. He can help you.
*The American Civil Liberties Union defends people's rights when they're violated.
I was gonna fight back again, but not with my fist this time.
That's a clear case of discrimination.
Let's try to put some pressure on the school to do what's right.
While I file a lawsuit on your behalf.
My crew gathered 280 signatures to support me.
The school claims Diamond wearing a gown will cause trouble.
That's crazy. It's not like Diamond's been hiding who she is!
Sign here if you're in support of Diamond wearing what she damn pleases.
You bet.
They think there's gonna be a riot if Diamond shows up in a dress.
Hahahah! There might be one if she don't!

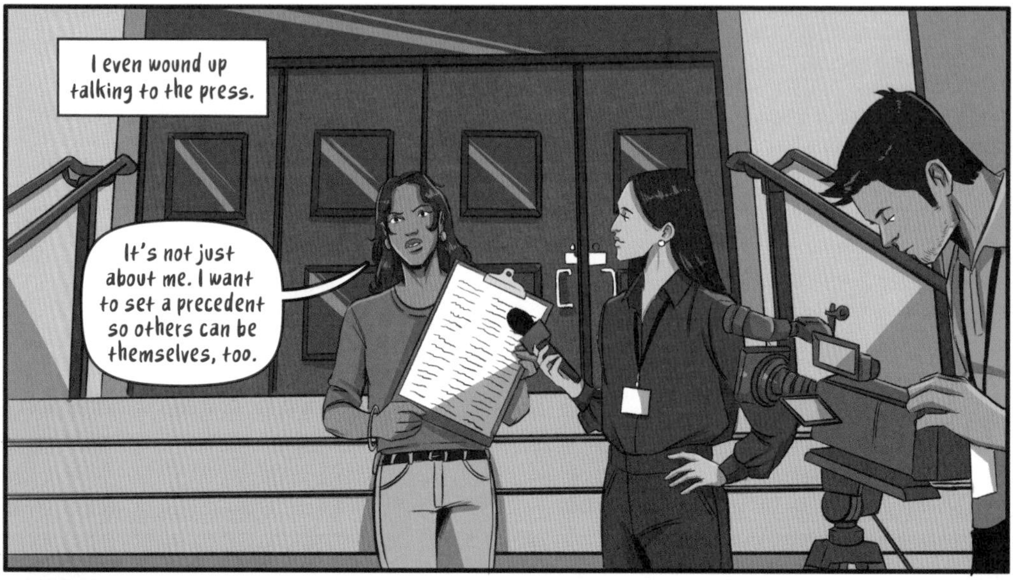
I even wound up talking to the press.
It's not just about me. I want to set a precedent so others can be themselves, too.

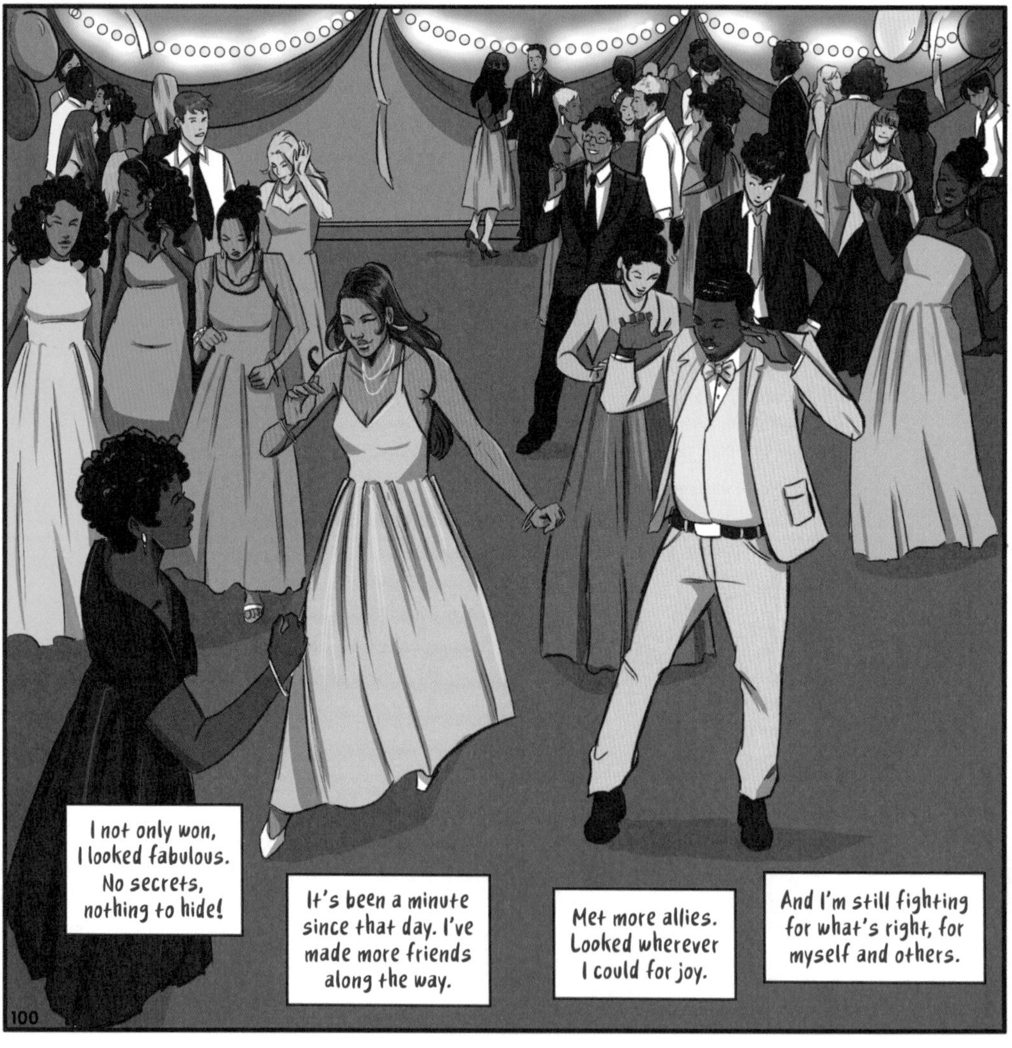
I not only won, I looked fabulous. No secrets, nothing to hide!
It's been a minute since that day. I've made more friends along the way.
Met more allies. Looked wherever I could for joy.
And I'm still fighting for what's right, for myself and others.

BECOMING MARLI WASHINGTON

Marli combined his love for innovation and design to start a company that designs binders and other transitional apparel. When not working on a new idea, Marli likes to hang with his wife and new baby, hike, and play sports!

WRITTEN BY SAMMY LISEL
ILLUSTRATED BY SAGE COFFEY

Sage Coffey (they/them) is a trans nonbinary cartoonist in Chicago. They're best known for their work in *The Washington Post*, *The New Yorker* and the video game *BUGSNAX*. They love their cats and peach oolong tea.

website: sagecoffey.com

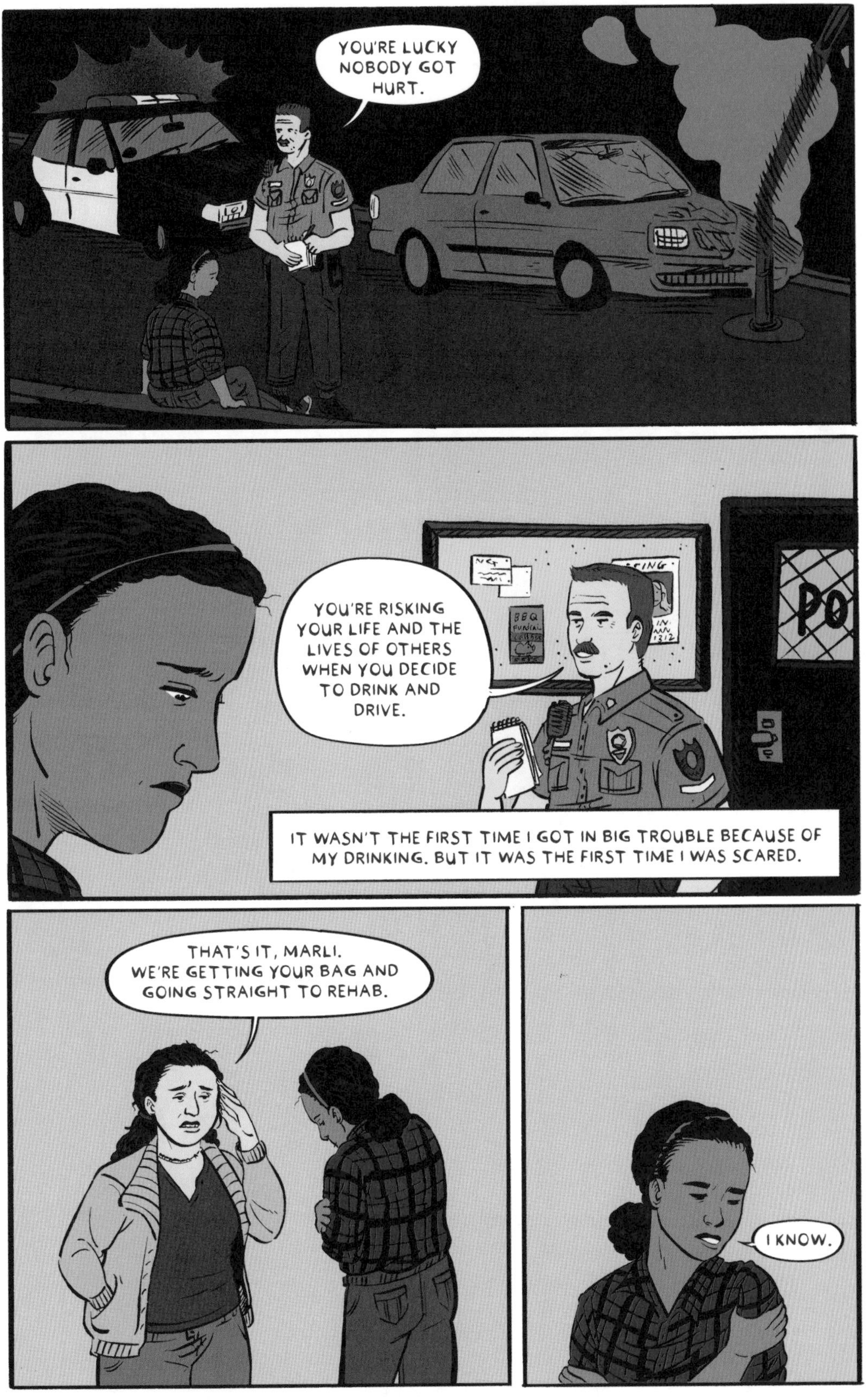
YOU'RE LUCKY NOBODY GOT HURT.
YOU'RE RISKING YOUR LIFE AND THE LIVES OF OTHERS WHEN YOU DECIDE TO DRINK AND DRIVE.
IT WASN'T THE FIRST TIME I GOT IN BIG TROUBLE BECAUSE OF MY DRINKING. BUT IT WAS THE FIRST TIME I WAS SCARED.
THAT'S IT, MARLI. WE'RE GETTING YOUR BAG AND GOING STRAIGHT TO REHAB.
I KNOW.

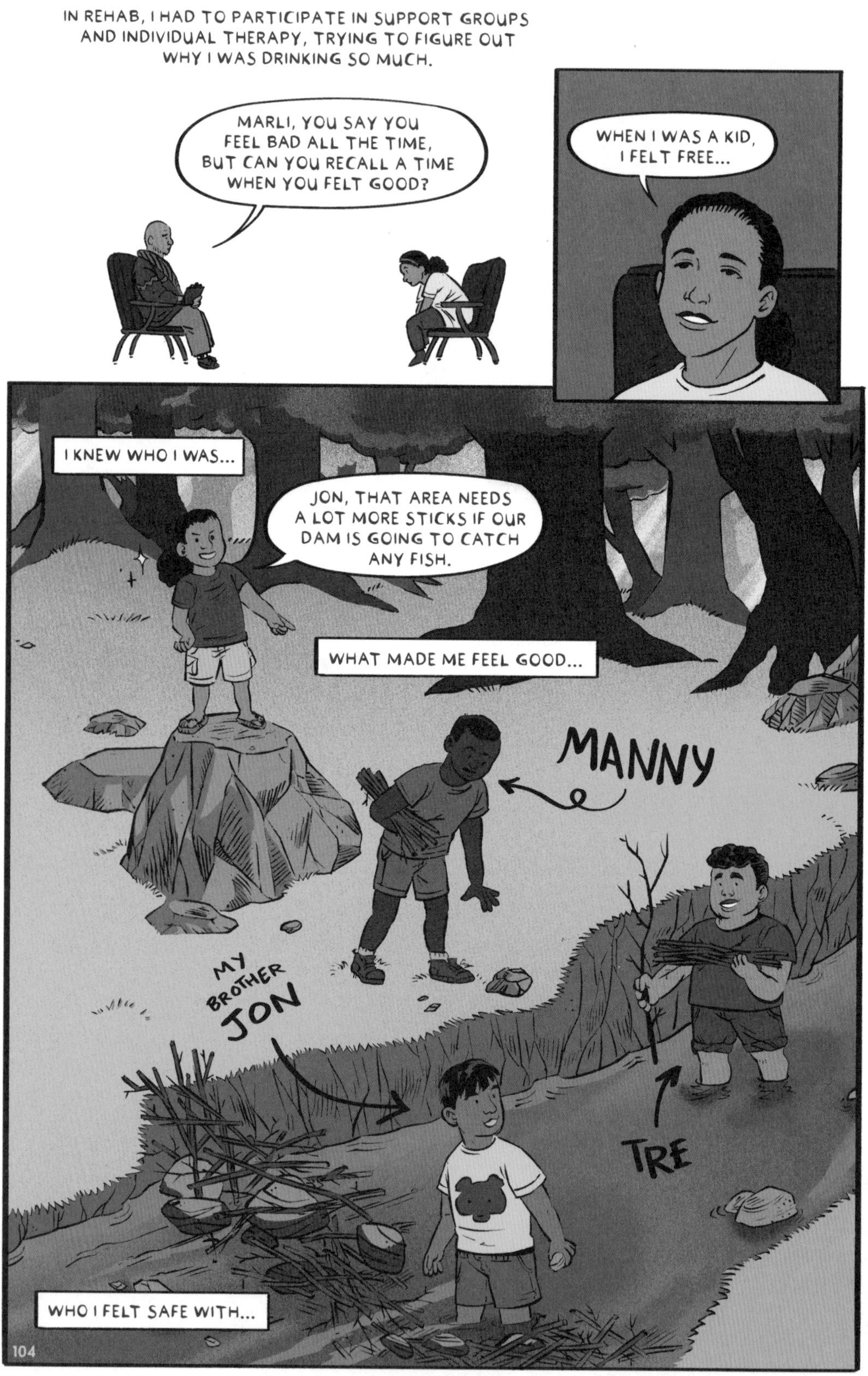
IN REHAB, I HAD TO PARTICIPATE IN SUPPORT GROUPS AND INDIVIDUAL THERAPY, TRYING TO FIGURE OUT WHY I WAS DRINKING SO MUCH.
MARLI, YOU SAY YOU FEEL BAD ALL THE TIME, BUT CAN YOU RECALL A TIME WHEN YOU FELT GOOD?
WHEN I WAS A KID, I FELT FREE...
I KNEW WHO I WAS...
JON, THAT AREA NEEDS A LOT MORE STICKS IF OUR DAM IS GOING TO CATCH ANY FISH.
WHAT MADE ME FEEL GOOD...
MANNY
MY BROTHER JON
TRE
WHO I FELT SAFE WITH...

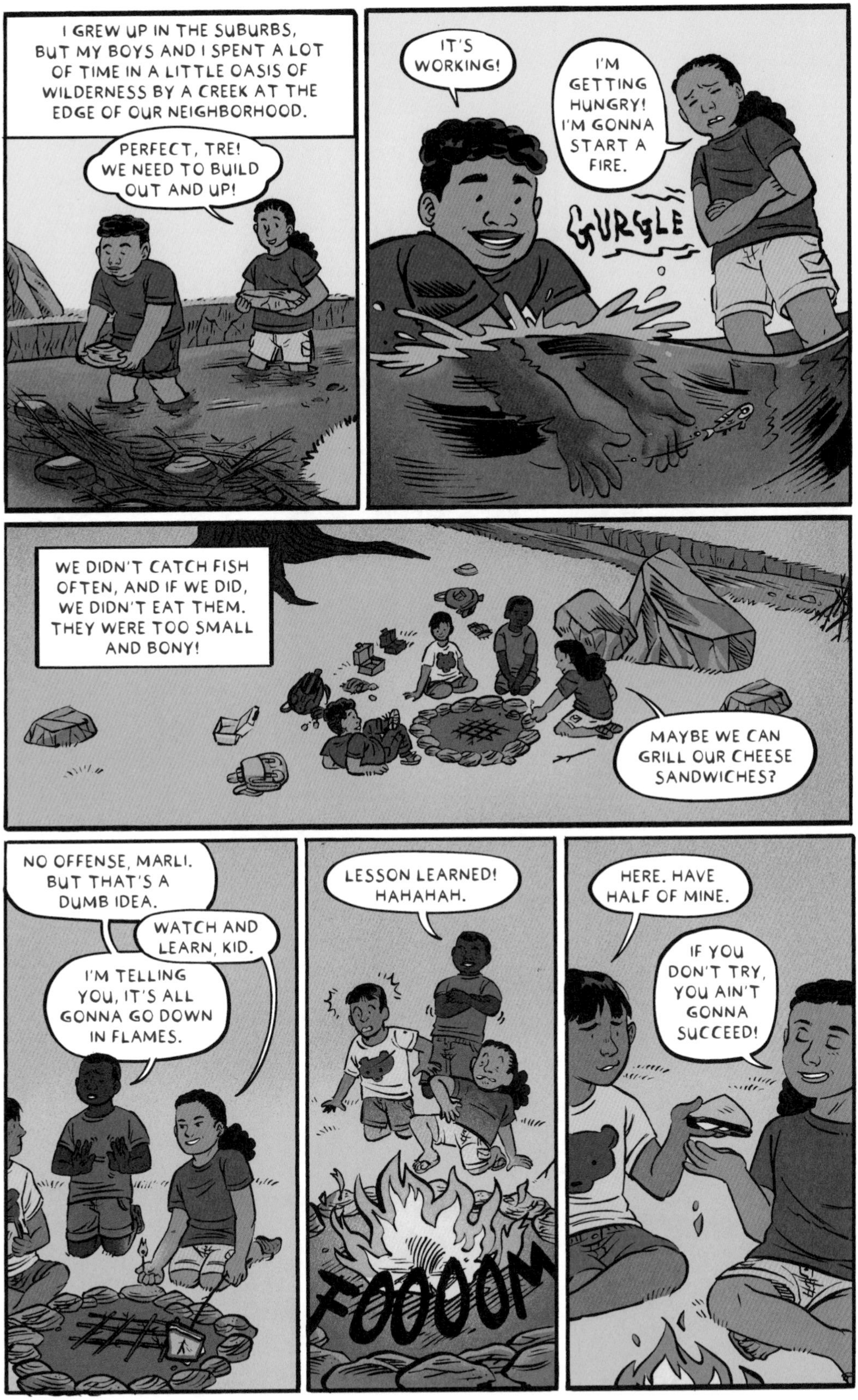
I GREW UP IN THE SUBURBS, BUT MY BOYS AND I SPENT A LOT OF TIME IN A LITTLE OASIS OF WILDERNESS BY A CREEK AT THE EDGE OF OUR NEIGHBORHOOD.
PERFECT, TRE! WE NEED TO BUILD OUT AND UP!
IT'S WORKING!
I'M GETTING HUNGRY! I'M GONNA START A FIRE.
GURGLE
WE DIDN'T CATCH FISH OFTEN, AND IF WE DID, WE DIDN'T EAT THEM. THEY WERE TOO SMALL AND BONY!
MAYBE WE CAN GRILL OUR CHEESE SANDWICHES?
NO OFFENSE, MARLI. BUT THAT'S A DUMB IDEA.
WATCH AND LEARN, KID.
I'M TELLING YOU, IT'S ALL GONNA GO DOWN IN FLAMES.
LESSON LEARNED! HAHAHAH.
FOOOOM
HERE. HAVE HALF OF MINE.
IF YOU DON'T TRY, YOU AIN'T GONNA SUCCEED!

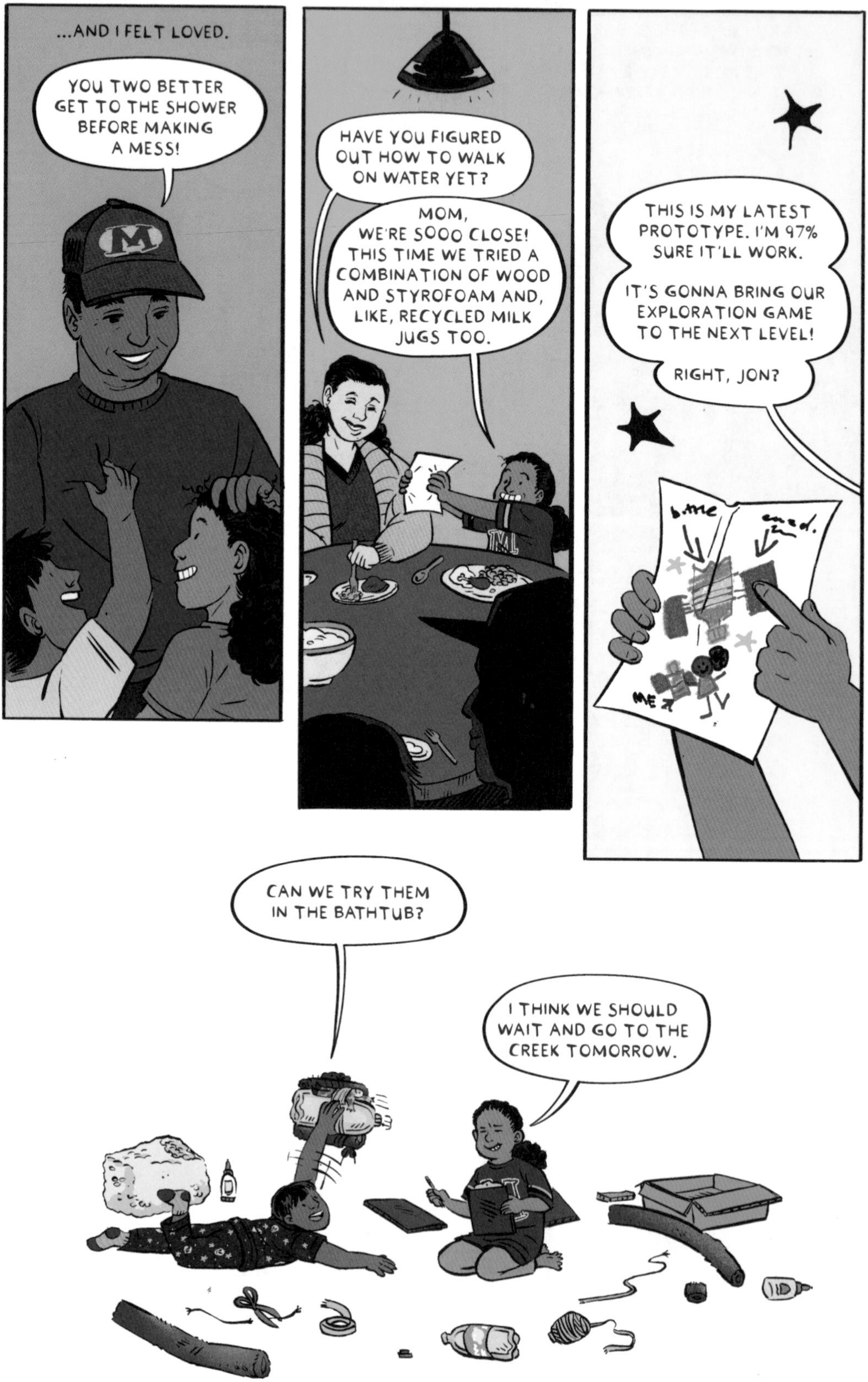
...AND I FELT LOVED.
YOU TWO BETTER GET TO THE SHOWER BEFORE MAKING A MESS!
HAVE YOU FIGURED OUT HOW TO WALK ON WATER YET?
MOM, WE'RE SOOO CLOSE! THIS TIME WE TRIED A COMBINATION OF WOOD AND STYROFOAM AND, LIKE, RECYCLED MILK JUGS TOO.
THIS IS MY LATEST PROTOTYPE. I'M 97% SURE IT'LL WORK.
IT'S GONNA BRING OUR EXPLORATION GAME TO THE NEXT LEVEL!
RIGHT, JON?
CAN WE TRY THEM IN THE BATHTUB?
I THINK WE SHOULD WAIT AND GO TO THE CREEK TOMORROW.

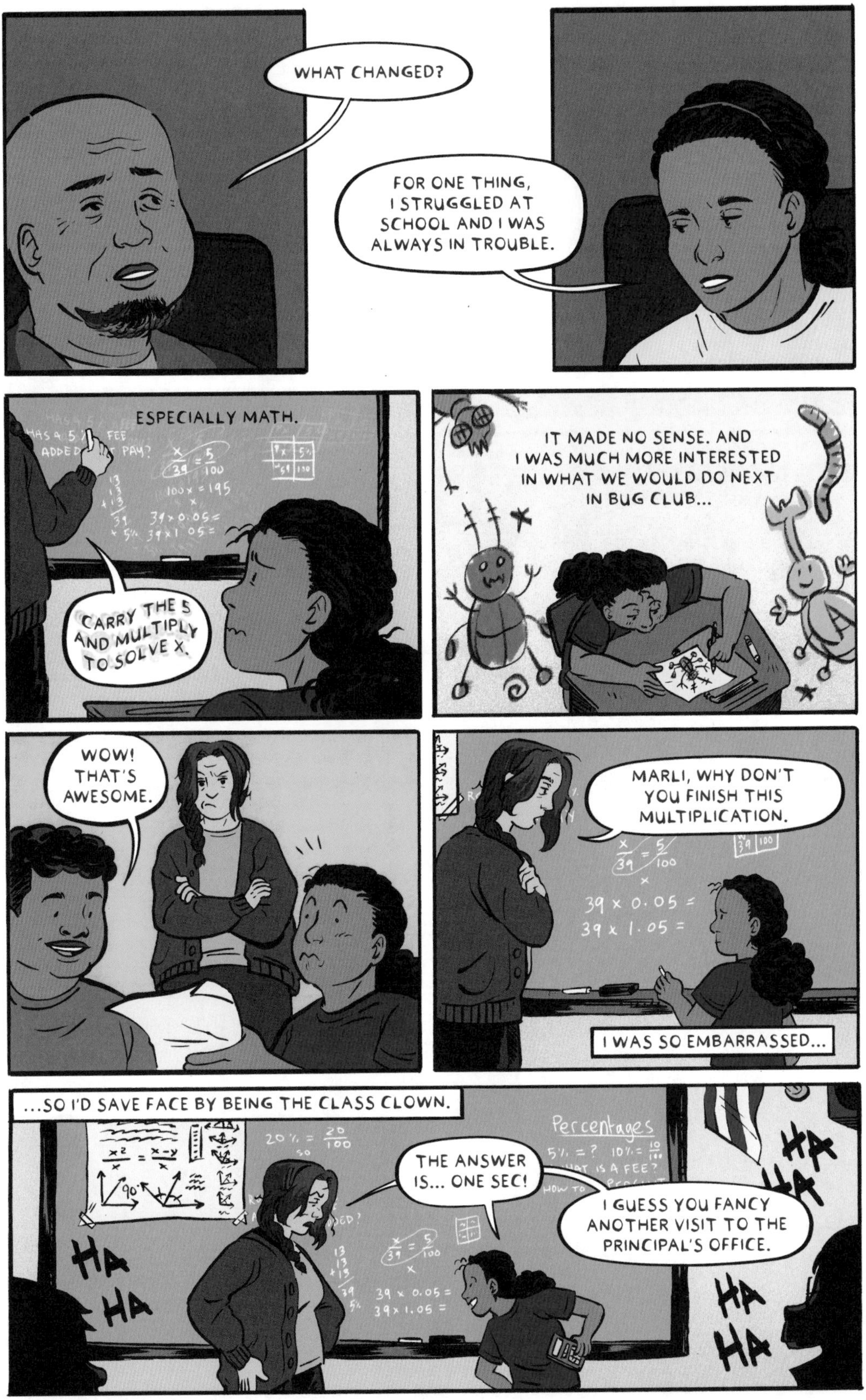
WHAT CHANGED?
FOR ONE THING, I STRUGGLED AT SCHOOL AND I WAS ALWAYS IN TROUBLE.
ESPECIALLY MATH.
CARRY THE 5 AND MULTIPLY TO SOLVE X.
IT MADE NO SENSE. AND I WAS MUCH MORE INTERESTED IN WHAT WE WOULD DO NEXT IN BUG CLUB...
WOW! THAT'S AWESOME.
MARLI, WHY DON'T YOU FINISH THIS MULTIPLICATION.
39 x 0.05 =
39 x 1.05 =
I WAS SO EMBARRASSED...
...SO I'D SAVE FACE BY BEING THE CLASS CLOWN.
Percentages
THE ANSWER IS... ONE SEC!
I GUESS YOU FANCY ANOTHER VISIT TO THE PRINCIPAL'S OFFICE.
HA HA
HA HA
HA HA

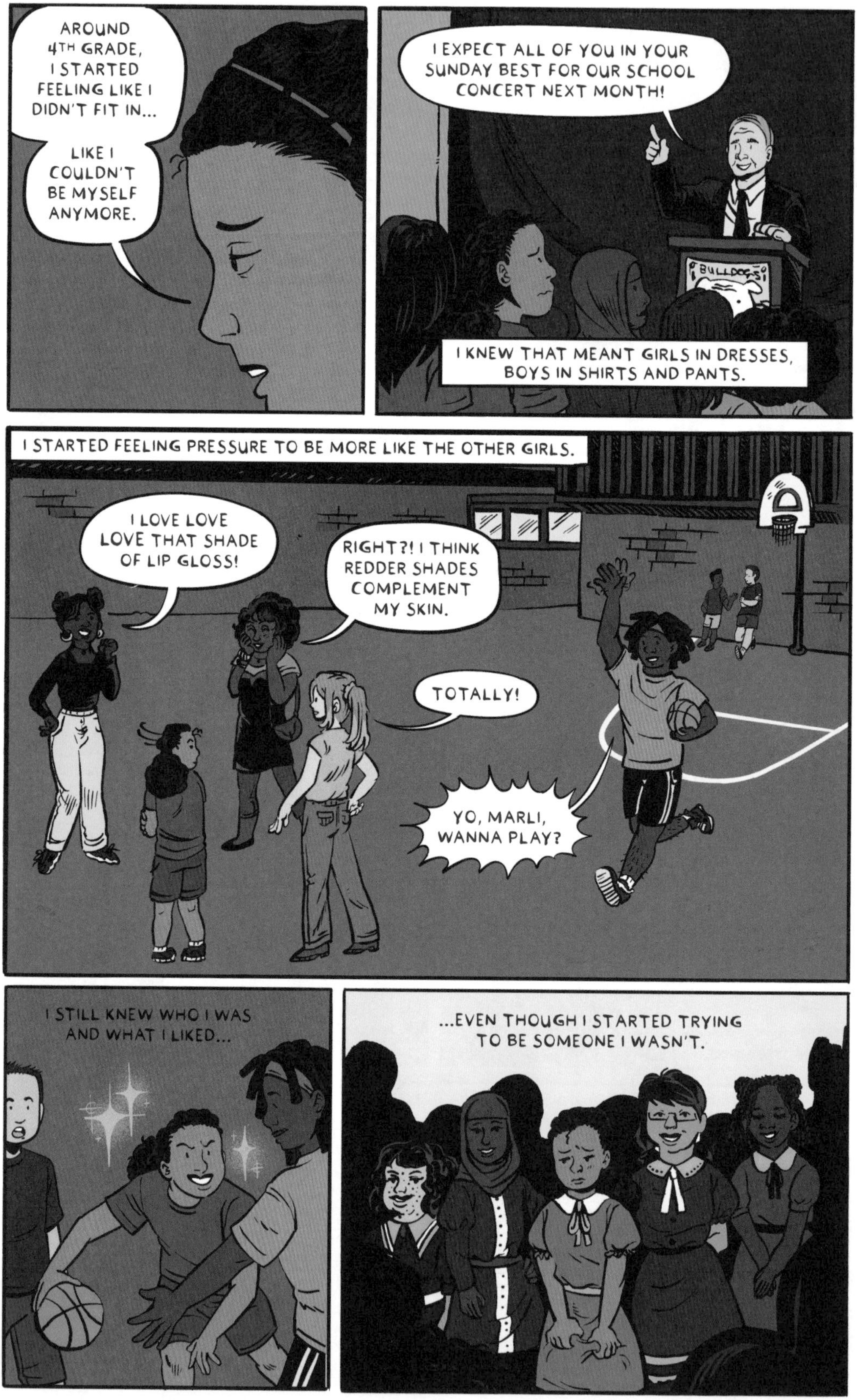
AROUND 4TH GRADE, I STARTED FEELING LIKE I DIDN'T FIT IN...
LIKE I COULDN'T BE MYSELF ANYMORE.
I EXPECT ALL OF YOU IN YOUR SUNDAY BEST FOR OUR SCHOOL CONCERT NEXT MONTH!
BULLDOGS!
I KNEW THAT MEANT GIRLS IN DRESSES, BOYS IN SHIRTS AND PANTS.
I STARTED FEELING PRESSURE TO BE MORE LIKE THE OTHER GIRLS.
I LOVE LOVE LOVE THAT SHADE OF LIP GLOSS!
RIGHT?! I THINK REDDER SHADES COMPLEMENT MY SKIN.
TOTALLY!
YO, MARLI, WANNA PLAY?
I STILL KNEW WHO I WAS AND WHAT I LIKED...
...EVEN THOUGH I STARTED TRYING TO BE SOMEONE I WASN'T.

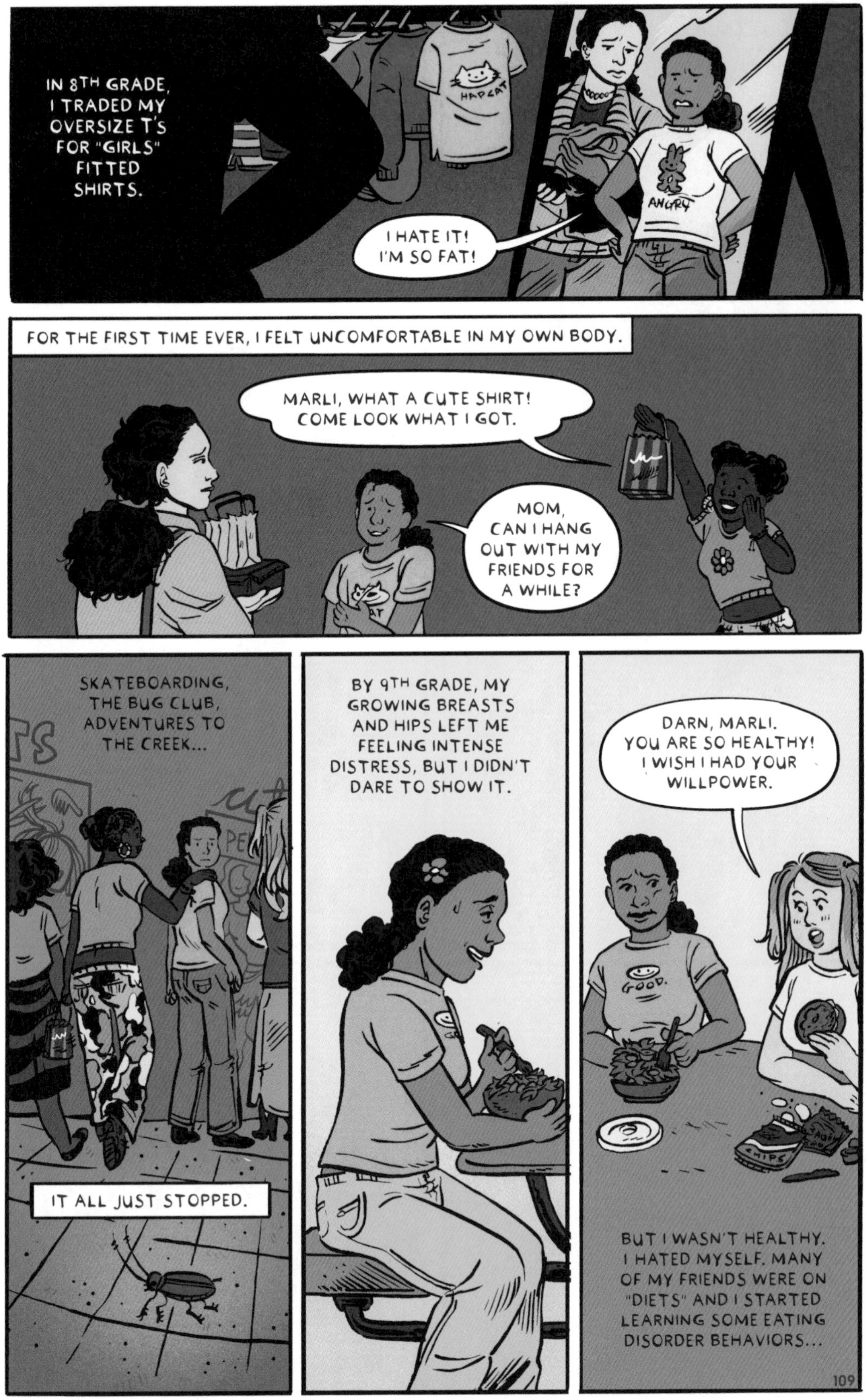
IN 8TH GRADE, I TRADED MY OVERSIZE T'S FOR "GIRLS" FITTED SHIRTS.
HAPCAT
ANGRY
I HATE IT! I'M SO FAT!
FOR THE FIRST TIME EVER, I FELT UNCOMFORTABLE IN MY OWN BODY.
MARLI, WHAT A CUTE SHIRT! COME LOOK WHAT I GOT.
MOM, CAN I HANG OUT WITH MY FRIENDS FOR A WHILE?
SKATEBOARDING, THE BUG CLUB, ADVENTURES TO THE CREEK...
IT ALL JUST STOPPED.
BY 9TH GRADE, MY GROWING BREASTS AND HIPS LEFT ME FEELING INTENSE DISTRESS, BUT I DIDN'T DARE TO SHOW IT.
DARN, MARLI. YOU ARE SO HEALTHY! I WISH I HAD YOUR WILLPOWER.
GOOD.
CHIPS
BUT I WASN'T HEALTHY. I HATED MYSELF. MANY OF MY FRIENDS WERE ON "DIETS" AND I STARTED LEARNING SOME EATING DISORDER BEHAVIORS...

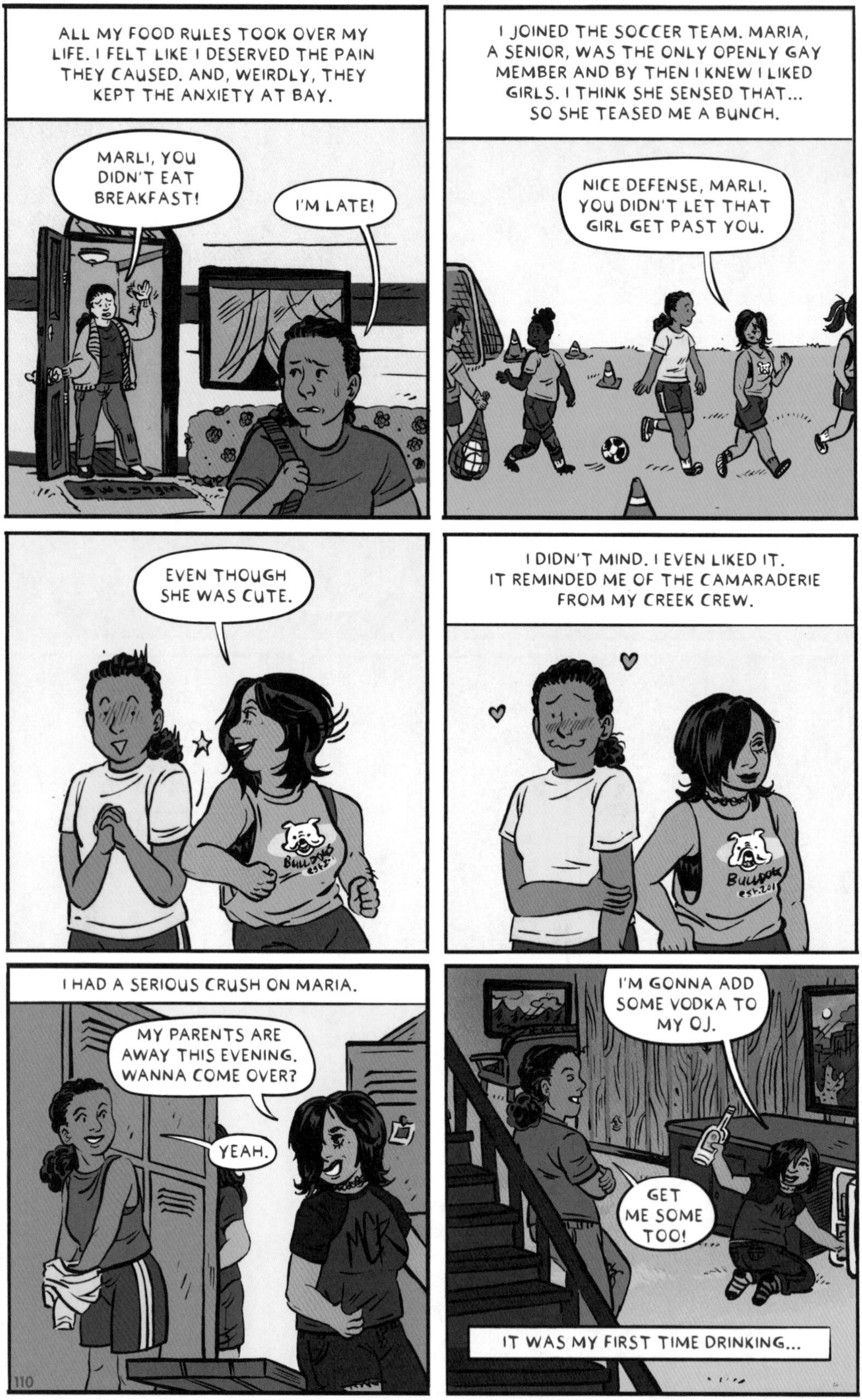
ALL MY FOOD RULES TOOK OVER MY LIFE. I FELT LIKE I DESERVED THE PAIN THEY CAUSED. AND, WEIRDLY, THEY KEPT THE ANXIETY AT BAY.
MARLI, YOU DIDN'T EAT BREAKFAST!
I'M LATE!
I JOINED THE SOCCER TEAM. MARIA, A SENIOR, WAS THE ONLY OPENLY GAY MEMBER AND BY THEN I KNEW I LIKED GIRLS. I THINK SHE SENSED THAT... SO SHE TEASED ME A BUNCH.
NICE DEFENSE, MARLI. YOU DIDN'T LET THAT GIRL GET PAST YOU.
EVEN THOUGH SHE WAS CUTE.
I DIDN'T MIND. I EVEN LIKED IT. IT REMINDED ME OF THE CAMARADERIE FROM MY CREEK CREW.
I HAD A SERIOUS CRUSH ON MARIA.
MY PARENTS ARE AWAY THIS EVENING. WANNA COME OVER?
YEAH.
I'M GONNA ADD SOME VODKA TO MY OJ.
GET ME SOME TOO!
IT WAS MY FIRST TIME DRINKING...

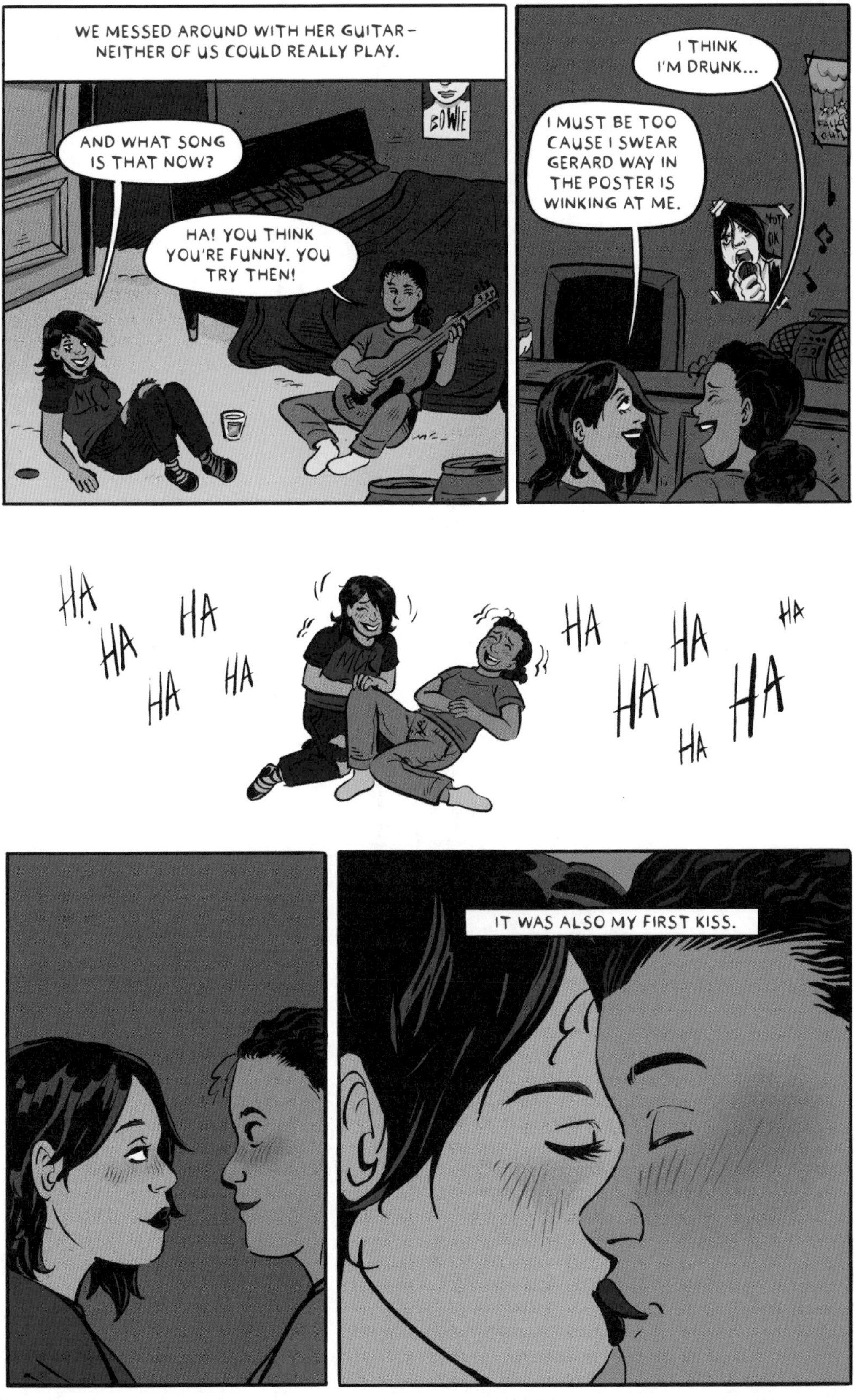
WE MESSED AROUND WITH HER GUITAR – NEITHER OF US COULD REALLY PLAY.
BOWIE
AND WHAT SONG IS THAT NOW?
HA! YOU THINK YOU'RE FUNNY. YOU TRY THEN!
I THINK I'M DRUNK...
I MUST BE TOO CAUSE I SWEAR GERARD WAY IN THE POSTER IS WINKING AT ME.
NOT OK
HA HA HA HA HA
HA HA HA HA HA HA HA
IT WAS ALSO MY FIRST KISS.

AS TIME PASSED, I WOULD DRINK MORE AND MORE. MY FRIENDS AND I WOULD MEET IN THE WOODS OR THE FIELD, MAKE A BONFIRE... THERE WAS A SENSE OF ADVENTURE THAT REMINDED ME OF BEING A YOUNG KID AT THE CREEK.

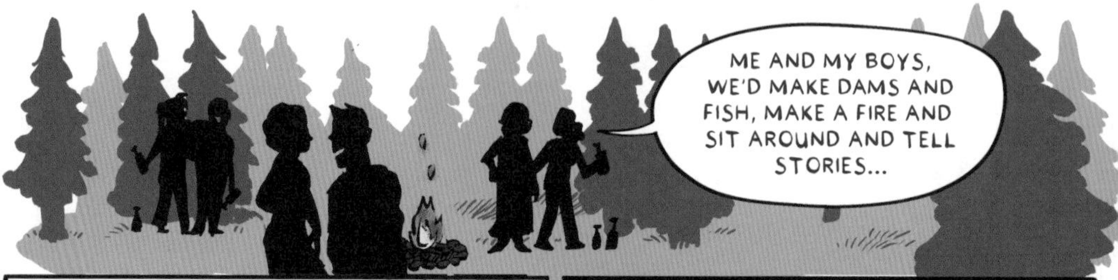
ME AND MY BOYS, WE'D MAKE DAMS AND FISH, MAKE A FIRE AND SIT AROUND AND TELL STORIES...

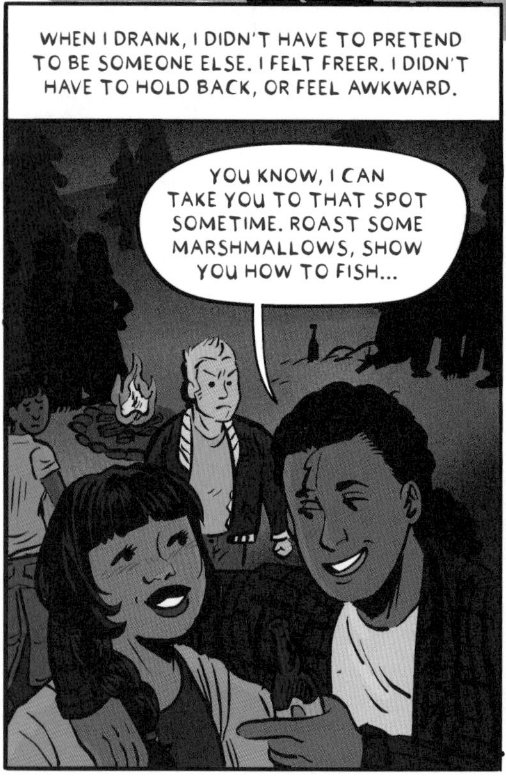
WHEN I DRANK, I DIDN'T HAVE TO PRETEND TO BE SOMEONE ELSE. I FELT FREER. I DIDN'T HAVE TO HOLD BACK, OR FEEL AWKWARD.
YOU KNOW, I CAN TAKE YOU TO THAT SPOT SOMETIME. ROAST SOME MARSHMALLOWS, SHOW YOU HOW TO FISH...

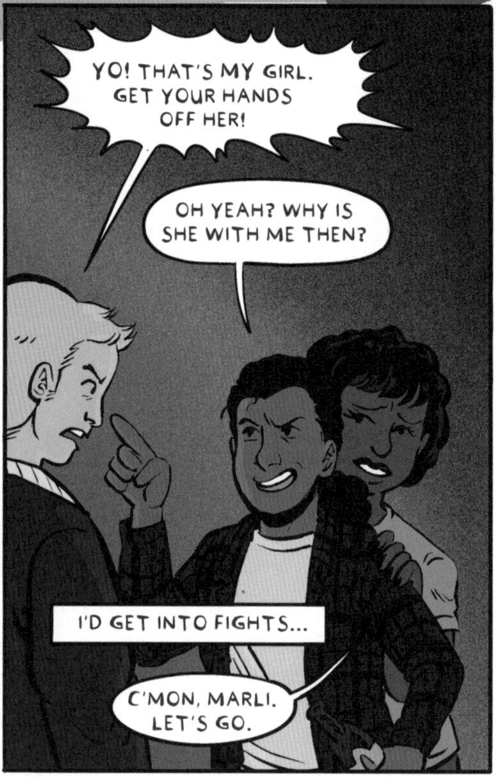
YO! THAT'S MY GIRL. GET YOUR HANDS OFF HER!
OH YEAH? WHY IS SHE WITH ME THEN?
I'D GET INTO FIGHTS...
C'MON, MARLI. LET'S GO.

...OR END UP PASSED OUT OR SICK. MY FRIENDS STOPPED WANTING TO GO TO PARTIES WITH ME.

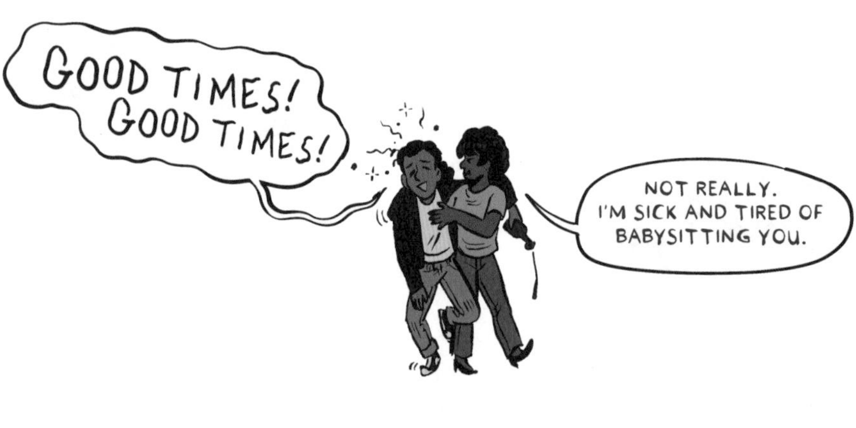
GOOD TIMES! GOOD TIMES!
NOT REALLY. I'M SICK AND TIRED OF BABYSITTING YOU.

SOUNDS LIKE DRINKING WAS THE ONLY WAY YOU FELT YOU COULD GET A SENSE OF INTIMACY, OF FEELING LOVED.

IT WAS MORE THAN THAT. IT WAS THE ONLY WAY I COULD FEEL LIKE WHO I REALLY AM. IT WAS... I'M JUST STARTING TO REALIZE SOMETHING...

I THINK I'M...

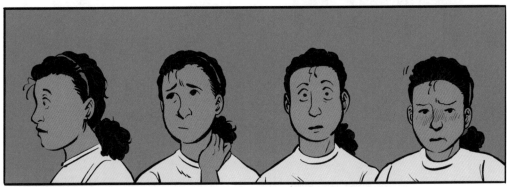

I'M TRANS!

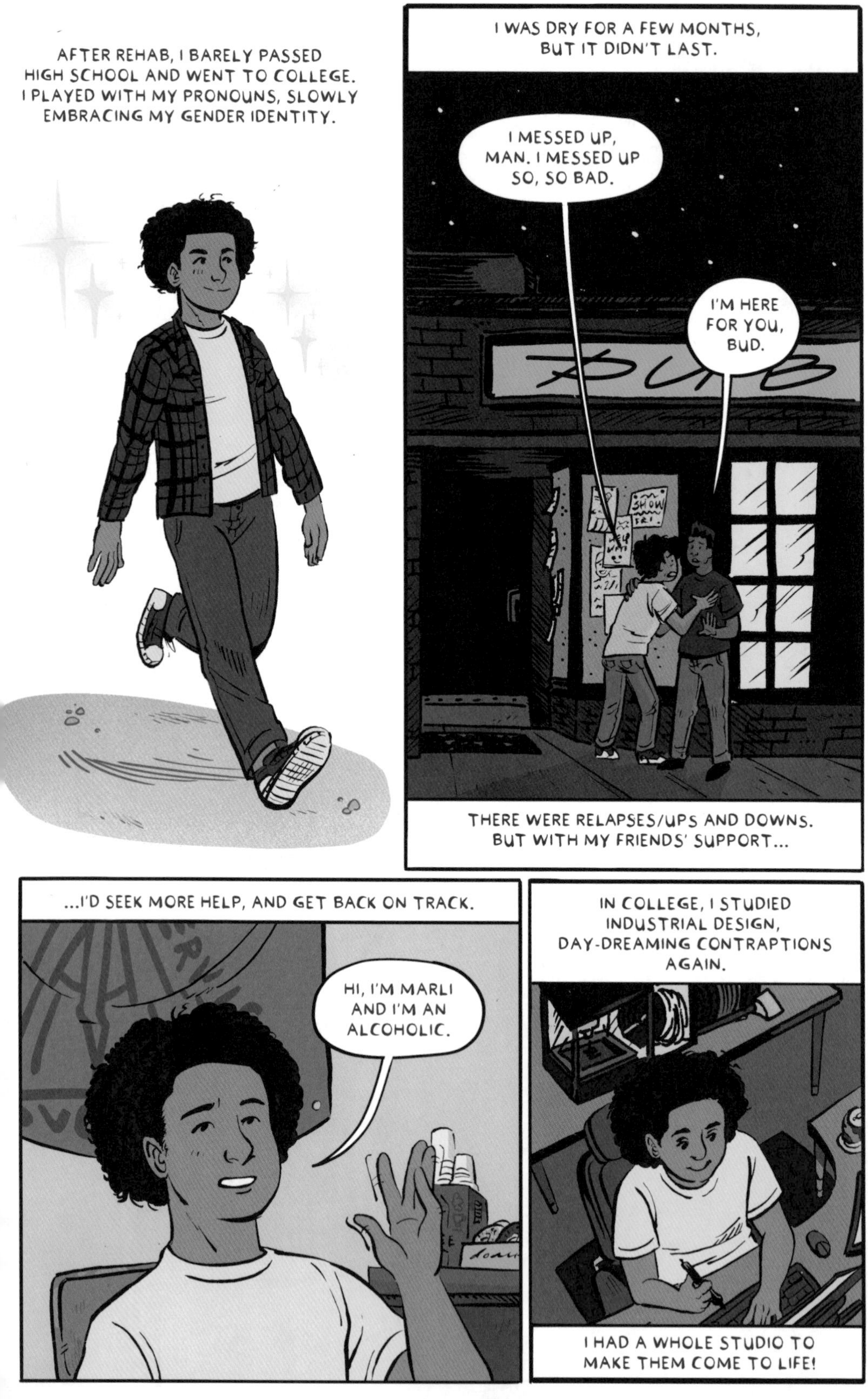
AFTER REHAB, I BARELY PASSED HIGH SCHOOL AND WENT TO COLLEGE. I PLAYED WITH MY PRONOUNS, SLOWLY EMBRACING MY GENDER IDENTITY.
I WAS DRY FOR A FEW MONTHS, BUT IT DIDN'T LAST.
I MESSED UP, MAN. I MESSED UP SO, SO BAD.
I'M HERE FOR YOU, BUD.
THERE WERE RELAPSES/UPS AND DOWNS. BUT WITH MY FRIENDS' SUPPORT...
...I'D SEEK MORE HELP, AND GET BACK ON TRACK.
HI, I'M MARLI AND I'M AN ALCOHOLIC.
IN COLLEGE, I STUDIED INDUSTRIAL DESIGN, DAY-DREAMING CONTRAPTIONS AGAIN.
I HAD A WHOLE STUDIO TO MAKE THEM COME TO LIFE!

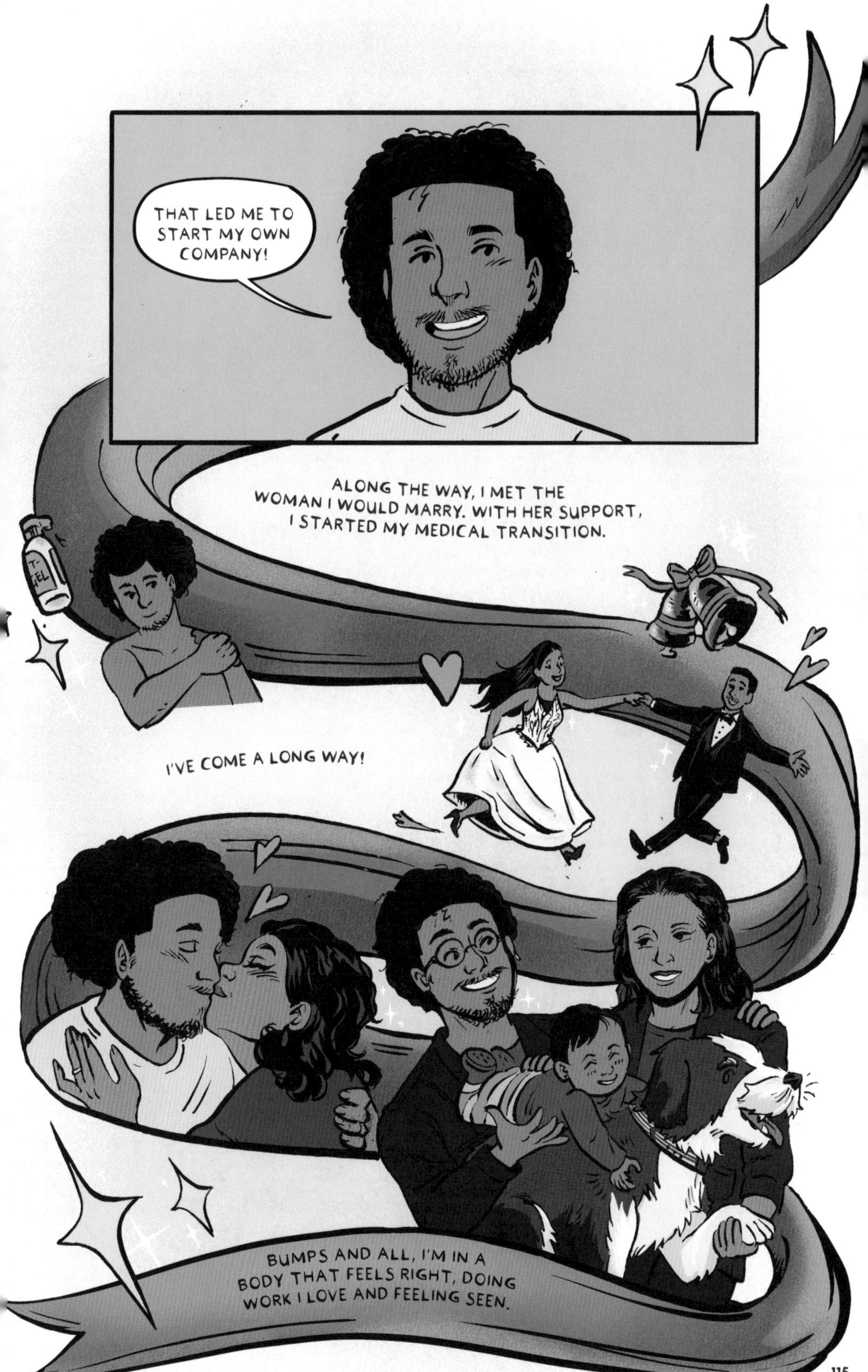

THAT LED ME TO START MY OWN COMPANY!
ALONG THE WAY, I MET THE WOMAN I WOULD MARRY. WITH HER SUPPORT, I STARTED MY MEDICAL TRANSITION.
T-GEL
I'VE COME A LONG WAY!
BUMPS AND ALL, I'M IN A BODY THAT FEELS RIGHT, DOING WORK I LOVE AND FEELING SEEN.

BECOMING ROBIN AGUILAR

Robin Aguilar (they/them/theirs) is a first-gen, genderfluid, and Latinx scientist who loves writing, drawing, sampling teas, and biking in nature around the Pacific Northwest.

Written by Sammy Lisel
Illustrated by Sunmi

Sunmi (they/them/theirs) is a queer & diasporic Korean cartoonist and illustrator. They always say hi to stray cats and are trying to get really good at grilling outdoors.

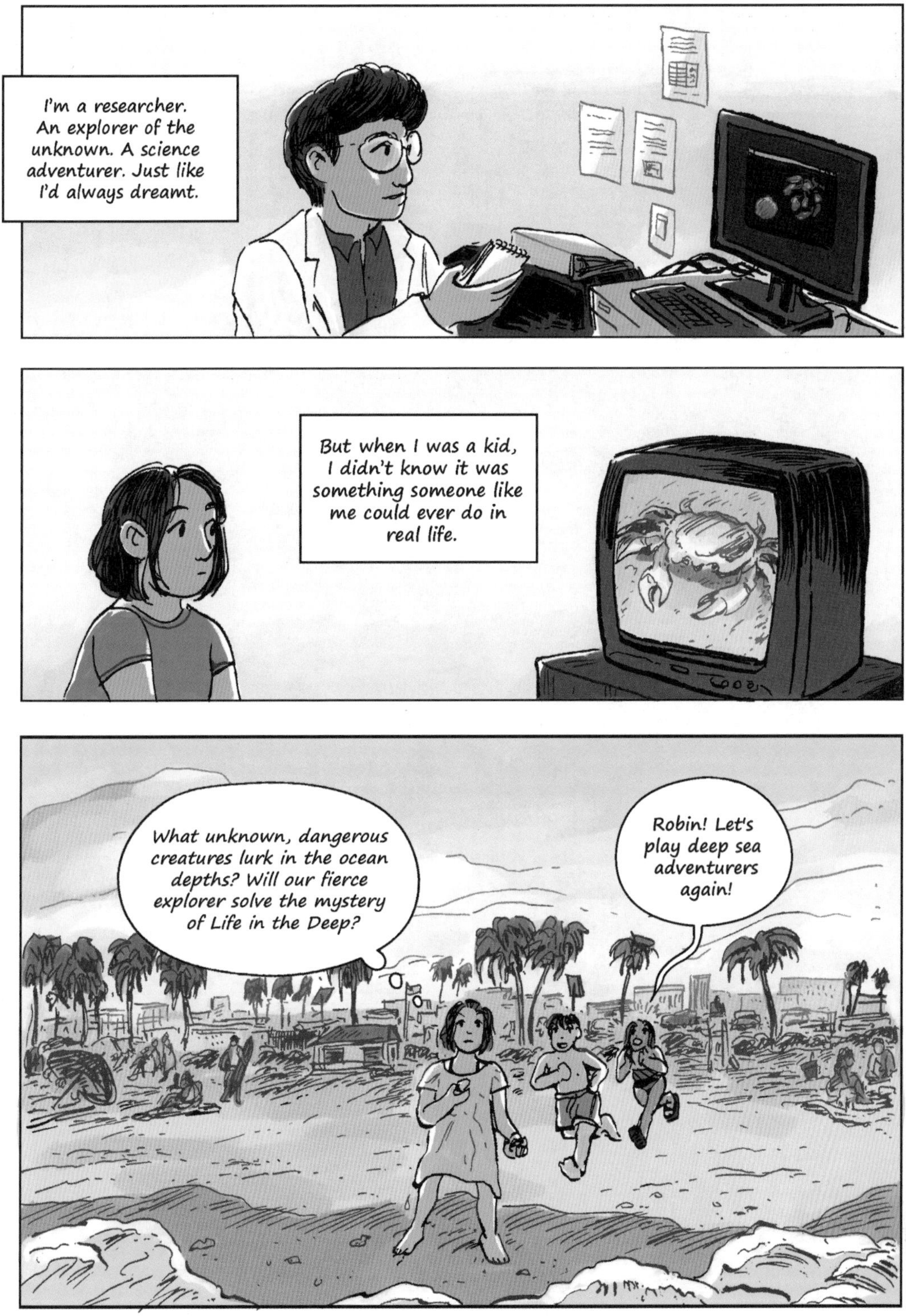
I'm a researcher. An explorer of the unknown. A science adventurer. Just like I'd always dreamt.
But when I was a kid, I didn't know it was something someone like me could ever do in real life.
What unknown, dangerous creatures lurk in the ocean depths? Will our fierce explorer solve the mystery of Life in the Deep?
Robin! Let's play deep sea adventurers again!

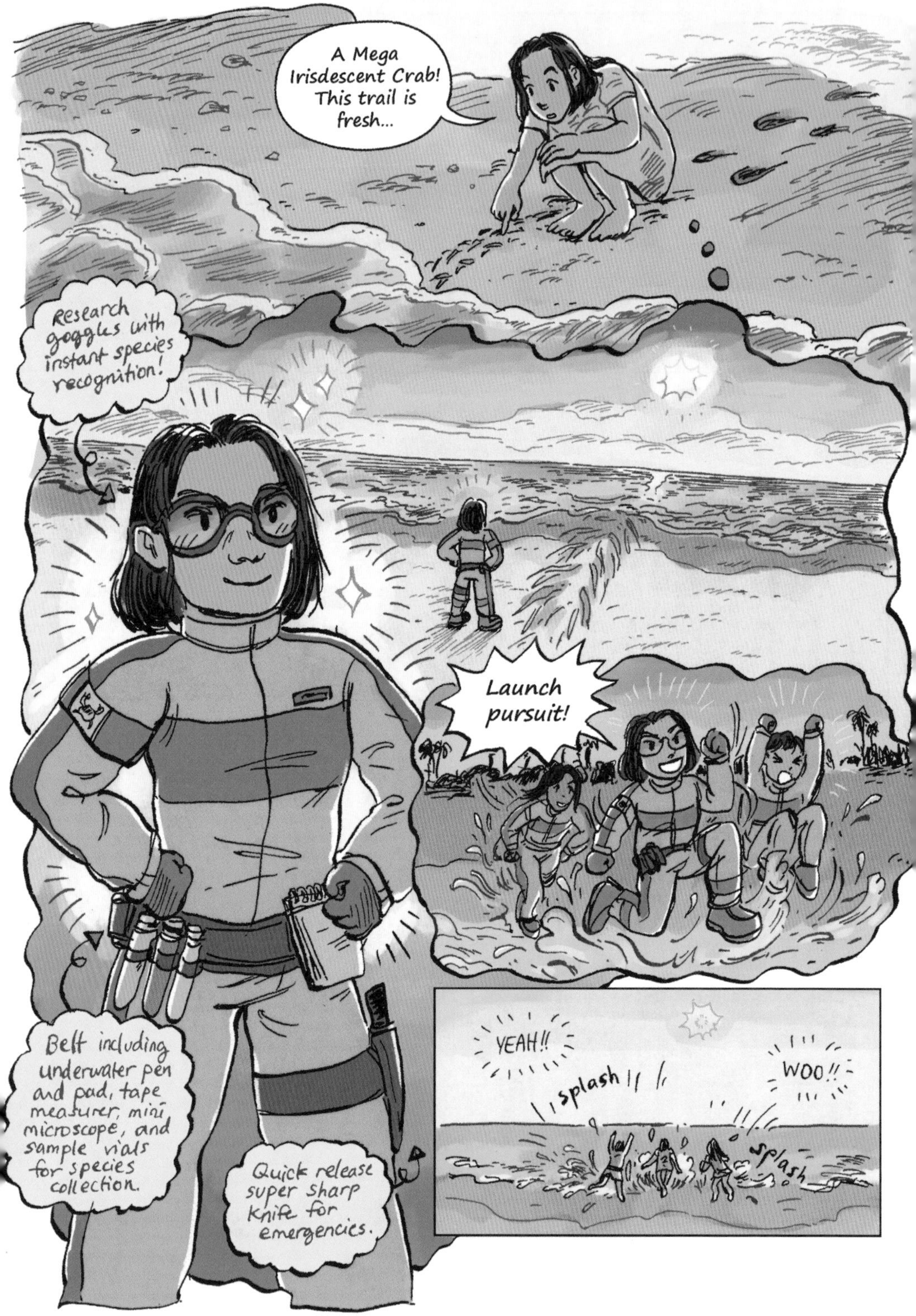
A Mega Irisdescent Crab! This trail is fresh...
Research goggles with instant species recognition!
Launch pursuit!
Belt including underwater pen and pad, tape measurer, mini microscope, and sample vials for species collection.
Quick release super sharp knife for emergencies.
YEAH!!
WOO!!
splash
splash

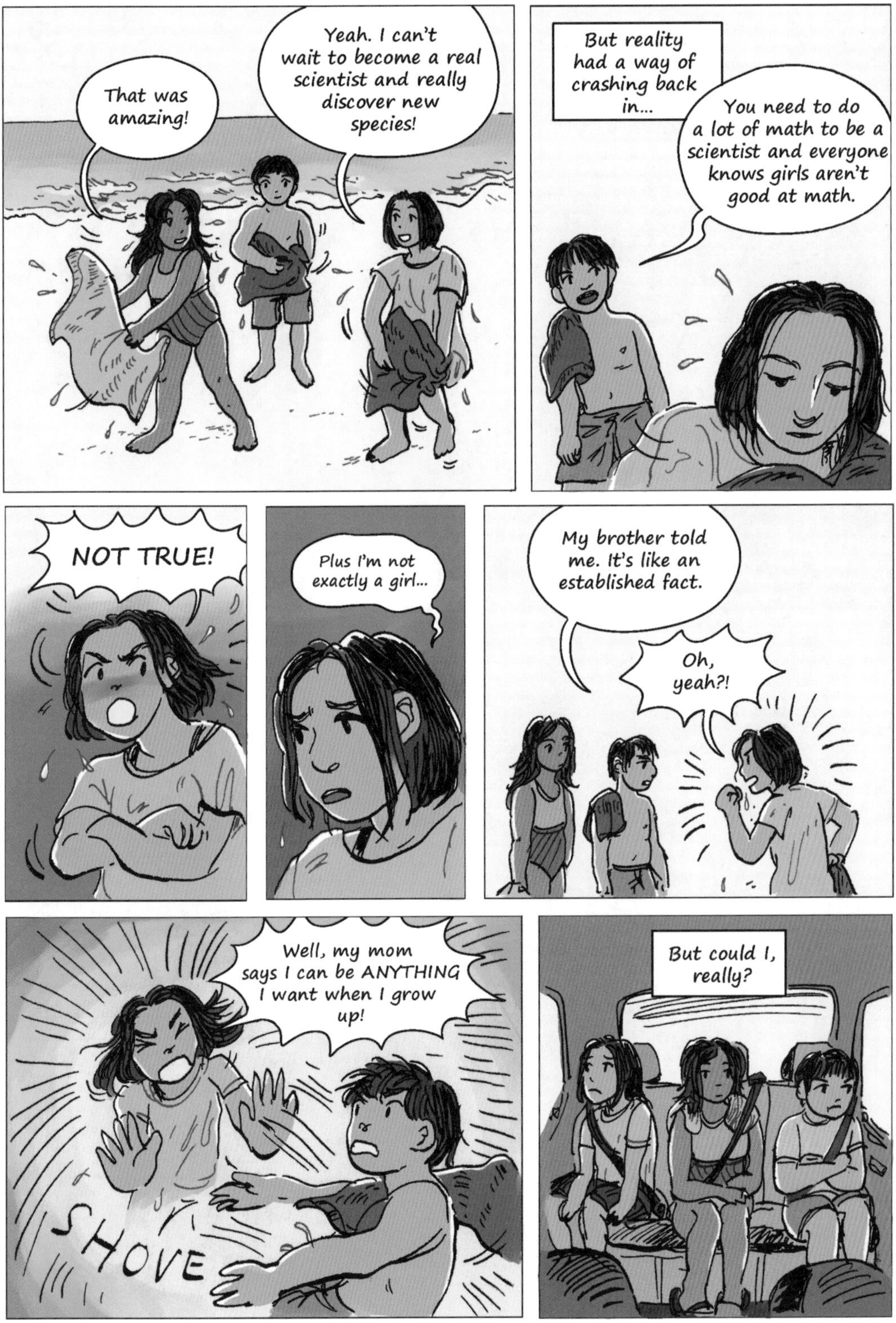

That was amazing!
Yeah. I can't wait to become a real scientist and really discover new species!
But reality had a way of crashing back in...
You need to do a lot of math to be a scientist and everyone knows girls aren't good at math.
NOT TRUE!
Plus I'm not exactly a girl...
My brother told me. It's like an established fact.
Oh, yeah?!
Well, my mom says I can be ANYTHING I want when I grow up!
SHOVE
But could I, really?

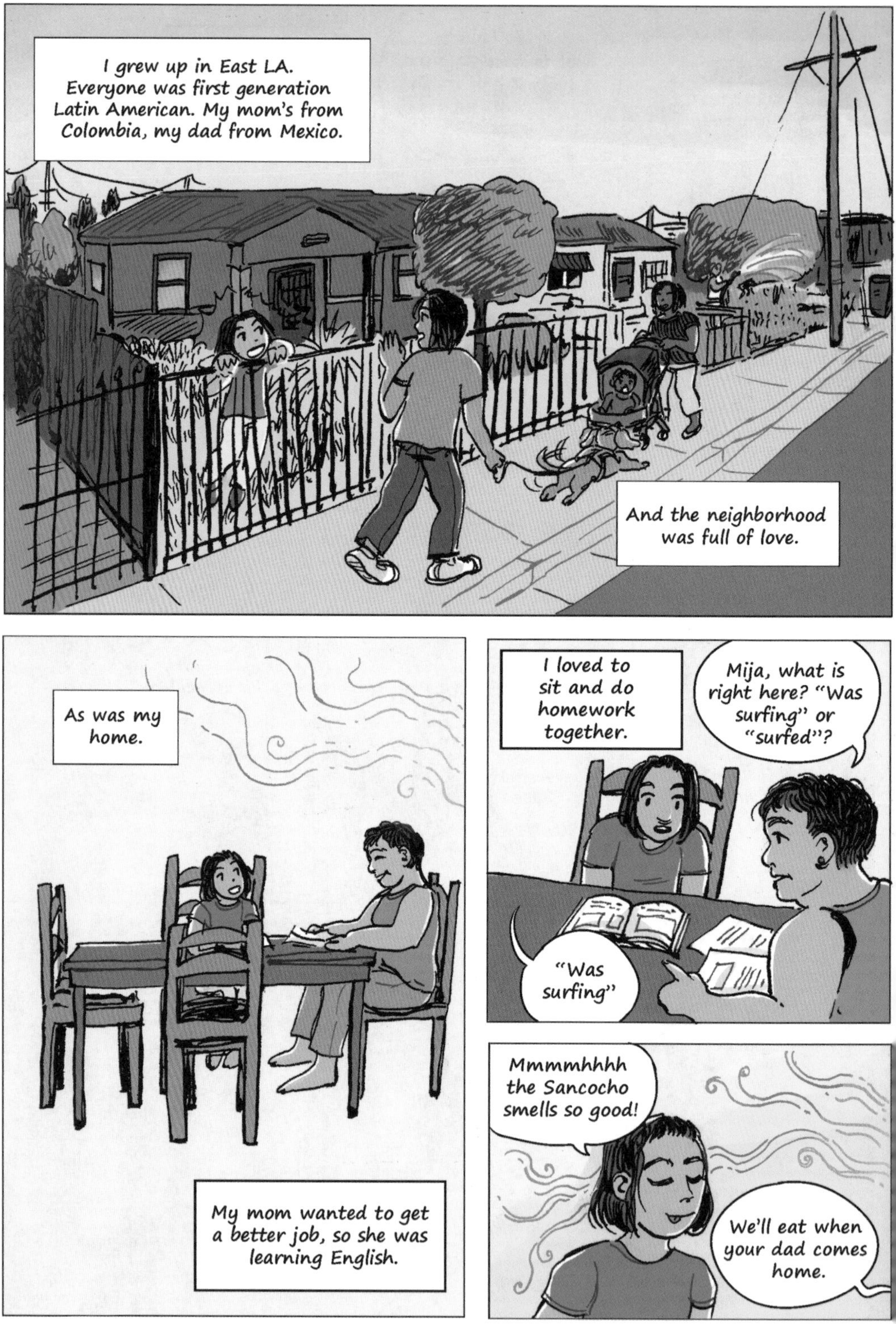
I grew up in East LA. Everyone was first generation Latin American. My mom's from Colombia, my dad from Mexico.
And the neighborhood was full of love.
As was my home.
My mom wanted to get a better job, so she was learning English.
I loved to sit and do homework together.
Mija, what is right here? "Was surfing" or "surfed"?
"Was surfing"
Mmmmhhhh the Sancocho smells so good!
We'll eat when your dad comes home.

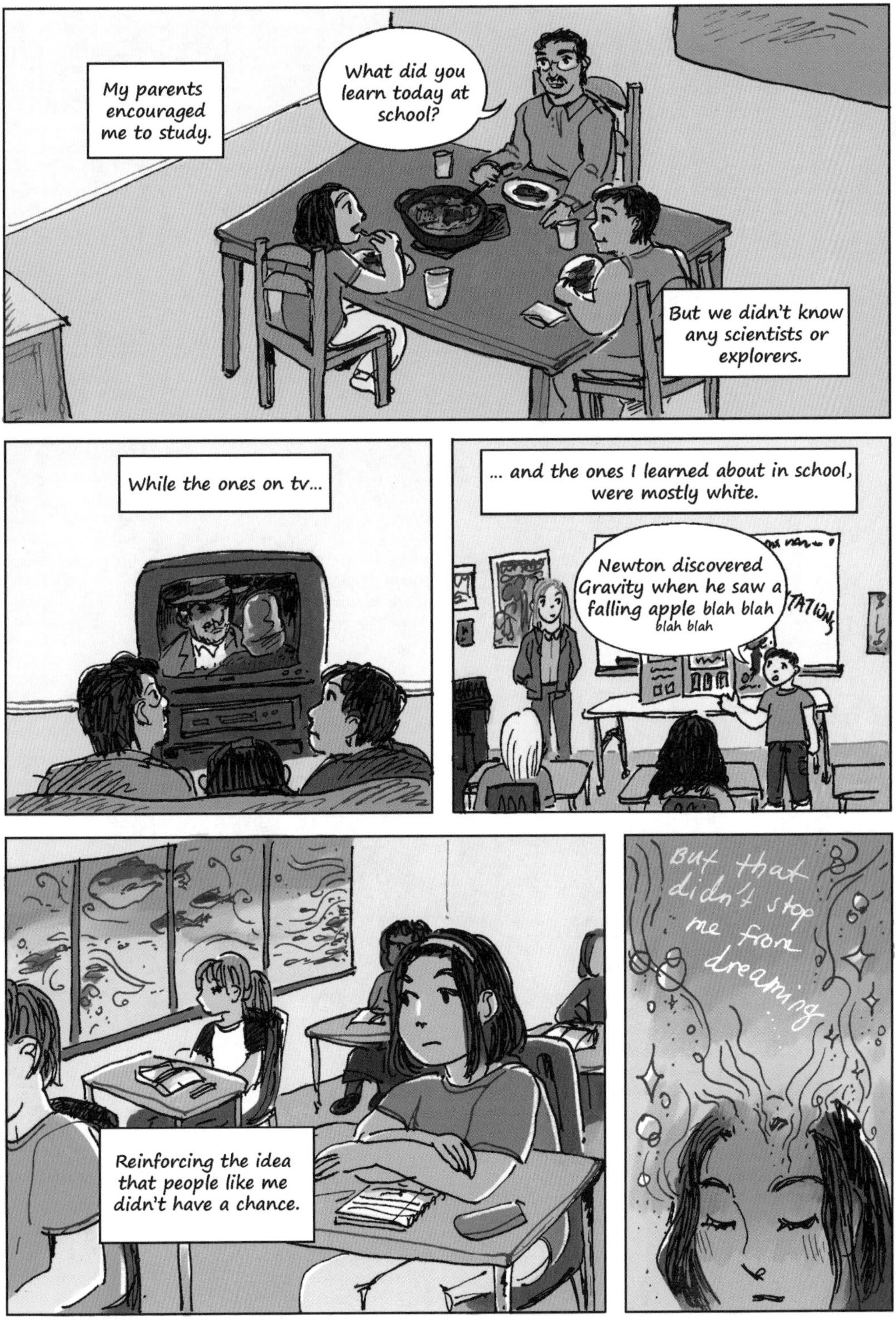
My parents encouraged me to study.
What did you learn today at school?
But we didn't know any scientists or explorers.
While the ones on tv...
... and the ones I learned about in school, were mostly white.
Newton discovered Gravity when he saw a falling apple blah blah blah blah
Reinforcing the idea that people like me didn't have a chance.
But that didn't stop me from dreaming...

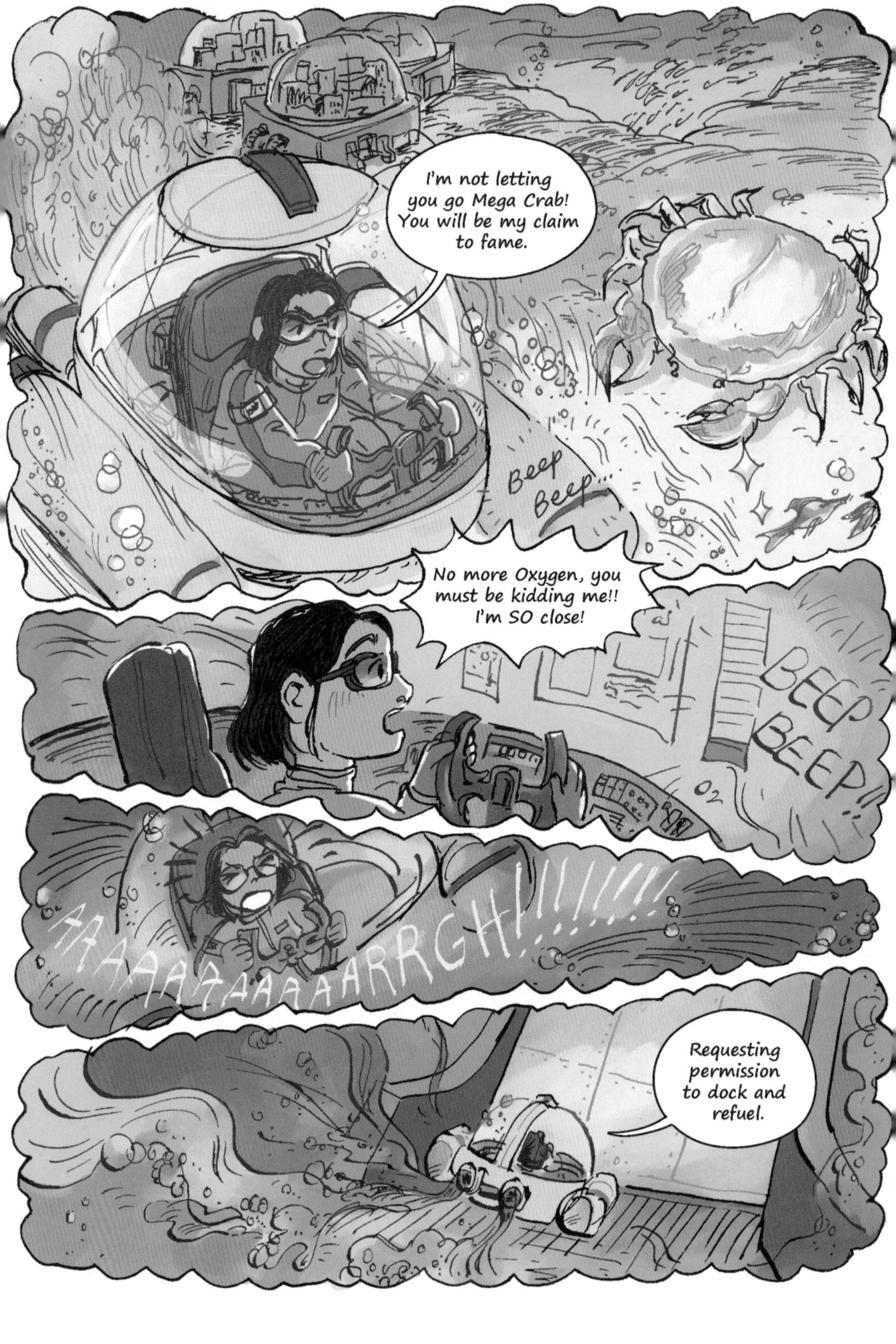
I'm not letting you go Mega Crab! You will be my claim to fame.
Beep Beep....
No more Oxygen, you must be kidding me!! I'm SO close!
BEEP BEEP!!
O_2
AAAAAAAAAARRGH!!!!!!!
Requesting permission to dock and refuel.

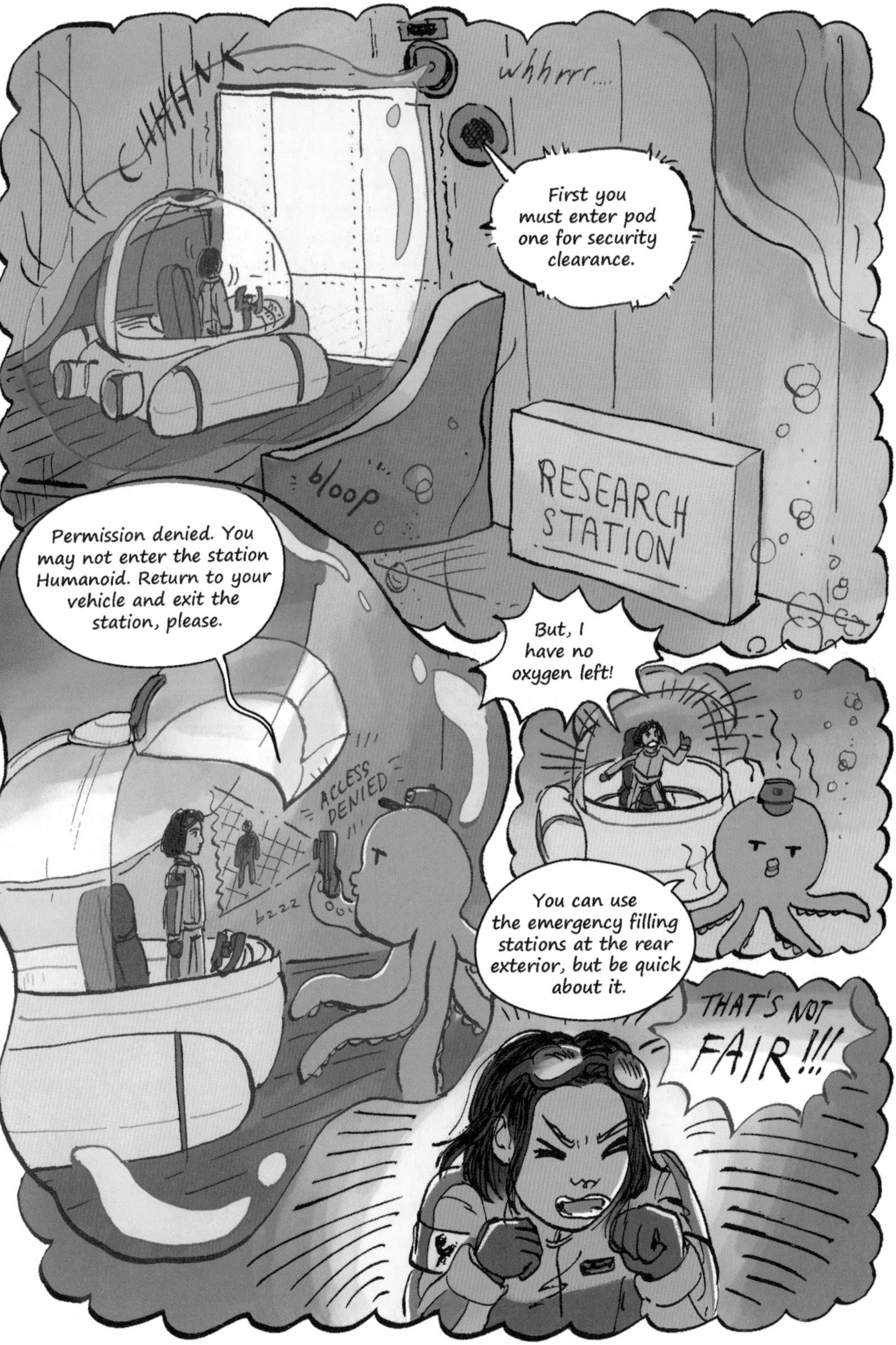
CHHHNK
whhrrr...
First you must enter pod one for security clearance.
bloop
RESEARCH STATION
Permission denied. You may not enter the station Humanoid. Return to your vehicle and exit the station, please.
ACCESS DENIED
bzzz
But, I have no oxygen left!
You can use the emergency filling stations at the rear exterior, but be quick about it.
THAT'S NOT FAIR!!!

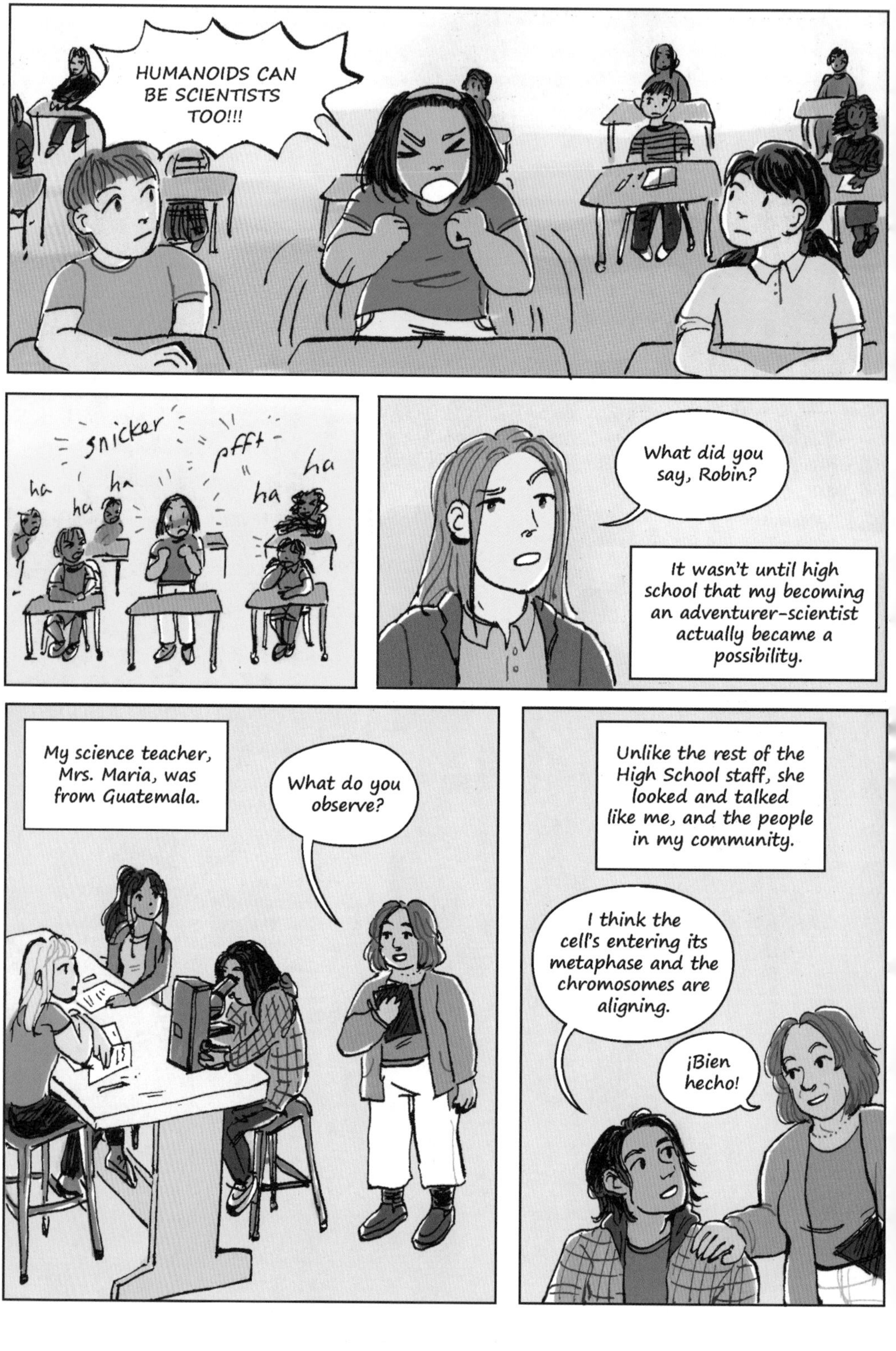
HUMANOIDS CAN BE SCIENTISTS TOO!!!
snicker
pfft
ha
ha
ha
ha
ha
What did you say, Robin?
It wasn't until high school that my becoming an adventurer-scientist actually became a possibility.
My science teacher, Mrs. Maria, was from Guatemala.
What do you observe?
Unlike the rest of the High School staff, she looked and talked like me, and the people in my community.
I think the cell's entering its metaphase and the chromosomes are aligning.
¡Bien hecho!

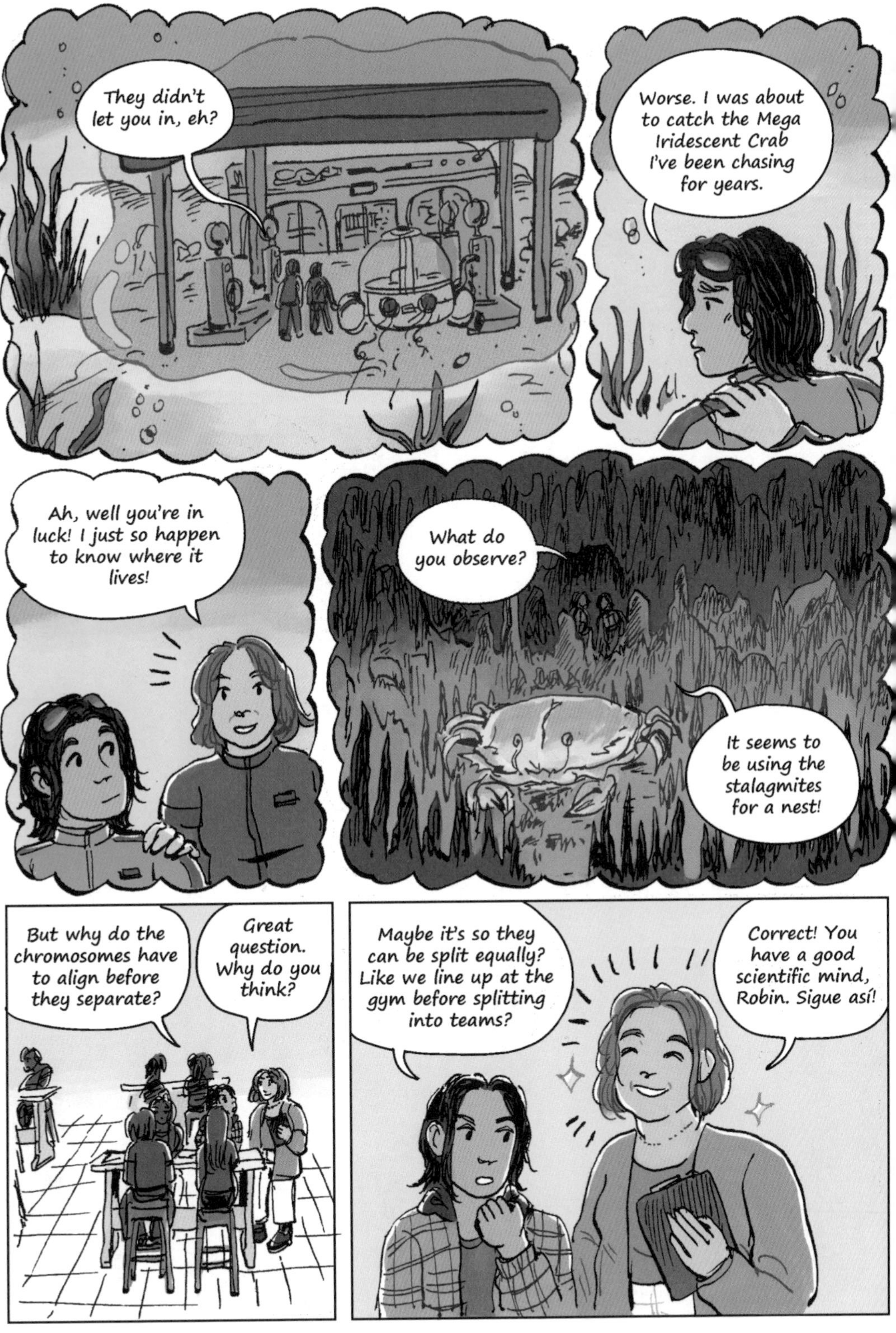

They didn't let you in, eh?
Worse. I was about to catch the Mega Iridescent Crab I've been chasing for years.
Ah, well you're in luck! I just so happen to know where it lives!
What do you observe?
It seems to be using the stalagmites for a nest!
But why do the chromosomes have to align before they separate?
Great question. Why do you think?
Maybe it's so they can be split equally? Like we line up at the gym before splitting into teams?
Correct! You have a good scientific mind, Robin. Sigue así!

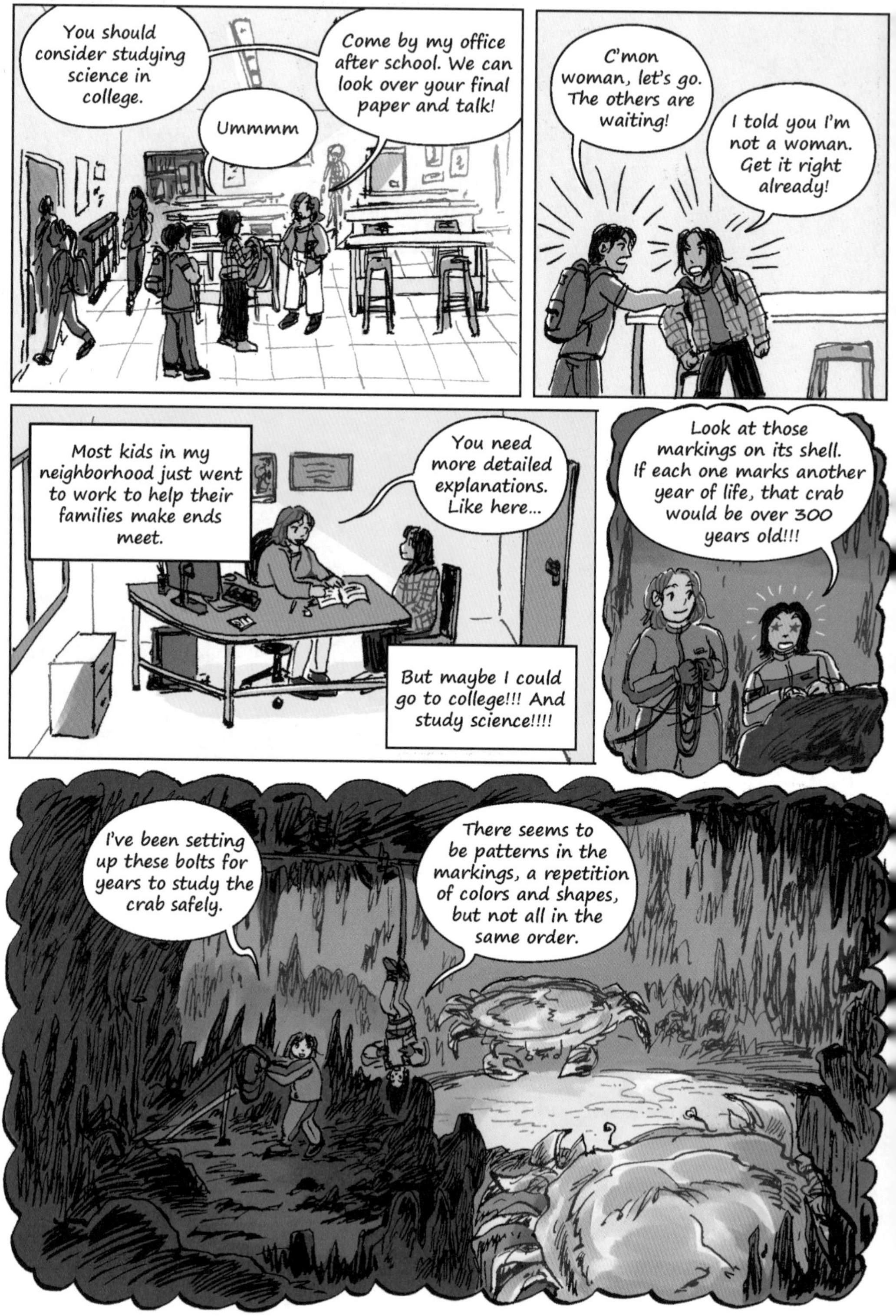
You should consider studying science in college.
Ummmm
Come by my office after school. We can look over your final paper and talk!
C'mon woman, let's go. The others are waiting!
I told you I'm not a woman. Get it right already!
Most kids in my neighborhood just went to work to help their families make ends meet.
You need more detailed explanations. Like here...
But maybe I could go to college!!! And study science!!!!
Look at those markings on its shell. If each one marks another year of life, that crab would be over 300 years old!!!
I've been setting up these bolts for years to study the crab safely.
There seems to be patterns in the markings, a repetition of colors and shapes, but not all in the same order.

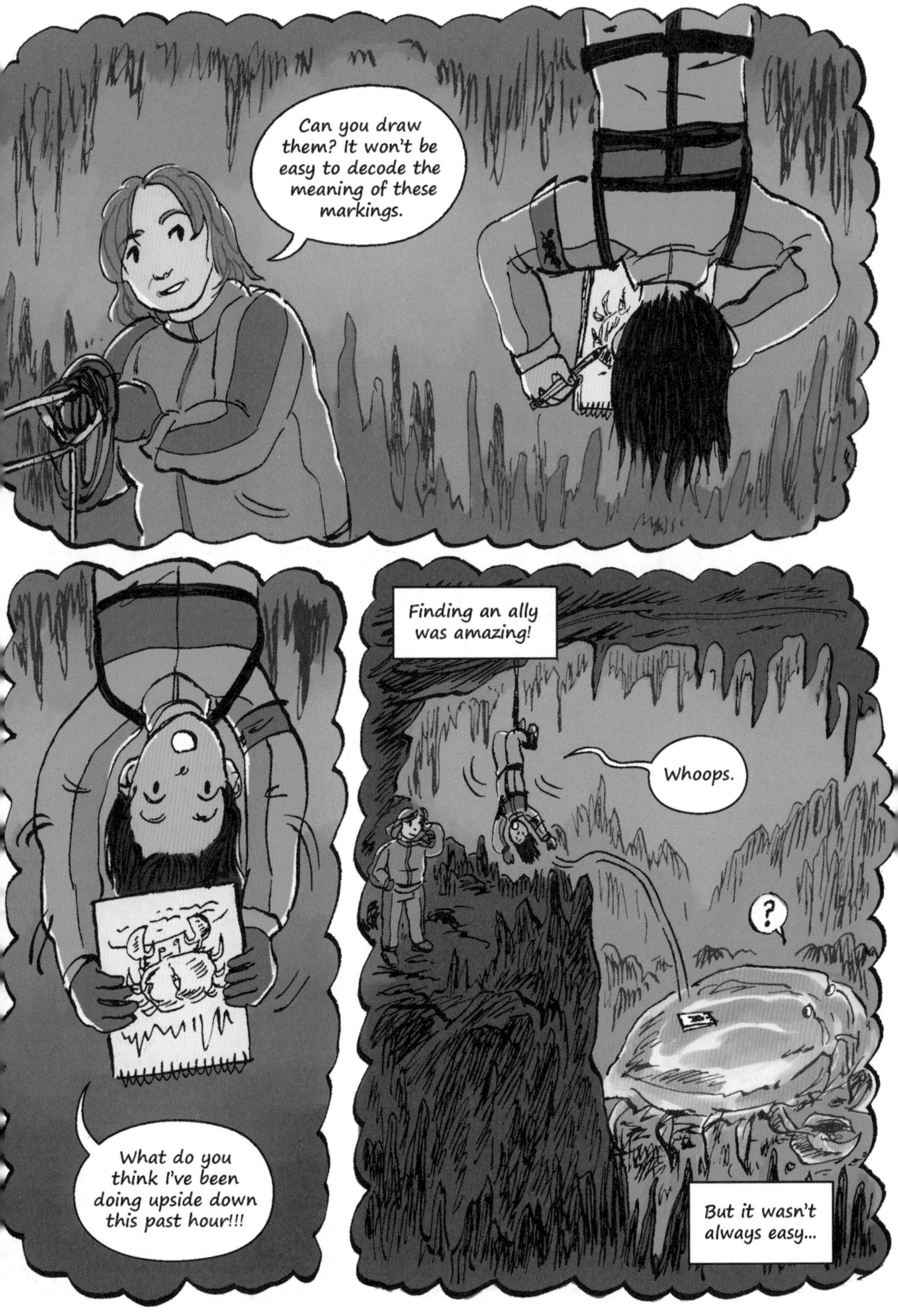
Can you draw them? It won't be easy to decode the meaning of these markings.
What do you think I've been doing upside down this past hour!!!
Finding an ally was amazing!
Whoops.
?
But it wasn't always easy...

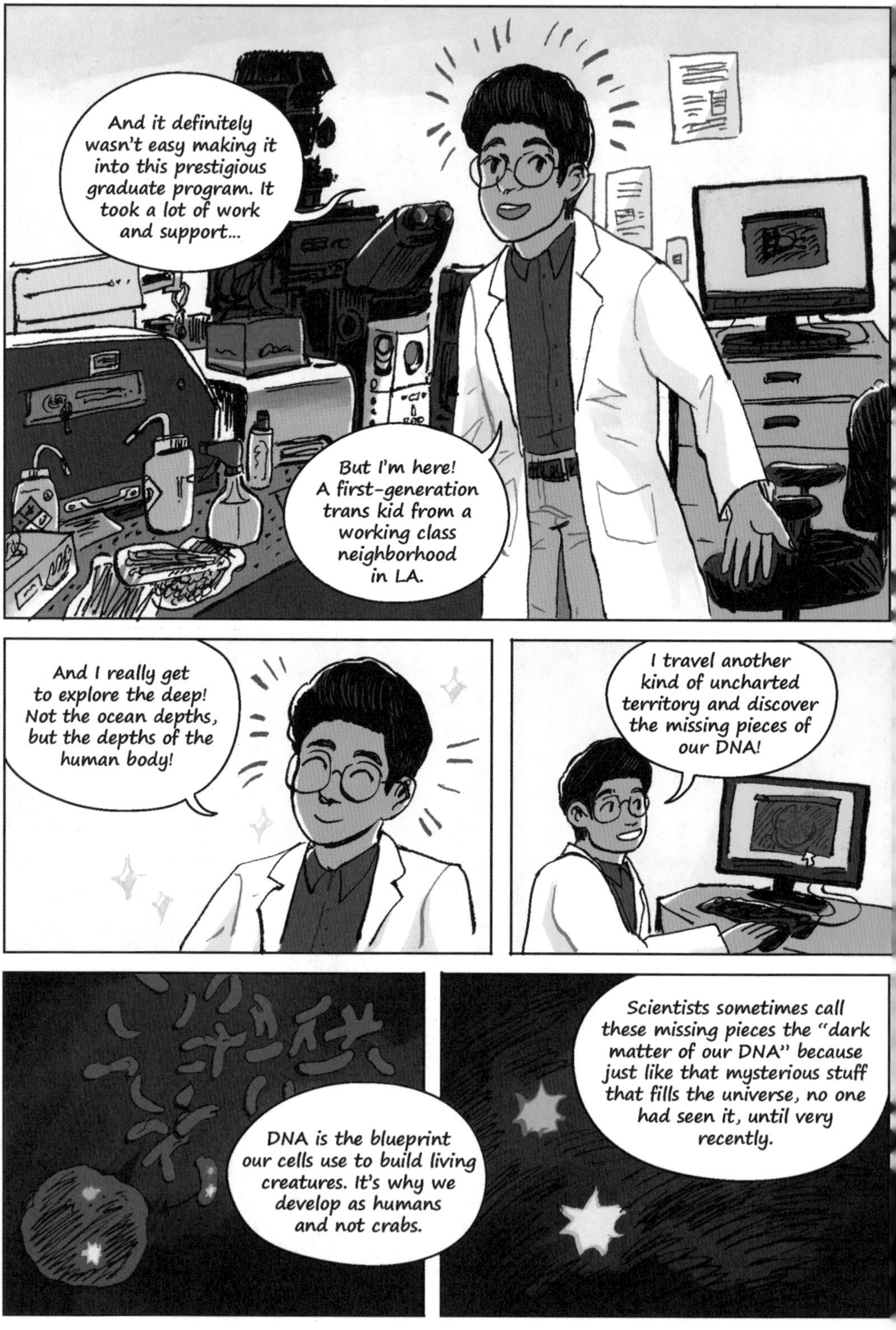
And it definitely wasn't easy making it into this prestigious graduate program. It took a lot of work and support...
But I'm here! A first-generation trans kid from a working class neighborhood in LA.
And I really get to explore the deep! Not the ocean depths, but the depths of the human body!
I travel another kind of uncharted territory and discover the missing pieces of our DNA!
DNA is the blueprint our cells use to build living creatures. It's why we develop as humans and not crabs.
Scientists sometimes call these missing pieces the "dark matter of our DNA" because just like that mysterious stuff that fills the universe, no one had seen it, until very recently.

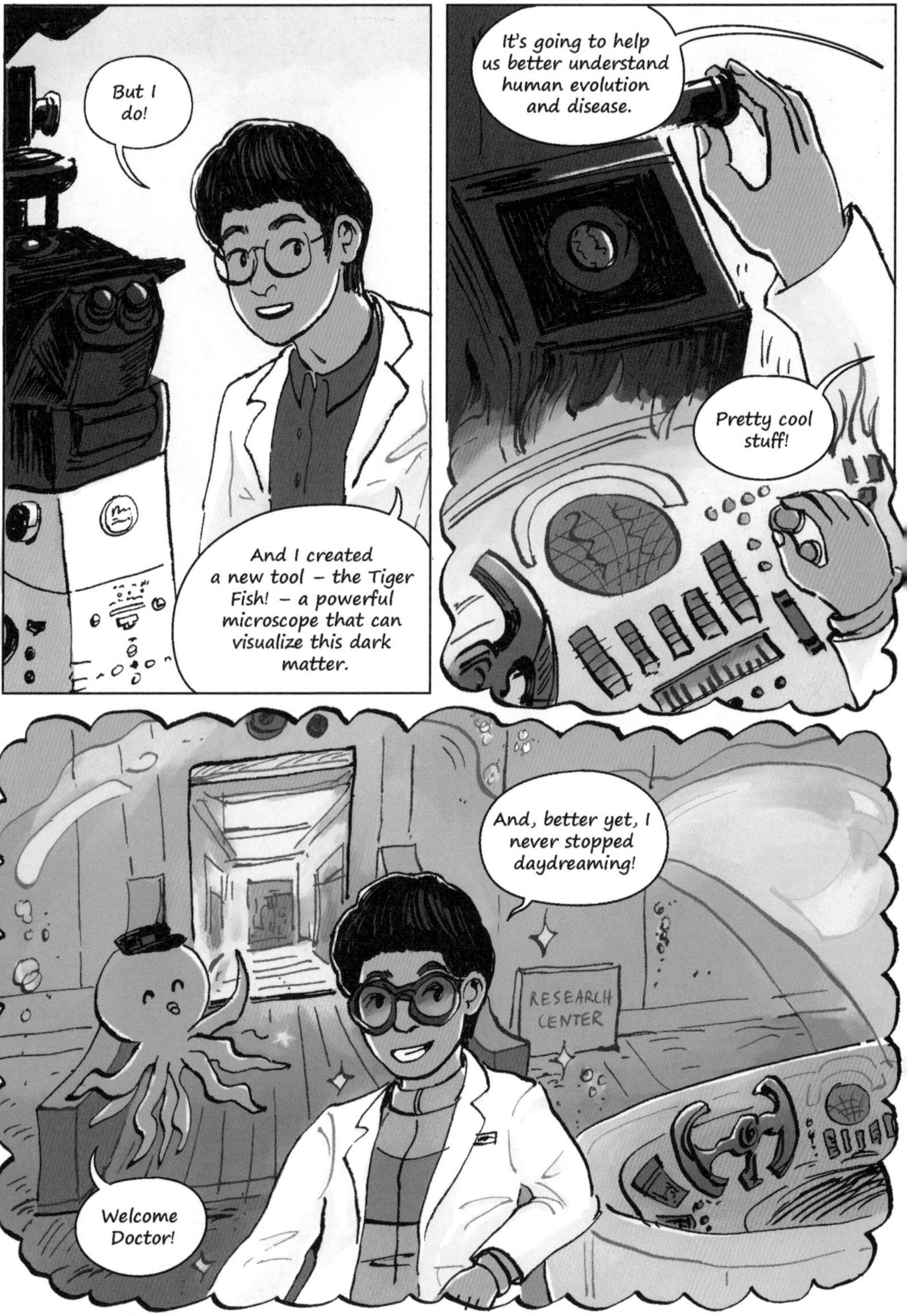
But I do!
And I created a new tool – the Tiger Fish! – a powerful microscope that can visualize this dark matter.
It's going to help us better understand human evolution and disease.
Pretty cool stuff!
And, better yet, I never stopped daydreaming!
RESEARCH CENTER
Welcome Doctor!

BECOMING REBEKAH BRUESEHOFF

Rebekah is an award-winning activist and author from New Jersey. Whether in meetings with legislators, on the field hockey field, hanging out with friends, or performing in the school musical, Rebekah inspires people of all ages and identities to show up authentically and dare to make the world a better place.

Written by Sammy Lisel
Illustrated by higu rose

higu rose is a queer Black illustrator and graphic novelist. When not drawing comics, higu likes to read shoujo manga and watch old Hollywood movies with handsome male leads.

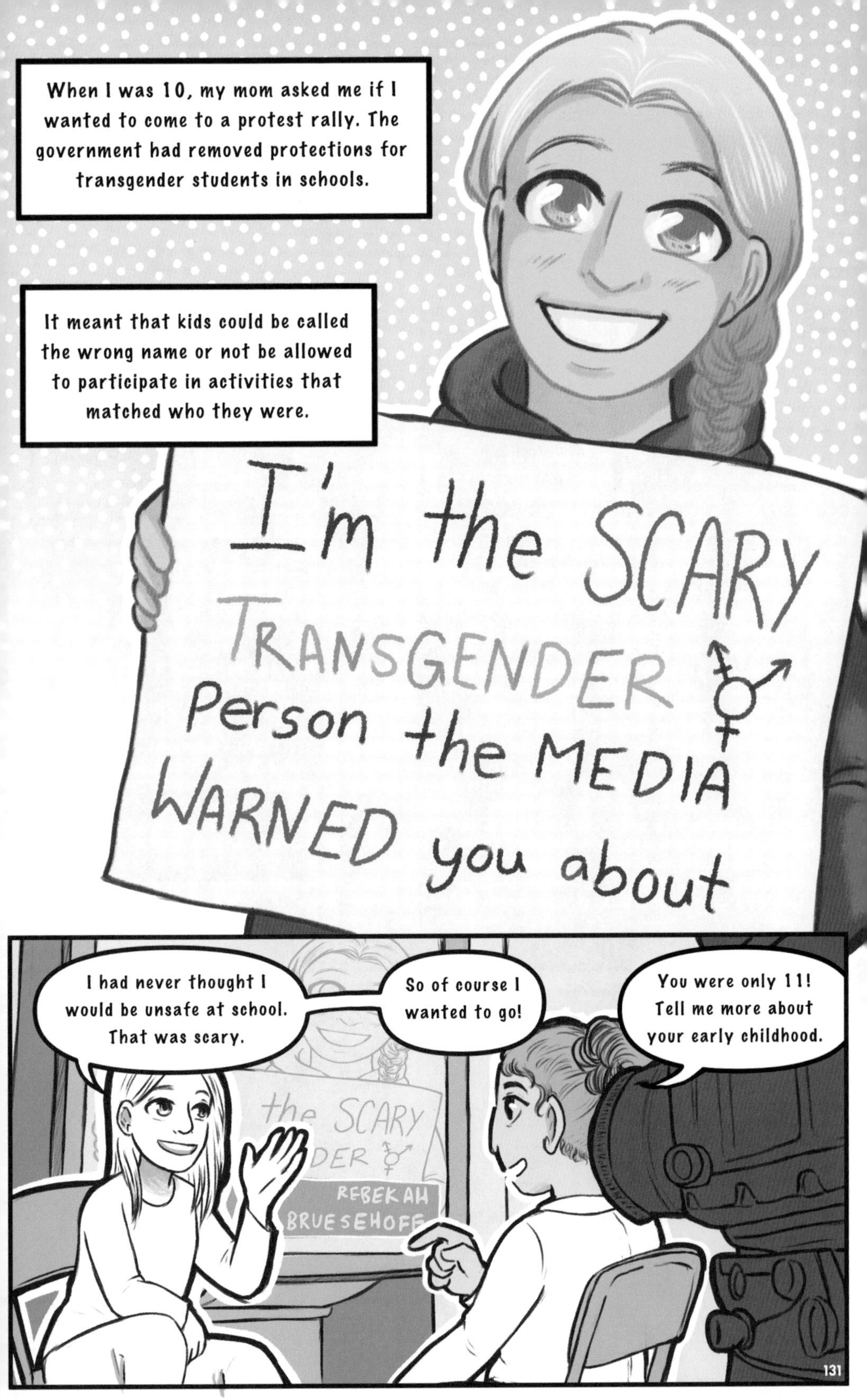
When I was 10, my mom asked me if I wanted to come to a protest rally. The government had removed protections for transgender students in schools.
It meant that kids could be called the wrong name or not be allowed to participate in activities that matched who they were.
I'm the SCARY TRANSGENDER Person the MEDIA WARNED you about
I had never thought I would be unsafe at school. That was scary.
So of course I wanted to go!
You were only 11! Tell me more about your early childhood.
the SCARY
DER
REBEKAH BRUESEHOFF

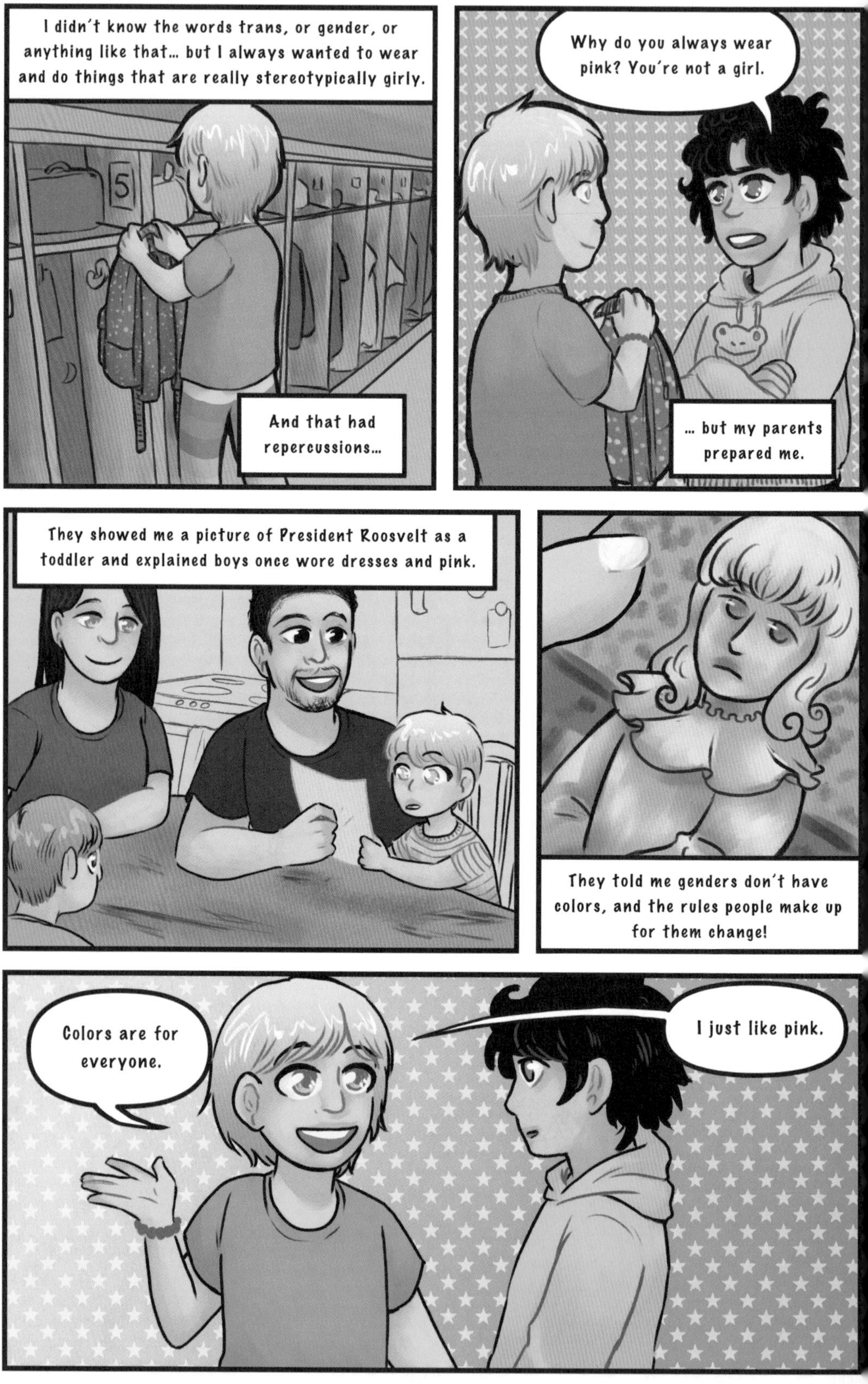
I didn't know the words trans, or gender, or anything like that... but I always wanted to wear and do things that are really stereotypically girly.
5
And that had repercussions...
Why do you always wear pink? You're not a girl.
... but my parents prepared me.
They showed me a picture of President Roosvelt as a toddler and explained boys once wore dresses and pink.
They told me genders don't have colors, and the rules people make up for them change!
Colors are for everyone.
I just like pink.

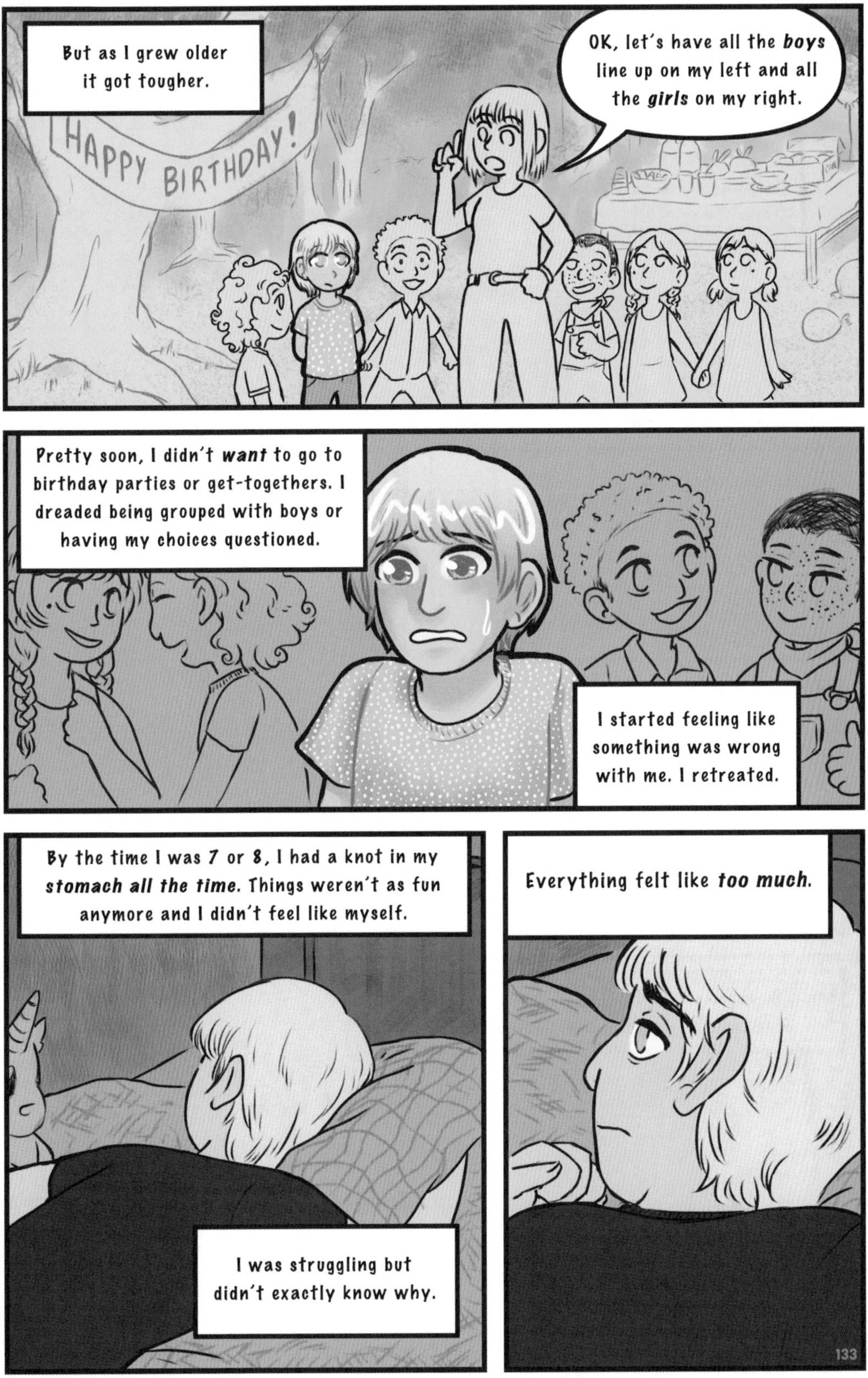

But as I grew older it got tougher.
OK, let's have all the ***boys*** line up on my left and all the ***girls*** on my right.
HAPPY BIRTHDAY!
Pretty soon, I didn't ***want*** to go to birthday parties or get-togethers. I dreaded being grouped with boys or having my choices questioned.
I started feeling like something was wrong with me. I retreated.
By the time I was *7* or *8*, I had a knot in my ***stomach all the time***. Things weren't as fun anymore and I didn't feel like myself.
I was struggling but didn't exactly know why.
Everything felt like ***too much***.

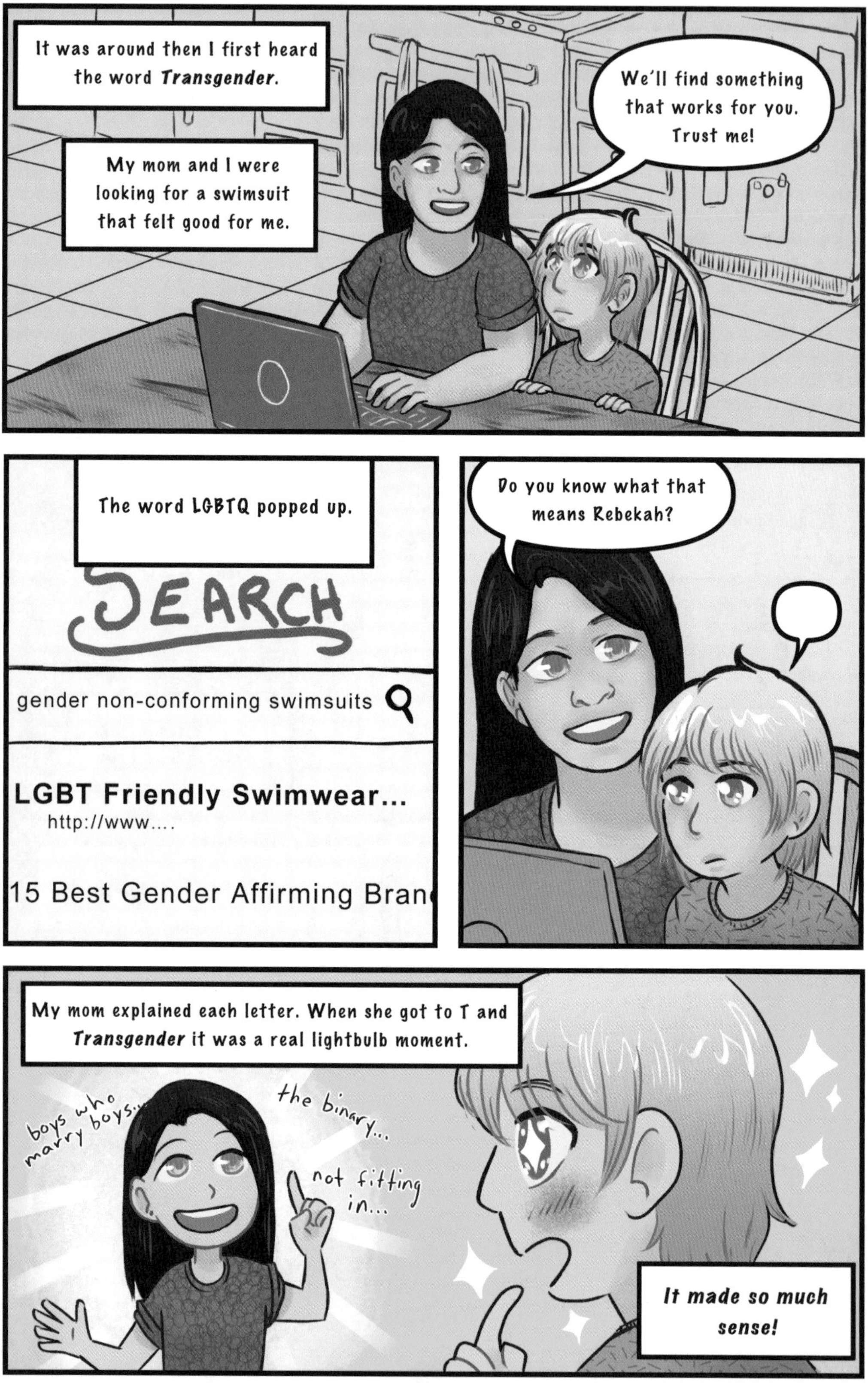
It was around then I first heard the word *Transgender.*
My mom and I were looking for a swimsuit that felt good for me.
We'll find something that works for you. Trust me!
The word LGBTQ popped up.
SEARCH
gender non-conforming swimsuits
LGBT Friendly Swimwear...
http://www....
15 Best Gender Affirming Bran
Do you know what that means Rebekah?
My mom explained each letter. When she got to T and *Transgender* it was a real lightbulb moment.
boys who marry boys...
the binary...
not fitting in...
It made so much sense!

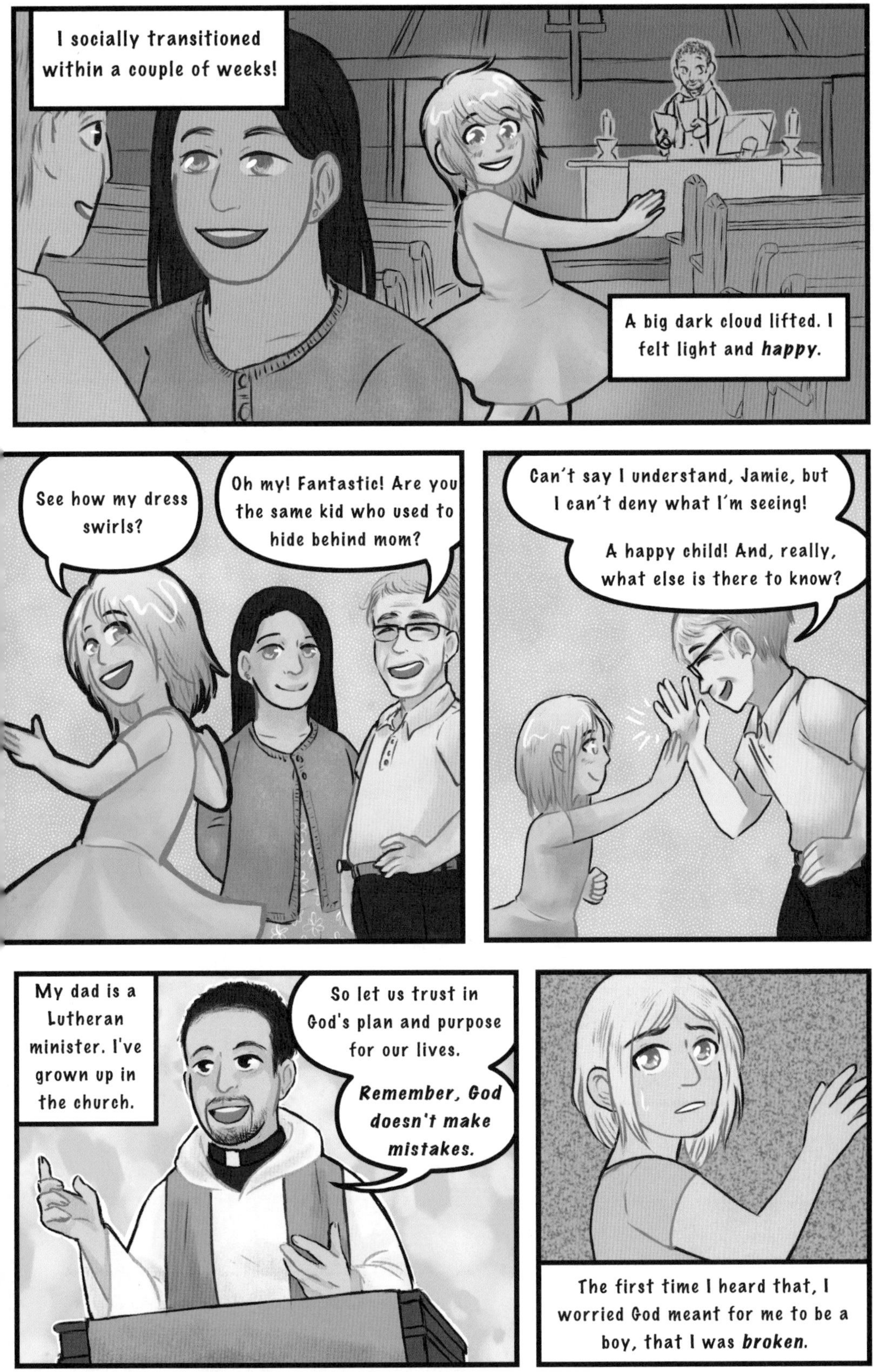
I socially transitioned within a couple of weeks!
A big dark cloud lifted. I felt light and *happy*.
See how my dress swirls?
Oh my! Fantastic! Are you the same kid who used to hide behind mom?
Can't say I understand, Jamie, but I can't deny what I'm seeing!
A happy child! And, really, what else is there to know?
My dad is a Lutheran minister. I've grown up in the church.
So let us trust in God's plan and purpose for our lives.
Remember, God doesn't make mistakes.
The first time I heard that, I worried God meant for me to be a boy, that I was *broken*.

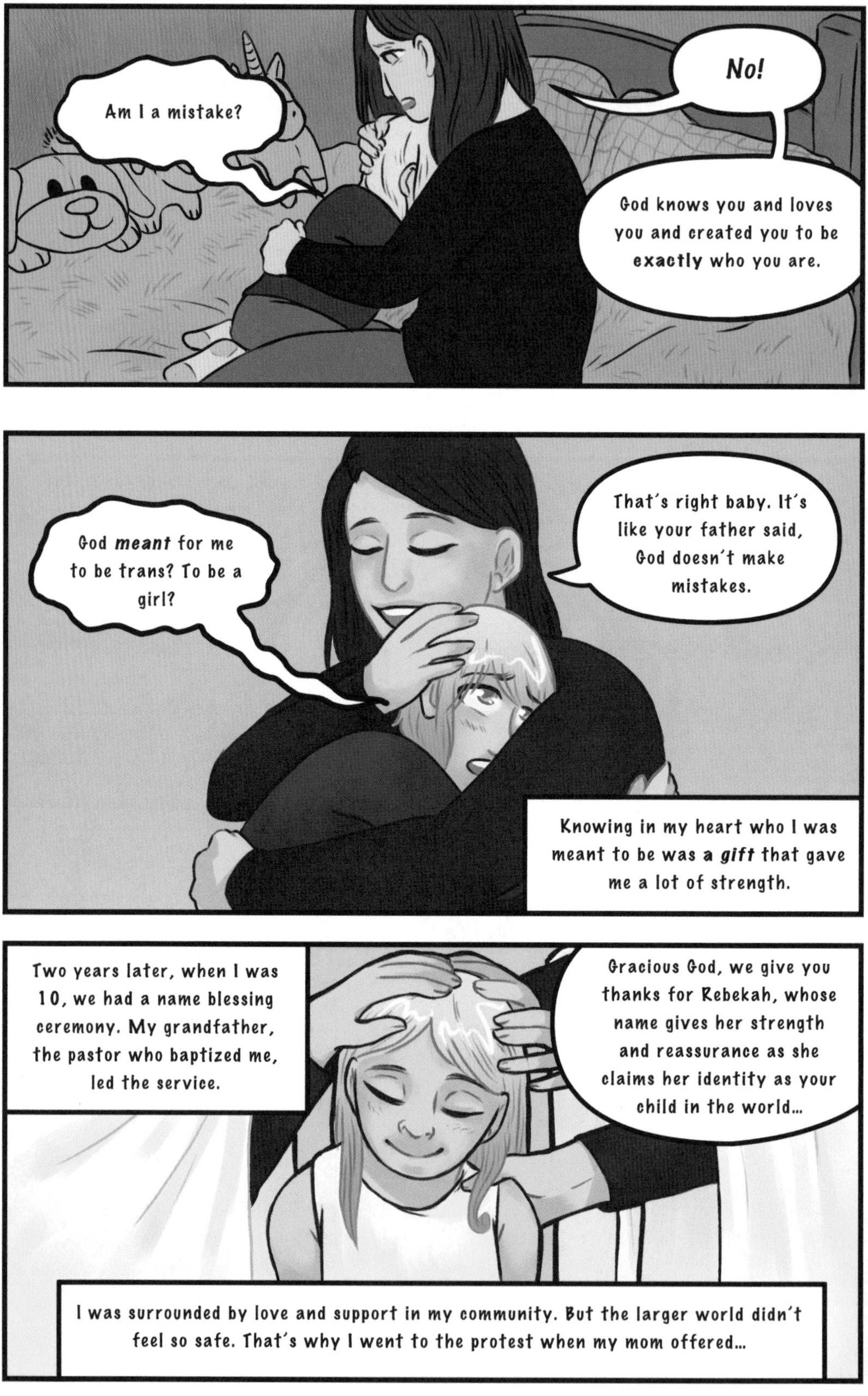
Am I a mistake?
No!
God knows you and loves you and created you to be **exactly** who you are.
God *meant* for me to be trans? To be a girl?
That's right baby. It's like your father said, God doesn't make mistakes.
Knowing in my heart who I was meant to be was a *gift* that gave me a lot of strength.
Two years later, when I was 10, we had a name blessing ceremony. My grandfather, the pastor who baptized me, led the service.
Gracious God, we give you thanks for Rebekah, whose name gives her strength and reassurance as she claims her identity as your child in the world...
I was surrounded by love and support in my community. But the larger world didn't feel so safe. That's why I went to the protest when my mom offered...

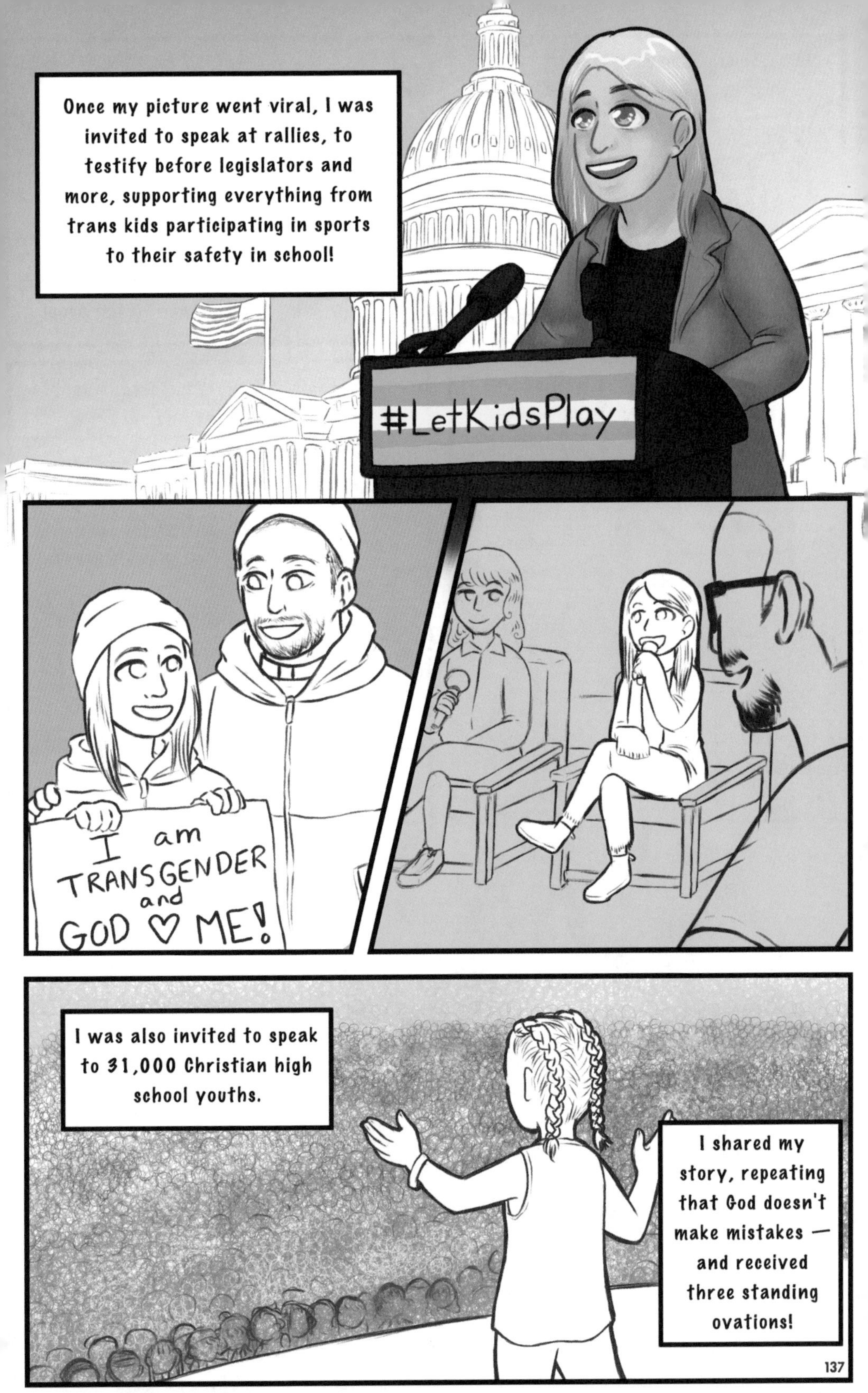
Once my picture went viral, I was invited to speak at rallies, to testify before legislators and more, supporting everything from trans kids participating in sports to their safety in school!
#LetKidsPlay
I am TRANSGENDER and GOD ♡ ME!
I was also invited to speak to 31,000 Christian high school youths.
I shared my story, repeating that God doesn't make mistakes — and received three standing ovations!

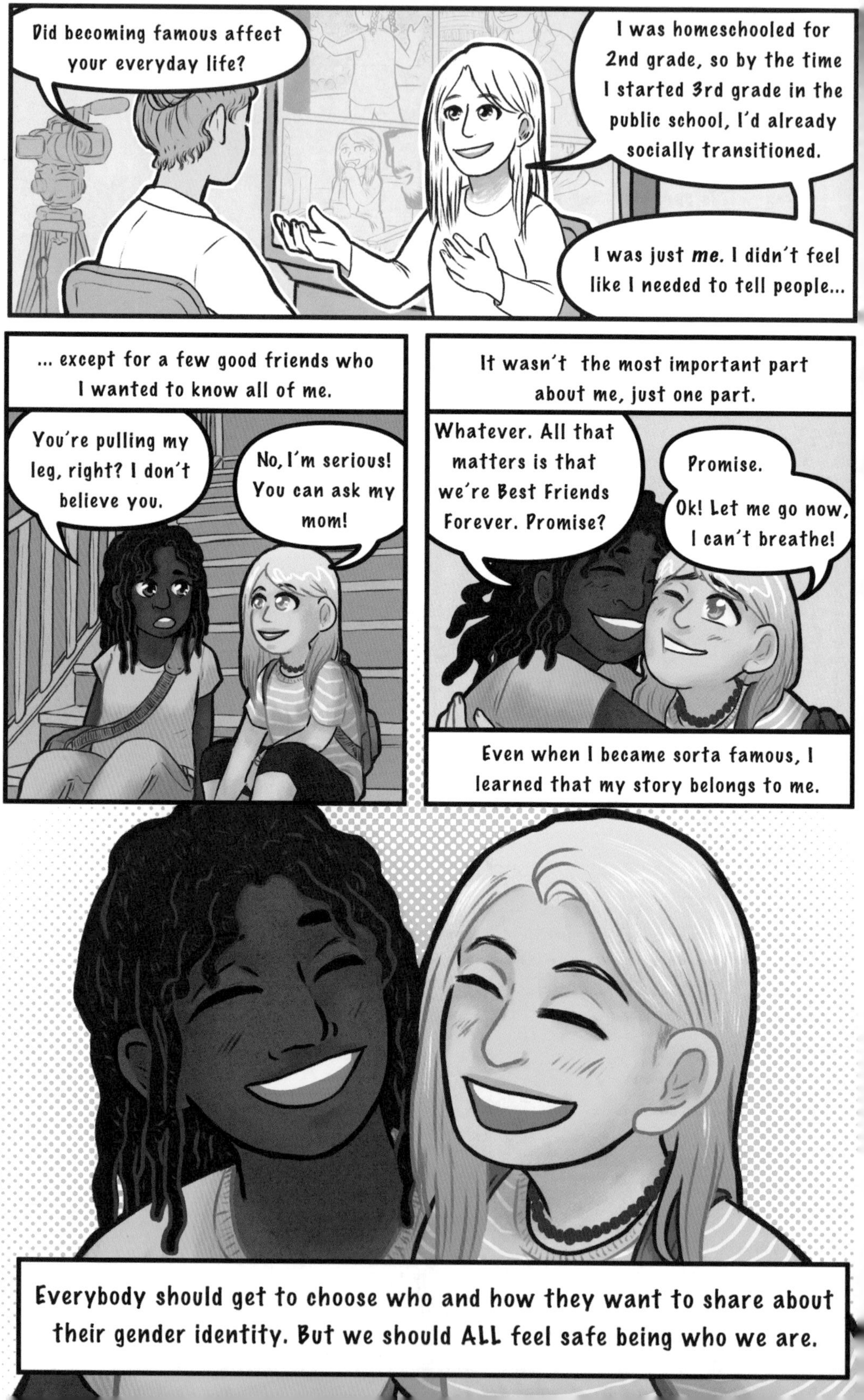
Did becoming famous affect your everyday life?
I was homeschooled for 2nd grade, so by the time I started 3rd grade in the public school, I'd already socially transitioned.
I was just *me.* I didn't feel like I needed to tell people...
... except for a few good friends who I wanted to know all of me.
You're pulling my leg, right? I don't believe you.
No, I'm serious! You can ask my mom!
It wasn't the most important part about me, just one part.
Whatever. All that matters is that we're Best Friends Forever. Promise?
Promise.
Ok! Let me go now, I can't breathe!
Even when I became sorta famous, I learned that my story belongs to me.
Everybody should get to choose who and how they want to share about their gender identity. But we should ALL feel safe being who we are.

RESOURCES

If you're in crisis, or just need someone
to talk to, help is out there!

THE TREVOR PROJECT
(866) 488-7386 • thetrevorproject.org/get-help

Crisis counselors are available to support LGBTQ+
youth by phone, text, or online chat, 24/7.

TRANS LIFELINE
(877) 565-8860 • translifeline.org

Trans Lifeline's Hotline is a peer support phone
service run by trans people. Call if you need
someone trans to talk to, even if you're not in
a crisis or if you're not sure you're trans.

NATIONAL RUNAWAY SAFELINE
1-800-RUNAWAY • 1800runaway.org

24/7 crisis services for youth. Connect with a
compassionate person who will listen and help you
create a plan to address your concerns.